Horse Sweat
and Powder Smoke

MILITARY HISTORY SERIES ☆ TEXAS A&M UNIVERSITY
66

Horse Sweat and Powder Smoke

The First Texas Cavalry in the Civil War

STANLEY S. McGOWEN

TEXAS A&M UNIVERSITY PRESS
College Station, Texas

Library of Congress Cataloging-in-Publication Data

McGowen, Stanley S., 1947–
    Horse sweat and powder smoke : the first Texas cavalry in the
Civil War / Stanley S. McGowen.
        p.   cm. — (Texas A&M University military history series ; 66)
    Includes bibliographical references and index.
    ISBN 0-89096-903-5
    1. Confederate States of America. Army. Texas Cavalry Regiment,
1st—History.   2. Texas—History—Civil War, 1861–1865—Regimental
histories.   3. United States—History—Civil War, 1861–1865—
Regimental histories.   I. Title.   II. Series.
    E580.6 1stM34   1999
    973.7'464—dc21   99-24705
                                                              CIP

CONTENTS

ILLUSTRATIONS

MAPS

PREFACE

I became interested in the 1st Texas Cavalry Regiment because my great-grand-father, William Joseph "Billy" McGowen, served with the regiment from the Texas plains to the Louisiana bayous. Cursory research revealed that histori-ans, by and large, had overlooked this rather unique regiment. I then deter-mined to write a comprehensive history of this atypical cavalry unit and the stalwart Texans who filled its ranks.

Many Texas units fought for the Confederacy, but the first regiment from the state mustered into Confederate service surpassed most others in length of service and in diversity of campaigns. From February, 1861, until the end of April, 1865, the 1st Texas Cavalry Regiment participated in campaigns from the far western frontier and the Gulf coast of Texas to the swamps and bayous of Louisiana. Few other Texas regiments could boast of fighting in such far-flung theaters or confronting such a variety of opponents. Indians, insurgent Unionists, bandits, and, of course, Federal soldiers all encountered the hard-riding, quick-shooting Texas cavalrymen.[1]

In December, 1861, the Confederate War Department officially designated the 1st Texas Mounted Rifles the 1st Texas Cavalry Regiment. Although the 1st Texas Mounted Rifles enlisted for only twelve months, an unbroken legacy of service existed among the men and units forming the 1st Texas Cavalry Regiment. In April, 1862, when the Mounted Rifles disbanded, four of its com-panies remained on active duty under the command of Regimental Surgeon Joseph Taylor. These four, with an additional company, formed the 8th Texas Cavalry Battalion. William O. Yager, adjutant of the 1st Mounted Rifles, left the regiment to form the 3rd Battalion of Texas Cavalry. In May, 1863, the Confederate government combined the 3rd and the 8th battalions to reconsti-tute the 1st Texas Cavalry Regiment.[2]

The officers of this regiment were unique among Texas commanders. Many who led mounted Texas units in the Civil War lacked self-control; as a result, their troops gained reputations as rowdy, undisciplined soldiers. Some regi-mental commanders allowed their men to wander away from camp almost anytime they chose. These men gambled freely, raced their horses, and became "a gambling, profane, brawling Lot." Henry E. McCulloch, Augustus Buchel, and William O. Yager, however, stood in strong contrast to the lackadaisical commanders who allowed their men to disregard regulations they deemed too restrictive. McCulloch, Buchel, and Yager were strong-willed, dedicated men who demanded discipline and "gentlemanly behavior" from their troops. Officers and men who deviated from prescribed regulations received punishments ranging from reprimand to court martial, depending on the offense. Regimental commanders were not martinets but empathic leaders who displayed genuine concern for their men. They were committed to providing the best training, equipment, and care for the regiment. All troops in the regiment received training in both mounted and dismounted tactics, as well as instruction in caring for their personal equipment, especially their horses. As a result of its colonels' energy and devotion to duty, the 1st Texas Cavalry achieved singular success in battle and became one of the few Texas cavalry units that retained its horses and fought mounted throughout the Civil War.[3]

The regiment's soldiers were a microcosm of Texas' prewar population. When the 1,083 members of the regiment mustered into service, men enlisted from all regions of the state and registered a panoply of occupations. Lawyers, doctors, and other professional men volunteered their services, but most who joined the 1st Texas Cavalry listed more ordinary vocations. Clerks, druggists, sailors, saddlers, and various tradesmen enlisted, but by far the majority of men enrolled were farmers and stock raisers. The 599 men associated with farming and stock raising comprised 55 percent of the regiment. The remainder of occupations listed on muster rolls included skilled laborers, 8 percent; unskilled laborers, 5 percent; professionals, 11 percent; and miscellaneous or unknown, 21 percent. Inconsistent with popular perceptions of Confederate soldiers, only two members of the unit considered themselves planters.[4]

Regimental enlistees also listed diverse places of birth and drew upon many traditions. Men came from every section of the United States. Of the 77 percent of the 1,083 men who listed a place of birth, 58 percent documented their places of birth as southern states and 8 percent as border states. Not a few (14 percent), however, specified their places of birth as northern states. Germany, Scotland, Ireland, England, Mexico, Canada, and France also contributed native sons to the regiment; a total of 21 percent were of foreign origin. German immigrants especially appeared in significant numbers on regimental rolls; of 175 foreign born, 103 were of German birth.[5]

The regiment exhibited characteristics both common and unusual in Texas Confederate units. Like most Confederate soldiers, Texans suffered the ravages of disease when brought together in close living quarters. The majority of the southern population lived in rural districts and had not developed immunities to common diseases; as a result, illness felled more men than enemy bullets. Like other Confederate organizations, the regiment carried a miscellany of weapons and received an assortment of clothing that always was in short supply and seldom uniform in color or style. Rations varied from good to nonexistent. Troops dined on anything from fresh beef to prairie dog or subsisted on a few handfuls of parched corn, depending on the stage of the war and where the regiment was posted at the time.[6]

Unlike most mounted Texas units, the 1st Texas Cavalry carried sabers and underwent training to fight as both cavalry and dismounted infantry. Although McCulloch, a frontier Indian fighter, believed the saber to be of dubious value, both Buchel and Yager were trained in conventional European tactics and regarded the saber as an essential weapon in a close-quarter cavalry fight. As a result, sabers usually hung from the saddles or hips of all regimental soldiers.[7]

The regiment also differed from other Texas units in the number of men who deserted. During the first year of service, the regimental desertion rate rose to less than 1 percent—in other Confederate units the number of deserters was much higher. As the war progressed, the number of desertions increased but still averaged only 3.8 percent for the entire war. Even when conditions at home worsened to the point that men were induced to return home and solve their domestic problems, most troopers requested a furlough through military channels rather than deserting their comrades without appropriate authority. In April, 1865, after Gen. Robert E. Lee surrendered in Virginia, many Confederate units disintegrated into leaderless, unruly mobs; but the 1st Texas Cavalry remained a cohesive organization, disbanding only when it received competent military orders.[8]

Several factors contributed to keeping the regiment's desertion rate low. Initially, regimental soldiers were assigned to protect fellow citizens from Indian raids and were posted near home and family; such assignments encouraged them to remain at their duties. Several company commanders sent patrols near troopers' homes or offered liberal leaves for their men. Strong leadership throughout the war, too, reduced desertions. All regimental commanders possessed considerable skill and experience leading men in combat. These commanders' strict moral codes and fair discipline inspired most of their subordinates to remain with their units even when far from home and enduring severe hardships. Notwithstanding fatalities from disease and combat, the 1st Texas Cavalry did not suffer the appalling casualties of some Confederate regiments serving east of the Mississippi River. Undoubtedly, the infrequency of losses encouraged these particular Texas horsemen to remain at their posts.

Despite shortages of money, men, and materiel, the 1st Texas Cavalry Regiment served with distinction throughout the war, confronting varied enemies from the sun-baked plains of Texas to the fever-ridden swamps of Louisiana. First to muster into Confederate service and one of the last Confederate regiments to deactivate, the regiment formed part of the barrier that prevented any major Union invasion of the state. Since Union forces failed to overrun Texas, the state never suffered the devastation that Federal armies wrought on other southern states. Because of the regiment's resolute horsemen, Indian war parties ventured into settled areas less frequently than they did when U.S. troops protected the frontier. Unique in many ways, the troops of the regiment committed themselves to stand in the path of those who assailed Texas and to defend their homes and way of life against all aggressors.[9]

ACKNOWLEDGMENTS

Completing a complicated project such as a book manuscript without sight required some very special assistance, and I wish to recognize those most significant in bringing my book to a successful completion.

Danay Carranza, Barbara Daughtry, Kelly Kinard, Susan Sopira, and Jennifer Zajicek were my eyes and, more often than not, my chauffeurs. I cannot thank these individuals enough for the long hours they spent in tedious research. Without their patience and dedicated assistance, I could not have accomplished anything.

Another person who deserves special thanks is Peggy Fox of the Confederate Research Center, Hillsboro, Texas. Her knowledge and cheerful assistance with diverse requests guaranteed that my research was completed accurately and as quickly as possible.

At Texas Christian University, I certainly must acknowledge the sage advice and direction of Dr. Grady McWhiney, who quietly but very effectively guided my research and writing. His expertise in organization and archival research proved invaluable. A few hints from Dr. McWhiney focused my attention on the major topic when I meandered into areas not necessarily related to my subject. Dr. Donald E. Worcester contributed his editing genius. By subtle suggestions he transformed my untutored efforts into readable passages.

The military history staff at the National Archives deserves considerable credit for their invaluable assistance. No matter what I needed, they provided it. No request was too insignificant to receive serious attention and a speedy response. The same must be said about the Center for American History, University of Texas, Austin, and the Texas State Archives.

Dr. Don Frazier, of McMurry University in Abilene, Texas, employed his not inconsiderable skills to produce the maps of Texas, Louisiana, and the Red River Campaign.

Gene Swinson of Baird, Texas, executed the pen and ink drawings that enliven this book. Many thanks to an old friend.

Another artist who I certainly must thank is Gary Zaboly, my cover artist.

Gary, a noted western and military artist, captured, in meticulous detail, the ferocity of a running fight between the mounted Texans and Comanche warriors.

Without question, I must thank the staff at Texas A&M University Press. Throughout a long and tedious process, they were always friendly, helpful, and open to questions and ideas from someone unfamiliar with publishing.

There are many other professors, colleagues, and friends who aided in research and reading; space prevents me from thanking them individually. They know who they are and, I hope, do not feel slighted.

My wife, Jolene, deserves very special thanks. She participated in every phase of my research and, most important, bolstered my morale or provided a swift kick in the pants when my motivation faltered.

Horse Sweat
and Powder Smoke

CHAPTER I

Genesis of a Regiment

Months before the crescendo of cannon fire and clouds of acrid powder smoke rolled across Charleston Harbor in South Carolina, Texas took significant steps to become an active participant in the coming Civil War. After Lincoln's election in November, 1860, several fragmentary groups coalesced to form two major factions vying for control of the state: one, to varying degrees, favored remaining in the Union, while the other, made up of both radical and moderate secessionists, sought to secede. As early as December, 1860, these secessionists moved to separate Texas from the United States.[1]

On January 30, 1861, the Secessionists, in a special meeting of the state legislature, formed a Committee of Public Safety before Texas officially ratified any ordinance of secession. The committee planned to oust all Federal troops from the state as soon as possible and appointed a commission with authority to negotiate with U.S. Bvt. Maj. Gen. David E. Twiggs for the surrender of arms, stores, and public property in Texas. His poor health and southern sympathies led the commission members to believe that Twiggs would surrender all Federal property without resistance.[2]

The committee also authorized units of armed volunteers to force the surrender of U.S. troops and military supplies if negotiations failed. On February 5, 1861, the committee appointed Henry E. McCulloch, a noted frontiersman and Texas Ranger, colonel of cavalry. His mission was to raise a sufficient volunteer force to effect the surrender of all Federal posts along that portion of the Texas frontier running from Fort Chadbourne, which was on Oak Creek approximately eleven miles northeast of Bronte in present Coke County, to the Red River in present Montague County. The committee designated McCulloch's volunteer companies the 1st Regiment of Texas Mounted Rifles.

This regiment formed the foundation of the unit that eventually became the 1st Regiment of Texas Cavalry.[3]

On February 5 and 6, 1861, Henry McCulloch, acting under directions from the Committee of Public Safety, sent letters to Capts. James B. "Buck" Barry, D. C. Cowan, Thomas C. Frost, R. B. Halley, and H. A. Hamner, authorizing them to raise companies of one hundred men each. He also wrote to Capts. George Harrison and Lawrence "Sul" Ross, both under service to Gov. Sam Houston, asking for their cooperation in protecting the frontier settlements. Several of these men had been members of Texas Ranger companies, and McCulloch knew that their experience would be valuable in forming his new regiment.[4]

On February 11, McCulloch, along with several of his hastily recruited troops, rode toward the outlying U.S. installations. Traveling through Austin and Gatesville, he reached Brownwood on the evening of the 17th. On the 22nd, Frost arrived with more than one hundred of his men. Halley and his officers had ridden in and were awaiting the arrival of the remainder of their partially filled company. An irregular civilian force under Lt. William Cunningham also joined McCulloch to act as spies and scouts. Still, McCulloch's entire column numbered fewer than two hundred horsemen. Cunningham's men provided current intelligence on the Federal movements at nearby Camp Colorado, six miles north of the Colorado River on Jim Ned Creek in present Coleman County.[5]

At 4 A.M. on February 16, Ben McCulloch, a veteran of the Mexican War, famed Texas Ranger, U.S. marshal, and Henry's elder brother, led over one thousand irregular Texas mounted volunteers into the center of San Antonio. His men quietly surrounded Twiggs's U.S. Army headquarters and arsenal, forcing a surrender of all Federal troops in the city. As a result of this strong show of force, Twiggs on February 18 issued General Order No. 5, directing the surrender of all U.S. military posts in the state. The order further directed all Federal forces to proceed to the Texas coast for evacuation, taking their arms and ammunition with them.[6]

On the morning of February 22, Henry McCulloch, unaware of the situation in San Antonio, rode alone into Camp Colorado and demanded total surrender of the post. He had instructed his commanders, as well as Cunningham, to gather their forces six miles from the camp and await word from him. McCulloch hoped for a peaceable surrender, but he and his men were prepared to fight if necessary.[7]

Meeting with the camp commander, Capt. Edmund Kirby Smith (West Point Class of 1841, Mexican War veteran, and commander of Company B of

fig. 1. Henry E. McCulloch received his Confederate commission from his brother Ben and formed the first regiment of Texas troops mustered into the Provisional Confederate Army. Courtesy Archives Division, Texas State Library, Austin

the 2nd U.S. Cavalry), McCulloch demanded the surrender of the entire post and all property "of every type and kind" belonging to the United States. McCulloch also offered to induct all of Smith's men into the Provisional Confederate Army. Smith declined both to surrender and to accept the offer of induction. Having tendered his services to his native state of Florida, he would not act until informed if his offer had been accepted. Smith did join the Confederate Army and, in October, 1862, became commander of the Trans-Mississippi Department. Thus he became McCulloch's commander. Other members of Company B expressed loyalty to the South but declined to join McCulloch. Smith made it plain that he was a friend of the South and Texas and would not use his force against either. He refused, however, to surrender his command's arms, horses, and individual property because such a capitulation would disgrace him as a soldier. He agreed to relinquish all else, keeping only sufficient provisions for his men. When McCulloch rejected these terms, Smith negotiated a compromise agreement allowing his command to keep their arms and horses until they reached the coast. At that point, all military property would be handed over to Texas authorities.[8]

During the deliberations, a messenger arrived bearing Twiggs's order to surrender all U.S. property to state officials. McCulloch and Smith then concluded the camp's surrender. The two officers jointly inventoried the camp and forwarded invoices to the Committee of Public Safety. According to Mc-Culloch, all negotiations and interactions between the two men were amicable. Smith later told a different story. He claimed that both men became belligerent and he would not have surrendered his command without a fight; only Twiggs's order changed his mind. Once negotiations were completed, McCulloch left Captain Frost's company at Camp Colorado to protect that area of the frontier.[9]

On the morning of March 26, McCulloch rode with his remaining men to accept the surrender of Fort Chadbourne, a large post in present Coke County. From there he reported delays in moving Federal troops to the coast because of a lack of available transportation. With McCulloch's concurrence, Lt. Col. Gouverneur Morris, Union commander of the post, held the fort with one company of infantry until sufficient conveyance for the troops arrived from San Antonio. Owing to the Texans' lack of supplies, Morris provided subsistence for both commands until the Federal troops left the post. McCulloch ordered Captain Halley to take possession of the fort and establish company headquarters there after the U.S. soldiers departed. He directed Halley to prepare for a scouting mission to the headwaters of the Colorado River as soon as possible. As he moved on toward Camp Cooper, on the Clear Fork of the Brazos River five miles west of present Albany-Throckmorton highway, McCulloch expressed regret at Morris's tenacious loyalty to the Union and his rejection of the offer to join the Confederacy.[10]

Halley could not comply with all of McCulloch's instructions. His company did not contain enough men to conduct both a long scout and occupation of Fort Chadbourne. He requested reinforcements of twenty-five men from Burleson and sent out recruiting officers to fill the company roster. He was short of fodder, and the available spring grass could not sustain his weary horses on a long scout. His experienced officers wanted to wait until the horses regained their strength before commencing patrols against marauding Comanche and Kiowa Indians. They realized that any Indians encountered could easily outdistance their weakened mounts. Near the end of March, Halley's troops completed a circuitous patrol that led them back to Camp Colorado to secure supplies before they moved into regular quarters at Fort Chadbourne.[11]

As the Texans rode north toward Camp Cooper, McCulloch knew he faced a situation unique among Federal posts. Before his arrival, the camp had surrendered to Col. William C. Dalrymple, an aide to Texas Gov. Sam Houston.

McCulloch expressed some hesitation about confronting state troops operating under a commission from the governor, while his orders were from the Committee of Public Safety. Arriving at Camp Cooper on March 7, McCulloch nevertheless demanded that Capt. E. W. Rogers, whom Dalrymple had left in command, surrender the facility. McCulloch's demand applied to all property previously under control of the United States. Rogers controlled everything that Capt. Stephen D. Carpenter, Company H, 1st U.S. Infantry, had surrendered to state troops. McCulloch's reluctance to take possession of the camp from a state officer left some doubt about the legitimacy of a transfer. Two days later, however, Rogers recognized McCulloch's authority under the state commissioners and gladly surrendered all property at Camp Cooper. McCulloch then ordered Barry to establish his forty-two man company base of operations at Camp Cooper. He also instructed Barry to organize quartermaster and commissary matters there. Federal troops had departed without inventorying camp property appropriately, and, because Rogers had improperly secured the stores, McCulloch feared that some supplies had been lost or ruined.[12]

Orders issued to McCulloch on February 5 to move Federal troops to the coast included responsibility for protecting the northwestern frontier of Texas from the Red River on the north to the confluence of the western and main branches of the Concho River on the south. A shortage of men made fulfilling this assignment arduous for McCulloch's small command. The task became easier in early March, when Capt. Aaron B. Burleson brought his company of state troops under McCulloch's command. Burleson placed his company on Home Creek about halfway between Fort Chadbourne and Camp Colorado. Several other modest-sized units of state troops also came under McCulloch's authority. These units had no official authorization, and McCulloch called them his "heel fly force"—they followed him around much as flies swarm around a herd of cattle.[13]

Problems other than Federal troops plagued McCulloch; he was critically short of funds as well as men. In correspondence back to Austin, he pleaded for funds to pay his men. He had left San Antonio without a dollar and in his own name had contracted debts amounting to about one thousand dollars. He had promised his creditors expeditious reimbursement and urged the committee promptly to forward sufficient funds to pay the debts. Of necessity, he appointed one man both regimental quartermaster and commissary officer. He also appointed assistant surgeons to take charge of medicines and medical facilities at the various frontier posts. Fort Chadbourne required quartermaster and commissary officers, but no qualified officers were available. McCulloch promised the commission to be as economical and efficient as possible in staffing the frontier posts, but he required personnel and funds "to do proper service to Texas." To compound his predicament, his regiment consisted of only four companies, none having a full complement of men. He allowed all commanders except Burleson to fill their ranks with recruits.[14]

Lacking sufficient arms and ammunition, McCulloch and his commanders protested any arrangement that allowed Federal troops to leave the state with their weapons. They knew the critical need for such materiel in Texas. McCulloch pointed out that most of the Federal troops would return to the U.S. to serve under a "Black Republican" president. He questioned why those troops should be allowed to leave with arms and munitions that his regiment desperately needed. If the choice were left to him, no troops would leave the state with their weapons. McCulloch offered, if necessary, to use force to keep the Federal arms for his own men.[15]

Upon completing the occupation of the northwestern U.S. posts, McCulloch requested state troops to relieve his regiment. He assured his men that they would remain on the frontier five months and then be mustered into the Confederate service. Some, like Captain Halley, had no desire to remain on permanent duty. McCulloch anticipated, however, that Lt. Sidney Davidson of Halley's company would be an able commander and designated him as captain of the remnants of Halley's and Burleson's companies. He also authorized Davidson to enlist men in sufficient strength to complete his unit roster. Captains Frost and Barry both exhibited the qualities of excellent company commanders. When time allowed, McCulloch planned to appoint an adjutant and sergeant major for the regiment.[16]

McCulloch mustered his men into the Provisional Confederate Army and was surprised when they were not relieved by state troops. It seemed logical that Texas outfits, and not Confederate cavalry, should garrison the frontier posts. Early recruiting efforts provided him sufficient men to take control of the frontier posts and replace U.S. troops with tough but poorly armed Texas volunteers.[17]

Unlike most commanders of Texas troops, McCulloch demanded "good order and conduct" from his volunteers as they traveled through the state. Under no circumstances did he condone taking liberties with citizens or their property. Cognizant of his men's personalities, he demanded discipline and strict adherence to regulations. He knew well that many Texas cowboys and frontiersmen exhibited boisterous, individualistic behavior and easily could get out of hand. He wanted a disciplined unit of which Texas could be proud and one that would continue to sustain a laudable reputation within the Confederate States.[18]

Although technically in command of Confederate soldiers, McCulloch officially could not be sworn into Confederate service until he returned to headquarters at San Antonio. After U.S. forces in Texas surrendered, the state government sent Henry McCulloch's brother Ben to Montgomery, Alabama, to accept a commission to form a cavalry regiment consisting of ten companies with sixty to eighty men each. Leroy Pope Walker, the Confederate secretary of war, apprised Ben McCulloch that, if he declined the commission, he had the authority to transfer it to whomever he chose. On March 24, deciding not to accept the commission, Ben transferred it to his brother Henry, who was still on the frontier with his regiment. Leaving three companies to occupy Fort Chadbourne, Camp Colorado, and Camp Cooper, Henry McCulloch returned to San Antonio to recruit the additional men needed to give the 1st Texas Mounted Rifles a full complement of ten companies. Departing his command on March 17, he designated Frost as temporary regimental commander and rode south toward San Antonio.[19]

When McCulloch arrived in San Antonio on March 24 to begin recruiting, he found it necessary to organize the state into a Confederate military department. Col. Earl Van Dorn, the assigned Confederate commander, had not yet arrived in Texas. McCulloch immediately began to organize the Department of Texas and search for officers and men qualified to fill his regiment. Although he was the highest-ranking Confederate military officer in the state, McCulloch could not muster his men into permanent Confederate service. For this purpose, Capt. C. L. Sayre, who possessed the authority formally to muster men into the Provisional Confederate States Army, came to Texas from Montgomery, Alabama.[20]

At this early stage, several perplexing issues made raising and training a military force in Texas extremely difficult. Desiring to move quickly, state officials recruited and organized units in a haphazard manner. Henry McCulloch left for the frontier with incomplete companies, hoping to fill the unit rosters later. Both the state and Confederate governments sent volunteer units to the Texas outposts, creating a predicament in terms of command. State lawmakers initially did not provide funding to pay salaries or transportation costs, and commanders were forced to pay for such expenses themselves. Conditions along the frontier and the attitudes of settlers also hampered recruitment, for men did not want to leave their families and property unprotected against Indian raids. Texas managed to station cavalry units on the frontier, but the state's leadership, both military and civilian, had only just begun to realize the magnitude of the responsibilities they had assumed.[21]

CHAPTER 2

"Good Riders and Crack Shots"

When Col. Henry E. McCulloch returned to San Antonio, he faced a monumental task. In the chaos and confusion of a country establishing a new government and preparing to defend its existence, he had to recruit and equip enough men to fill his regiment. Handbills appeared around San Antonio and in several counties in East Texas encouraging men to join McCulloch's command.[1]

McCulloch managed to raise ten companies of mounted volunteers from three distinct sections of Texas. From the area neighboring San Antonio and Austin came Capts. Travis Hill Ashby (Gonzales County), Governor H. Nelson (Bexar County), William A. Pitts (Travis County), and William G. Tobin (Bexar County). James B. "Buck" Barry (Bosque County), Sidney Green Davidson (Bell County), and Thomas C. Frost (Comanche County) enlisted their men from western frontier regions. Milton M. Boggess (Rusk County), James H. Fry (Burleson County), and Milton Webb (Lamar County) answered the call from posters circulated in East Texas. Most company commanders had acquired considerable military experience on the Texas frontier or during the Mexican War and were known by McCulloch. Boggess, Fry, Nelson, Pitts, and Tobin received instructions to form their companies and report to San Antonio by April 15, 1861. Webb took his company to Camp Cooper to await instructions. Barry, Davidson, and Frost, respectively, remained at Camp Cooper, Fort Chadbourne, and Camp Colorado to patrol the frontier.[2]

As these men formed their units, McCulloch sent them his instructions on organization and the caliber of men to be recruited for the regiment. He wanted each company to be composed of one hundred men, organized under a captain, one first lieutenant, two second lieutenants, four sergeants, four corporals, two buglers, a farrier, a blacksmith, and forty-four to sixty-four privates.

The men were to elect their officers, and the newly elected captains would se-
lect the noncommissioned officers. The ranks of lieutenants would be determined by drawing lots. McCulloch told the officers to fill their company rosters
with "hardy men in good health, between eighteen and forty-five years of age."
He favored men who were "good riders and crack shots." He also demanded
men with excellent moral character and "steady, sober habits." Professional
gamblers, drunkards, and "ne'er-do-wells" were not to be enrolled because they
were "unworthy of service." In a newspaper notice, McCulloch flatly stated, "I
do not expect any but gentlemen will be found in the regiment."[3]

He also expressed his very definite opinions concerning the horses and equipment required by his troops. The men needed horses of "good size, health, and
between five and ten years old." Each volunteer must possess or purchase a
good, strong saddle of the "Texas style" along with a blanket and single-reined
bridle and curb bit. He instructed the men to arm themselves with Colt revolvers and serviceable short rifles or double-barreled shotguns if rifles were
not available. Each trooper was to carry a cloth-covered tin canteen that held
at least a half-gallon of water. For sleeping on the ground during long scouts,
each man needed a good, heavy blanket.[4]

McCulloch established his headquarters at San Antonio and selected his
regimental staff. He appointed Capt. Washington "Wash" L. Hill (Travis County)
quartermaster; Capt. John R. King (Wilson County) commissary; Capt. William O. Yager (Guadalupe County) adjutant; and Dr. Henry P. Howard (Bexar
County) surgeon and temporary medical officer at San Antonio. On July 20, Joseph Taylor (Harrison County) became permanent regimental surgeon. Unwilling to command volunteers without their consent, McCulloch stood for election
along with others in the regiment. The men elected him colonel; Thomas C. Frost
lieutenant colonel; and Edward Burleson major. McCulloch instructed his commanders to conduct elections in their companies, if they had not previously done
so, to confirm their captaincies. During the voting, the men of Frost's company
elected James M. Homsley to replace their promoted commander.[5]

At least two of McCulloch's companies had been organized several weeks
before his call for troops. Under an act of the state legislature, Webb formed
his company for frontier defense in December, 1860. Initially mustering only
thirty-seven men, he increased the enrollment to seventy-three by March 20,
when the unit was accepted by the state secession convention. Most of the men
had horses, but not all had arms, even though Lamar County had appropriated funds to equip the company. By April 21, Webb had filled his full complement of one hundred men with volunteers from surrounding counties and was
on his way to Camp Cooper.[6]

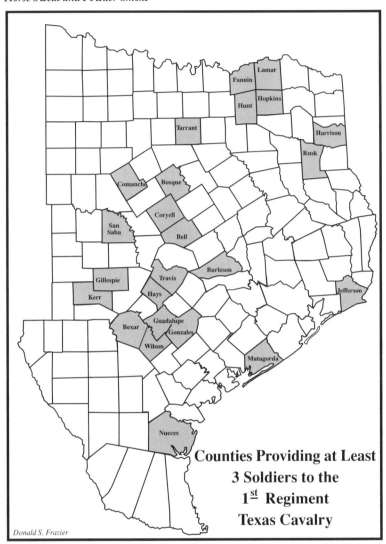

map 1. Counties Providing at Least Three Soldiers to the 1st Regiment of Texas
Cavalry. Map prepared by Don Frazier

Ironically, although Webb's company was organized before most of the regiment, it was the last company accepted into service. On June 15, 1861, although
his company had been patrolling actively for several weeks, Webb finally enlisted the last of his men into the Confederate army at the Hubbard Creek
Station of the Butterfield Stage Line that passed west of Camp Cooper on its
way to California. McCulloch added organized companies to his regimental
roster in the order in which he received letters from prospective commanders.

fig. 2. William J. "Billy" McGowen joined the 1st Texas Cavalry Regiment at the age of nineteen and served throughout the Civil War, rising to the rank of second sergeant. Collection of Stanley McGowen, San Antonio, Texas

He already had incorporated ten companies into the regiment when Webb's company was accepted. William A. Duke, from Jefferson, however, failed to secure a full complement of men. Although Duke stationed some of his troops at Camp Cooper, McCulloch accepted Webb's one hundred men into the regiment and dropped Duke's company from the regimental roll. Because Duke failed to meet his commitment, Webb's unit brought the regiment to full strength with ten companies.[7]

Boggess also formed his company before the call to arms. On January 29, 1861, the chief justice of Rusk County certified that Milton M. Boggess had been elected captain of a company of light infantry numbering sixty men. This was the first of several companies organized from Rusk County, but the Confederate government did not request that the company be called into service until April. By April 6, Boggess had reorganized his unit into a cavalry company, increased the ranks to eighty-one men, and ridden to join McCulloch's regiment. An Austin reporter, inspired by wartime enthusiasm, described the company's April 12 entry into Austin: "As the sun was brightly shining in the heavens," the company entered the city riding their "fine steeds" and had a "beautiful flag unfurled at the head of the company. A heartier or more skillful body of fighting men we have rarely seen." The company paraded down an avenue "under fine discipline," sending a "thrill of delight through every beholder." All of Boggess's men came from Rusk County and furnished their own equipment, except for a small number who were compelled to draw arms from the government.[8]

McCulloch sought men from all regions of Texas for his regiment. His personal reputation certainly enhanced his ability to draw fighting men to his cause. Born in Rutherford County, Tennessee, in December, 1816, McCulloch first came to Texas in 1835 with his brother Ben. He returned to Tennessee to aid his father on the family plantation but in 1838 was back in Texas, joining his brother at Gonzales. In Guadalupe and neighboring counties, McCulloch worked as a surveyor and Texas Ranger. As a lieutenant in John Coffee "Jack" Hays's company, he fought the Comanche Indians in the famous battle at Plum Creek in 1840, and Mexican soldiers retreating from San Antonio at the Battle of Salado Creek in 1842. Henry served as sheriff at Gonzales in 1843 and, during the Mexican War, commanded a volunteer company serving along the frontier. In 1850, he again commanded a force of volunteers protecting the pioneers west of San Antonio from Indian depredations. His reputation led to his election to the state legislature as a representative from Guadalupe County in 1853 and as state senator in 1855. In 1859, McCulloch received an appointment as United States marshal of the Eastern District of Texas. He served in this position until appointed colonel of cavalry in Texas in 1861. Before being offered the commission of colonel, McCulloch concluded that he would remain as marshal "until secession relieves me of it [the position of marshal]"; then "I shall resign at all hazards and take such position in her [Texas] service as her interest and my duty may require."[9]

Like McCulloch, several of the regimental officers were no strangers to the smell of burning powder. They had fought in the Mexican War or against raiding Indians. Some, such as Pitts, had served previously under McCulloch's command. Born in Washington County, Georgia, on October 30, 1830, Pitts moved to Texas with his father, William C. Pitts, in 1846. In April, 1847, he settled at San Marcos, Hayes County, where he worked clearing farmland. On November 5, 1850, he enlisted for twelve months in Henry McCulloch's company of Texas Rangers, where he quickly was promoted to sergeant. Pitts fought in several skirmishes with Indians until a rambunctious horse broke his leg and he went to Seguin to recuperate. For two years, he occupied minor county offices in Guadalupe County. Reenlisting in the Rangers, he served with Capt. James H. Callahan along the Rio Grande in 1857–58. As adjutant, he accompanied Callahan's "Piedras Negras Expedition" into Mexico. In this action, Callahan cited him for devotion to duty and calm under fire. When his messmate fell from his horse with a severe head wound, Pitts lifted the wounded man to his own horse and carried him twenty-seven miles to an army surgeon at Fort Duncan. In 1858, with McCulloch's support, Pitts became sergeant-at-arms of the Texas State Senate. At the end of his term, he again joined the Rangers under John S. Ford and accepted a commission as a lieutenant. On May 12, 1858, Pitts commanded one of four detachments of the force that killed the famous Comanche chief Iron Jacket. Ford complimented Pitts for skill and bravery in the melee. In 1861, McCulloch called on Pitts to raise a company for his regiment. Pitts remained with the regiment until it disbanded in April, 1862, then served the remainder of the war as an ordnance officer at the arsenal in Marshall, Texas.[10]

Davidson came to the regiment with a reputation as one who never shirked his duty to protect Texas' settlers. In 1859, he led a squad of twelve men of the Bell County Minutemen, a small, unpaid volunteer unit that patrolled western Bell and Coryell counties. On September 24, 1859, Davidson joined the Bell County Rovers as a second lieutenant and saw action against Indians later that year. He joined Halley as a lieutenant but soon became captain of his own 110-man company, which was mustered into Confederate service on May 10, 1861.[11]

At least two company commanders had fought in the Mexican War. The first, Webb, was born in Tennessee on June 3, 1812, and married Elizabeth M. Henry on November 7, 1838. In 1846, he moved his family to Texas and fought in the War with Mexico. He later settled in Paris, Texas, and operated a livery stable there until his death in 1901.[12]

In addition to his Mexican War experience, Barry brought to the regiment his vast experience as a frontiersman and Indian fighter. Son of Bryant Buckner Barry and Mary Murill Barry, he was born on December 16, 1821, in North Carolina and came to Texas in 1845. Barry served with a Ranger company under the command of "Jack" Hays and later worked as a surveyor locating headrights in the Robertson land district. Barry again joined the Texas Rangers during the Mexican War and was wounded at Monterrey. After the war, he returned to North Carolina, married Sarah A. Matticks on February 24, 1847, and returned to Texas to settle at Bazette Bluff on the Trinity River. Elected sheriff of Navarro County in 1849, he moved to Corsicana and served two terms as sheriff there before being elected county treasurer and sheriff for another term. In 1856, he moved to Bosque County and settled near Meridian on the Bosque River. In 1847, he clashed several times with Indian bands while attempting to secure the return of property stolen by raiding Indians. In 1859, he joined a minuteman company and was elected lieutenant. This company joined in the effort to force all reservation Indians out of Texas. In October, 1860, Barry organized a company of Meridian volunteers to pursue raiding Indians far out on the Texas plains. When he returned home in 1861, he found a commission from Governor Houston authorizing him to raise a company of state troops for frontier defense. He mustered in his men at Fort Belknap, located at present-day Newcastle in Young County, and assisted in confiscating the fort from Federal troops. He then accepted McCulloch's offer to join the 1st Texas Mounted Rifles and moved his company to Camp Cooper. Barry remained with the regiment until 1862, when he joined a battalion of horsemen organized for frontier defense.[13]

Burleson, whose father served with Sam Houston at the Battle of San Jacinto, had long years of hard-won experience as a Texas pioneer. Born in Tipton County, Tennessee, on November 26, 1826, Burleson moved to Texas in 1830 with his father, Edward Burleson, Sr., and his mother, Sarah Owen. The family first settled in Bastrop County and then moved to Hays County in 1848. Burleson served with Ben McCulloch and the Texas Mounted Volunteers during the Mexican War. In 1856, he joined the Texas Rangers and served two years under the command of John S. "Rip" Ford. Burleson rose to the rank of major in the Rangers before joining the 1st Texas Mounted Rifles in 1861.[14]

Also experienced in frontier warfare, Thomas Claiborne Frost knew the perils of the Texas plains. Born at Bellefont, Alabama, in November, 1833, he came to Texas after earning a law degree from Irving College in Tennessee. Following his arrival in the state in 1854, Frost received a professorship in Latin at Austin College in Huntsville. Having spent a short time reading law in Sam Houston's office, Frost moved westward, where he busied himself as a surveyor in and around Comanche County. In 1856, he was admitted to the bar and practiced law in Belton and San Antonio. He joined the Texas Rangers in 1856 and, as a lieutenant, during the next two years participated in several frays with hostile Indians. As a delegate to the Secession Convention, he signed the Texas Articles of Secession. Because of his experience, character, and fame, Frost was one of the first men McCulloch sought to form a company for his fledgling regiment.[15]

In addition to qualified men, McCulloch urgently needed arms and ammunition for the regiment. As temporary commander of the Department of Texas, he persuaded Gov. Edward Clark and the members of the Military Commission—Samuel Maverick, Dr. Phillip N. Luckett, and Judge Thomas J. Devine—to allow him to manage the disposition of all U.S. arms and ammunition surrendered at San Antonio and the northern frontier posts. He used these supplies to equip his own regiment, as well as other units as they came into service. The arsenal at San Antonio contained 862 rifled muskets, 732 Harper's Ferry rifles, 18 Colt army revolvers, 385 Colt navy revolvers, 213 Sharps carbines, 78 "rifle carbines," 171 artillery sabers, 412 cavalry sabers, and a small

fig. 3. Thomas C. Frost. After the Civil War, Frost became a successful businessman and founded the Frost Bank, which remains an important financial institution in South Texas to this day. Courtesy Frost Bank, San Antonio, Texas

quantity of small-arms cartridges, powder, and ammunition. These stores did not include the quartermaster, ordnance, and medical supplies left at the frontier posts by the departing Federal forces. The sabers did not enthrall Mc-Culloch, as he thought them virtually useless. He said that they might be more useful to the Texas Rangers in rattlesnake-infested country. He did admit that the sabers might be useful if Texas ever trained a regular army.[16]

Even with stores taken from Federal troops, shelter for the men and feed for their horses remained in short supply. Camp Cooper lost some equipment because state troops failed to secure the storehouses. Fire destroyed tents, mice ruined grain, and the Butterfield Stage took most of the feed for its horses. With only a modicum of ammunition and shortages in the areas of shelter and fodder, the regiment lacked sufficient stores in nearly all classes of supply.[17]

During April and May, 1861, McCulloch continued to organize his companies and prepare them to meet the exigencies of rigorous patrolling. On April 22, the staff drew lots to assign company letter designations. These letters also determined the order of rank for the company commanders. Aware that many rank-and-file members of his command were sorely deficient in mounted and dismounted drill, McCulloch appointed training officers for the regiment.[18]

He named Lt. William O. Yager and Lt. I. D. McFarland as primary and assistant regimental training officers. He also warned all officers and men to "lay aside" any prejudices against drill and discipline and to follow instructions issued by these officers. Commanders were encouraged to lead by example and ensure their men's compliance with directives and attention to detail. McCulloch knew that trained horsemen would be indispensable in conducting efficient operations against wily, mounted adversaries. He realized that the training officers were in a thankless position. Many of his men would resist their instructions, and he wanted to make the trainers' work as effective as possible.[19]

Before McCulloch concluded the formation and training of his regiment, Colonel Van Dorn ordered him to deploy his men to protect the frontier settlements west and northwest of San Antonio. Following Van Dorn's instructions, McCulloch planned to station Companies G, I, and K, as well as an artillery battery, at the Red River Camp; Companies B and C at Camp Cooper; Companies D and F at Fort Chadbourne; and Companies A and E at Concho Junction, soon to be known as Camp Concho (present-day San Angelo). Company H was to journey to Fort Phantom Hill, near the junction of Elm Creek and the Clear Fork in present Jones County, while the regimental headquarters initially began operation at Camp Cooper. Service records indicate that Companies D and E established a joint detachment at Fort Mason, on Post Oak Hill in present Mason County, from June through September, 1861. Although all units were not in place until July, by the end of April, 1861, three companies of the 1st Texas Mounted Rifles had begun extended scouting on the frontier. Furthermore, commencing with Van Dorn's order, the regimental area of operations was expanded several hundred miles. The regiment's area of responsibility began at the confluence of the Big Wichita River with the Red River in the north and extended to the meeting of the west and main branches of the Concho River in the south. By the fall of 1861, the patrol area extended south of Fort McKavett, near today's Menard, to Camp Verde, near present Kerrville, in Kerr County, west of San Antonio. The extended patrol line covered well over five hundred statute miles and encompassed more than thirty thousand square miles—a formidable assignment for a single regiment.[20]

Before the remainder of the 1st Texas Mounted Rifles left San Antonio, Van Dorn assigned it an additional mission. After the events at Fort Sumter and Lincoln's call for seventy-five thousand volunteers, both the Confederate War Department and Texas authorities agreed to abrogate all agreements made with Brevet Major General Twiggs. Confederate Secretary of War Leroy Pope Walker transmitted orders to capture all remaining Federal troops in Texas, disarm them, and treat them as prisoners of war. Several companies of Union troops were marching overland from Fort Bliss and the far western areas of the state, attempting to reach the coast for evacuation. Van Dorn ordered McCulloch's six companies of cavalry who were mustering in at San Antonio to intercept and capture these Federal forces. On May 9, Col. I. V. D. Reeve, leading over three hundred men of the 8th U.S. Infantry, confronted by McCulloch's mounted Texans, surrendered his command at San Lucas Springs, sixteen miles west of San Antonio. State troops assumed responsibility for the Union prisoners, and the 1st Texas Cavalry moved on toward fulfilling its primary mission—protecting northwestern Texas from marauding Indians and Federal incursions from north of the Red River.[21]

As McCulloch moved his units to the far-flung posts of Texas, Van Dorn issued an order commending Texas volunteers for their spirit in supporting the Confederacy. On May 13, Van Dorn singled out McCulloch and his commanders for possessing "the true spirit of brave men who know how to appreciate a soldier's honor." He stressed that their quick marshaling of troops to take command of the Federal posts had prevented unnecessary bloodshed among the Federal troops who had protected Texas' settlements for many years. Van Dorn lauded the Texans for their lack of exultation over the departure of the Federal forces. He knew that, if the volunteers of Texas were "called out under arms to contend with an invading force sent against them from the north," there would be "no regrets, no affection, and no disparity of numbers"; "death to the foe and victory after the fight" would be the aims of every true Texan. Van Dorn's words proved prophetic for the 1st Texas Mounted Rifles. Men of the regiment were beginning a tour of duty that would pit them against Indians, as well as against Union troops bent upon invasion, rapine, and destruction of Texas and its people.[22]

CHAPTER 3

"Chastising the Ruthless Savages"

On June 2, 1861, McCulloch and Burleson rode from Red River Station to Fort Cobb Indian Reservation, Indian Territory, to convene a council with the native inhabitants. They sought to reassure the Indians about the reasons for the presence of Texas troops along the Red River. The Texans defined their regiment's mission as protecting Texas from invasions of hostile forces and assured the Indians that it did not pose a threat to them as long as they remained peaceful. As the two grim-faced officers explained, however, the 1st Texas Mounted Rifles would protect Texans against any Indian raiders from across the Red River and would follow their trails onto the reservation. McCulloch promised not to make indiscriminate attacks but to seek out the "actual depredators." He affirmed his friendship and protection for friendly Indians but vowed that his men unhesitatingly would "administer merited chastisement to hostiles." He explained this in a letter to Van Dorn on June 8.[1]

Because departing United States troops had told the Indians that the Texans would massacre all who remained on the reservation, McCulloch continued, most tribal members had fled with their women and children. Only a few Tonkawas and Comanches remained at Fort Cobb. Several Tonkawas offered to serve as scouts for McCulloch, who planned to use them on future patrols. About 2,500 Indians roamed freely across the reservation, but agents had no real idea of the true number moving on and off Fort Cobb, he told Van Dorn.[2]

McCulloch considered the tribes "dirty and lazy" and unimproved by white contact. In McCulloch's opinion, life at Fort Cobb had failed to civilize them because of the agents' malfeasance; most Indian agents and white men associated with the tribes lacked character. According to his view, men of "moral worth" and officers who would trust and treat the Indians with consideration, while conducting themselves properly, should be appointed as agents. He believed that men who would ferret out and destroy what he called "villainous establishments stuck away in the bushes" freely selling liquor to the Indians should be placed in positions of authority on reservations. Only agents who would perform their duties without favoritism and thought of personal gain could keep the Indians satisfied. He wrote confidently that men of this caliber would apply fair measure and weights in food contracts. "Only sober honest men should be appointed among them" instead of men who gratified their sensual appetites, "losing themselves in whisky and adultery with the squaws." Indians sorely needed Christian guidance, not lessons in becoming "drunkards and whores."[3]

Regulations required that Indians residing on the reservation receive regularly scheduled rations of beef, corn, salt, and flour, but the Indians claimed to be shortchanged on all provisions issued. McCulloch agreed that the Indians were being swindled and believed they would hunt freely to feed their families. Both McCulloch and Burleson knew that, most certainly, some of these bands would ride south to hunt and raid in Texas. A large party of "wild Comanches" recently had stopped at Fort Cobb and pilfered scrap iron, steel, and files from the blacksmith shop for arrowheads and other weapons. Their young, belligerent leader spoke of hunting buffalo along the Brazos River in Texas and raiding south into Mexico for horses. Armed with rifles, these well-mounted warriors had numerous prisoners. They also had helped themselves to ammunition from reservation stores before riding off to the southwest. Because of these stories, McCulloch warned Van Dorn, he did not believe that the Comanches intended to live on any reservation. His guide, Mr. Lyons, had lived with Comanches for many years and asserted that Comanches stayed on reservations only at their convenience. According to Lyons's experience, Comanches raided into Texas whenever they pleased.[4]

While the two Texans remained at Fort Cobb, several tribes, including Chickasaws, Choctaws, Wacos, Wichitas, and some smaller bands, signed a mutual friendship treaty. The treaty supposedly included Texas and the other Confederate states. McCulloch nevertheless harbored doubts as to any serious intent on the part of the Indians. In his letter, McCulloch promised Van Dorn to treat Indians as they deserved, "hostile or friendly."[5]

McCulloch added that his main concern was protection of the Texas frontier. He firmly believed that a provisioning program for Indians, if properly administered, would be the cheapest and best mode of protecting vulnerable Texas settlements. He cautioned that more effective and honest men had to be put in charge before such a plan could work at Fort Cobb. The present reservation administration was a farce, with Indians debased and mistreated instead of being "moralized, Christianized or civilized," he concluded.[6]

White denizens of the Texas plains knew that roving bands of Comanches and Kiowas inhabited the headwaters of the Colorado, Brazos, and Canadian rivers. These nomadic raiders followed the small canyons of that country to infiltrate raiding parties into the settlements. Indian war parties used the Wichita and Pease rivers along the northern frontier for the same purpose. When pressured, large war parties scattered in the broken, irregular country and lost their pursuers. These Indians so devastated the frontier that horses could not be found to provide remounts for the regiment.

Wily horse thieves also raided the regiment's *remudas.* Milton M. Boggess reported a stampede and three horses missing from his Phantom Hill post. Protection and conservation of all available remounts became increasingly important. Long campaigns over rough, dry terrain broke down even the best horses, especially in the blistering heat of Texas summers. McCulloch repeatedly exhorted his commanders to exercise prudence and vigilance in posting guards. He advised them to apply "great caution and care" to prevent horses and mules from being stampeded and stolen.[7]

In another letter to Van Dorn, McCulloch listed the profusion of Indian bands his Mounted Riflemen faced in northwestern Texas. Using information gained from his trip to Fort Cobb, he described the various Comanche bands and their probable locations:

- "Uts-is-tib-e-way" (probably Kutsueka, or Buffalo Eaters), living on the upper Canadian and Arkansas rivers, estimated at between 4,000 and 5,000 men, women, and children.
- "No-co-mies" (Noyika or Noconee, Antelope Eaters), listed as 1,500 to 2,000 strong, lived around the headwaters of the Red and Brazos rivers, sometimes drifting south to the Rio Grande.
- "Cast-ta-ta-kers" (possibly Kwahihekehnuh, or Sun Shades on Their Backs, part of Antelope Eaters); 2,000 to 2,500 lived interspersed with the previous group and the "Fu-nu-mas."
- "Tunumas" or "Funumas" (probably Taniama, or Liver Eaters) numbered 1,200 to 1,700.
- "Pene-takeres" (Penateka, or Honey Eaters); about 600 of an ¡estimated 1,500 dwelled at Fort Cobb.
- "Yappies" (Yapparikas, or Root Eaters); about 1,000 lived high up on Rio Pecos.

- "Po-ho-hies" (possibly Pohoi, or Wild Sage), Wind River Shoshones who joined western Comanche bands.
- "Oquiu" or "Oquiax" (possibly a subgroup of the Honey Eaters) contained many young warriors.

To this list of Indians whom his regiment confronted, McCulloch added the "Ki-o-ways" (Kiowas), a large and very "manlike tribe"; other smaller tribes; and renegades. Because of the Indians' propensity for fighting, Texas had to fear the nomadic warriors who "depredated on Texans in a most rapacious manner."[8]

To counter such numerous and widely dispersed adversaries, McCulloch deployed his meager forces among the far-flung posts on the northwestern frontier. He distributed his companies to all recently abandoned Federal posts, including the old 2nd U.S. Cavalry fort at Phantom Hill, far out on the western plains. Filling a gap in his patrol line, he established a twenty-five man garrison at Fort Mason, commanded by 1st Lt. Samuel G. Ragsdale of Tobin's Company D. To protect the widely scattered Texas settlements against marauding Indians, McCulloch issued specific patrol directives to his unit commanders. He ordered Barry at Camp Cooper to establish a patrol line to Willow Springs, about halfway along the road to Red River Station. He directed Company C to establish a camp at a water source two or three miles north of the Brazos. The regimental commander further directed that a detachment of twenty men and a lieutenant should occupy the camp and be relieved by similar detachments every two weeks. Weekly scouts, beginning on Friday mornings, left both stations to meet the next day. McCulloch added that the detachment should send a squad to Willow Springs every Sunday, where it would spend the night with scouts from the Red River camp, at the junction of the Red and Big Wichita rivers in Montague County. McCulloch ordered Webb to change the name of Red River Station to Camp Jackson, honoring a Confederate officer killed in Virginia. In addition to patrolling to Willow Springs, Webb's orders included repulsing Indian or Federal incursions from north of the Red River.[9]

The remaining companies of the regiment received similar orders. Lacking sufficient forces for large punitive expeditions, McCulloch instructed all of his commanders to coordinate their patrols and pursuits of Indians with commanders of other camps, with the senior officer to command any joint force. McCulloch charged his captains to "throw out" scouts from the northwest to the southeast, to prevent Indians from penetrating the regimental patrol line.

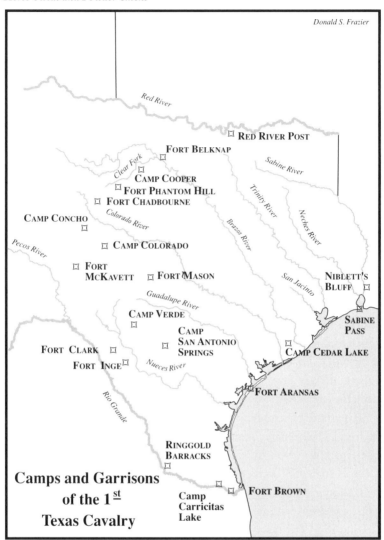

Donald S. Frazier

**Camps and Garrisons
of the 1ˢᵗ
Texas Cavalry**

map 2. Camps and Garrisons of the 1st Texas Cavalry. Map prepared by
Don Frazier

He encouraged his command to "severely chastise" any Indians found—that
is, shoot them on sight. His company commanders also were responsible for
the safety of any wagons or wagon trains passing through their area of operations, and detachments from various camps provided security escorts for wagons moving from one post to another. In this manner, both civilian and military
traffic passed along the entire length of the regimental area of operations with
enough firepower to guard against Indian attacks.[10]

Following McCulloch's instructions, the regiment spared no effort in pursuing hostile Indians and in protecting frontier settlers. Orders stressed that officers and detachment commanders should never abandon pursuit of Indians as long as men and horses were able to continue. "Hostiles" guilty of any aggression should be caught "at all hazards." Directives often reiterated the necessity of following all Indian trails, no matter where they led. Officers also were instructed to investigate any reports of stolen horses and mules taken into Indian Territory. McCulloch believed that any success against livestock raiders lay in relentless pursuit, and he warned officers that they would be held in neglect of duty if they failed to seek out fleeing Indians. He added that he would accept no excuse for failure to comply with his orders. He reminded his men that the only reason they had for crossing the Red River was in actual pursuit of raiders.[11]

In deploying the Mounted Rifles, McCulloch reassigned some critical personnel away from patrol duties. Although he needed all his officers afield, he realized that his quartermaster and commissary officers needed to be present at regimental headquarters. He relieved Hill and King of company duties and ordered them to San Antonio, while he gave 2d Lt. J. M. Frost the responsibility for all supply wagons headed for Red River Station. The lieutenant's supply column included forty-two pack mules, wagons, and other equipment. When Van Dorn arrived in San Antonio, he countermanded McCulloch's order and sent Hill and King back to their companies. Apparently Van Dorn thought his own logistical staff efficiently could supply all units in his department.[12]

Most patrols produced only horse sweat and saddle sores, but tenacious pursuit of Comanche raiding parties occasionally placed the Mounted Riflemen in great danger. From Fort Chadbourne, Capt. Sidney Green Davidson wrote his wife that he had plenty to do, as the Indians were "thick" in his section. On June 23, Lieutenant Colonel Frost led a combined detachment of seventy-five men from Davidson's and Tobin's companies to an area five miles south of Big Spring. As the men trailed a party of cattle-stealing Indians along the headwaters of the Colorado River, they spied at least eight Indians riding away from a recently abandoned camp. Frost immediately formed his men into line and charged the retreating Comanches. The chase covered "six or seven miles." Because of fatigued horses, the command became strung out over the prairie. Davidson, better mounted than most, spurred his lathered horse into a run and closed the gap between himself and the Indians. As he neared the dodging warriors, he began firing rapidly with his revolver, forcing a pair of them to dismount and fight. In the melee, one of the Comanches shot Davidson through the heart; as the dying officer raced past, the other fired two arrows into his back. According to William N. Alexander of Tobin's company, "Only about a dozen of our men were able to come up to the Indians." Several of these men following the captain opened fire, killing one of his assailants and wounding the other, who managed to escape on Davidson's horse. Nearby, Pvt. Andrew J. McCarty of Tobin's company, according to some reports, died in a similar action during the skirmish. He and three others chased a "young chief" for six or seven miles. When McCarty closed on the young Comanche, he turned and shot the trooper out of his saddle.[13]

In 1908, Alexander recounted a rendition of McCarty's death that differed from other sources. Alexander wrote that the young Indian was wounded and "several of the boys took in after him," forcing the young warrior "to run into a thicket." Failing to "get a glimpse" of the Indian, McCarty shouted, "Boys there is only one way to get him and that is to go in after him. I'm going into this thicket and get him." As McCarty approached the thicket, the Indian "darted out and rushed upon him." With an arm broken by a bullet, the Indian could not draw a bow and charged the Texan with only an arrow in one hand. McCarty, known to be "a excellent marksman and endowed with wonderful nerve," emptied his revolver at the onrushing Indian. After his last shot, the private hurled his useless pistol at the Indian's head. "With the frenzy of a dying savage," the warrior seized his antagonist and "drove his arrow threw [*sic*] the heart of brave Mike [*sic*] McCarty." Both men fell dead, side by side. Surprised by the Indian's sudden action and with their line of fire blocked by McCarty, the other men failed to shoot during the Indian's rush.[14]

After the fray, Frost's command counted the casualties on both sides and buried their dead. His men reported only two Indian bodies found but assured their commander that several others must have died of wounds. According to the men, many of the warriors rode away supported by their companions and clutching bloody wounds. The cavalrymen sorrowfully buried both Davidson and McCarty near Big Spring. With only a hatchet as a tool, the troopers scratched out shallow graves and tenderly wrapped their dead in blankets for burial. They piled "a heap of rude stones" over the graves as the only monument to their fallen comrades.[15]

Confrontations with this aggressive band of Comanches did not end until the next day. Because his command's horses were exhausted, Frost returned to Big Spring and established a temporary camp. Shortly before dark, seventeen Indians appeared on a small rise south of the camp and, in broken Spanish, "gave us an all around cussin" and challenged the Texans to fight. The leader of this group rode Davidson's stolen horse. Frost, with a few others, rode to a rise north of the Texans' camp. From this vantage point, they observed a large party of Indians to the east of their position and a larger number behind the rise on which the taunting Comanches sat astride their prancing ponies. Frost's guide, Jim Mulkey, estimated the entire party of Indians at between 125 and 150—a number sufficient to annihilate a patrol of about forty fatigued troopers. Alexander claimed that he prevailed on Frost to allow him "to take one shot at the Painted Scoundrel" who rode Davidson's horse. Alexander explained that he and Frost estimated the distance at 700 yards. "I dismounted, raised my gunsight to 500 yards, took good aim, and cut him down." Alexander missed, however, as his minié ball "knocked up the dust almost under his horse." After this incident, Frost prudently returned to camp and prepared for the worst. During the night, the Indians fired sporadically into the camp, failing to inflict any damage. A small party of Comanches attempted to infiltrate the perimeter and steal the pack mules; but alert guards, with a heavy volley of well-aimed fire, persuaded the Indians to remain away from the herd.[16]

The Texans had traveled across the sun-scorched plains for six days, forcing their horses to live on shriveled grass and little water. Low on ammunition and with his mounts in poor condition, Frost could only return to Fort Chadbourne and hope for better results at a later date. McCulloch lauded Frost's decision and "moral courage" not to be taunted into pursuing a well-mounted party of Indians that outnumbered his command by at least four to one. He later commented that, while not a brilliant engagement, it had driven the Indians away from the settlements and reminded the Comanches that they could not raid with impunity.[17]

A few days later, a small patrol rode into another desperate situation with dire consequences. On June 26, a ten-man patrol from Company C, led by Cpl. Thomas J. Erkenbreck, clashed with forty-one Comanches near the Little Wichita River between Camps Cooper and Jackson. All the warriors carried rifles and had tied themselves to their horses to prevent capture if they were killed or wounded. The Indians charged the Texans across the open plain, but concentrated fire repulsed their initial attack. Erkenbreck's men took cover, either in a shallow depression or behind their horses, fighting off sporadic attacks for over five hours. The patrol exhausted most of its ammunition during the fight, and only the Comanches' distaste for protracted engagements saved the small detail. The war party finally rode away, leaving the cavalry with seven men and one horse wounded and five horses killed. The corporal's men could account for only two Indians definitely killed, but they suspected that several others rode away with mortal wounds. McCulloch congratulated the troopers for the "noble and gallant manner" in which they had conducted themselves. He also offered his sympathy and hope for a speedy recovery to those wounded

fig. 4. Comanche warriors such as these contested the encroachment upon the Texas plains of an ever-increasing number of white settlers. The Comanches were not forced onto reservations until 1874. Courtesy Gene Swinson, Baird, Texas

in the fray, but James McKee and William Kelly later succumbed to wounds received during the encounter. McCulloch later chided his entire command for wasting ammunition needlessly; he assured his men that more Indians might have been killed if the patrol had not run short of cartridges. Shortages of ammunition plagued the regiment during its entire service.[18]

McCulloch remained extremely busy with duties other than regimental command. To protect the frontier settlements and Rio Grande crossings, Van Dorn placed all forces in the field, including infantry and artillery, under McCulloch. During the summer, McCulloch constantly shuttled from post to post and back to San Antonio. From early August to mid-September, he again temporarily assumed command of the Department of Texas, as Brig. Gen. Paul O. Hebert replaced Van Dorn. During his absences, McCulloch allowed Frost and Burleson unfettered authority to conduct regimental operations.[19]

In late June, McCulloch ordered Burleson to lead an extended reconnaissance to the north and west, to push Indian raiders away from the line of camps. The regimental commander augmented Burleson's force at Camp Jackson with forty men from each of Boggess's and Barry's companies. These well-equipped men arrived with thirty days' rations and ammunition, riding the best mounts available. McCulloch cautioned Burleson that the government wanted to cultivate good will on the part of any Indians displaying friendly intentions. The major's instructions included "being as prudent as possible with Indians who professed friendship." According to his orders, however, the Fort Cobb Reservation inhabitants lacked permission to cross the Red River into Texas. Burleson's extensive instructions included seizing any horse herds discovered during the reconnaissance and considering any Indians on Texas soil to be enemies. His force was to "chastise any and all parties of Indians found." As previously promised, Burleson recruited a band of thirty to fifty friendly Tonkawas as scouts. He had no authority to pay them, but he provided them rations and ammunition, along with spoils taken from hostile Indians.[20]

McCulloch, hoping to treat with hostile Comanche and Kiowa bands, decided to accompany the expedition. On June 28, McCulloch and Burleson departed from Camp Jackson with an effective strength of 230 soldiers and Tonkawas. Guided by Charles Goodnight, the noted tracker, Ranger scout, and pioneering stock raiser, who led the Indian scouts, the command traveled up the Red River and crossed over to the Washita above Antelope Butte. Along the way, scouts discovered three hundred abandoned indigenous camps that had been deserted for several days. From the campsites, McCulloch's force continued down the Canadian to the Washita and then on to another major trail some fifteen miles below the buttes. According to the Tonkawas, the trails indicated that Comanche and Kiowa war parties traveled at will between the reservation and Texas.[21]

As with most military operations, everything did not proceed as planned. A private accidentally shot himself, and the patrol was forced to halt while a detail evacuated him. Other unforeseen events prevented Burleson from returning all the stolen horses found on the patrol. In late July, his men discovered a Comanche camp with about a thousand horses that Burleson suspected of being stolen from Texas. These Comanches possessed a letter stating that they should not be disturbed, as they "someday intended to make peace." Brig. Gen. Albert Pike, Confederate Indian Commissioner and commander of the reservation, had given the wandering Comanches a letter of protection. He also had sent offers of protection to roving bands of Kiowas. Burleson ordered the Comanches to return to the Fort Cobb Reservation immediately. In Burleson's opinion, Pike indicated his prejudice against Texas by aiding the Indians. Burleson did not believe the Indians intended to make peace. In a report to McCulloch, he wrote, "The red devils go on and off the reservation at will to kill and scalp. A scout is a waste of time if Pike keeps Indians posted on our movements." He also found that the reservation agents often furnished the Indians with ammunition, supposedly for hunting. Referring to the Indian agent's conduct, McCulloch retorted to Burleson, "General Pike has blocked the game on us as far as Indian operations are concerned." Disgusted, Burleson turned back toward Camp Jackson. With his horses and mules almost broken down and his weary men ill with fever, Burleson had no choice but to end the expedition. The patrol discovered good winter campsites along the Washita, the only positive accomplishment of the long scout.[22]

During the early summer, protected by several of his companies, McCulloch managed to meet with several Comanche and Kiowa chiefs but, because of long-standing animosity between the Indians and Texans, concluded no agreements. Comanche chiefs Red Bear and Eagle Chief, as well as Lone Wolf, Satank, and Satanta of the Kiowas, refused to agree to any terms with the Confederacy. These Indian warriors plainly stated that they were preparing to fight the Texans and steal from them.[23]

On July 29, Barry and thirty-two men rode to meet Burleson northwest of Camp Cooper. In the shimmering heat, his men ran headlong into about seventy Comanches, and a running fight ensued. The pursuit covered over fifteen miles, and at least twelve Indians were killed. Although well-armed and painted for war, the warriors scattered when the Texans killed the war party's leader, who wore a coat taken from a Federal soldier. Barry lost Pvts. E. J. Weatherby, "Tiff" Conneley, and Bud Lane, and seven more men were wounded. Private McKay later died of wounds. Barry's detachment dug graves with butcher knives and buried their fallen comrades in frontier graves. The skirmishes caused the Comanches and Kiowas to move northward, away from the aggressive Texans. Comanches and Kiowas, nevertheless, continued to send small raiding parties into the state. From Montague County in the north to San Saba and Mason counties in the south, horses and mules continued to disappear.[24]

During their raids on Texas settlements, Comanche and Kiowa war parties killed and scalped numerous isolated civilians. In early May, thirty Comanches burned the stage station on Grape Creek thirty-five miles west of Fort Chadbourne, badly wounding Joel Pennington in the process. A warrior fired a shotgun loaded with slugs into Pennington's face at point-blank range. The tough frontiersman, though horribly wounded, survived after being treated by Dr. Jesse Denson, Fort Chadbourne's physician. The same month, ten Indians, driving a "caballada" of stolen horses, discovered two men, named Carmeans and Tankersley, riding near Clear Creek in Brown County some twenty miles from Camp Colorado. These men had refused a military escort and, as a result, died when the Indians surrounded and killed the two hapless travelers.[25]

As 1861 passed, other settlers fell victim to Indian war parties. During the late summer, a raiding band of nine Comanches came upon William Youngblood splitting rails near his ranch south and west of Jacksboro. Soon a bloody scalp adorned the bridle of a young warrior. A hastily gathered band of nearby ranchers trailed the Indians for several miles and, although several ranchers received slight wounds, avenged Youngblood's death. They killed at least two of the raiders and brought the rancher's scalp home to be buried with his body.[26]

In two separate instances along Grindstone Creek, in the vicinity of Youngblood's ranch, stray bands of warriors killed John Killen and wounded his companion with several well-placed arrows. A few days later, Mrs. John Brown was killed, probably by the same marauders, as she strolled toward a neighbor's farm. Another band of roving Indians killed Samuel Kuykendall of Erath County when he left home with a friend to search for wandering oxen. The raiding party chased the unarmed Kuykendall into a bog, "filled his body with arrows," and scalped and stripped the hapless stockman.[27]

McCulloch had too large an area of responsibility; despite his most carefully conceived stratagems, some warriors managed to escape his patrols. Moses Jackson and almost his entire family became victims of Indian raiders in the fall of 1861. Jackson and two neighbors, Mr. Kirkpatrick and Mr. King, had agreed to meet on Pecan Bayou in Coleman County for a group picnic and to cut planks from the abundant large pecan trees there. The next day, Jackson's friends heard several shots near their meetingplace but thought them to be fired by hunters. Searching for cattle the following afternoon, Jackson's friends happened upon his wagon, standing in the road near the bayou. Jackson and two of his children lay dead in the wagon, while the bodies of his wife and daughter were found a short distance away. The raiders first had shot Jackson and then dragged his wife and fourteen-year-old daughter from the wagon and cut their throats. The Indians then cut the throats of his four-year-old daughter and seven-year-old son and left their heads hanging outside the wagons with their bodies draped inside. All had been scalped. The raiders rode off with Jackson's eleven-year-old son and nine-year-old daughter as captives but, for some unaccountable reason, left them in a stand of trees. Several days later, a rescue party found the children walking back home.[28]

On October 14, John Williams and several "cowhands" rode through the northern sections of Llano County, gathering cattle to fill a beef contract for the Confederate army. As the Texans separated, searching for cattle, a large group of Indians attacked the horsemen and chased the cowboys through the brush.

Most of the men escaped, but Ed King, riding a mule, fell behind the others. Williams wheeled his mount around and raced to aid his employee, who was attempting to fight off several warriors. Amid the swirling dust and war cries, the Indians shot down both Texans and rode away brandishing fresh scalps.[29]

Five days later, twenty-two Comanches struck another party of Texans riding near the headsprings of the Lampasas River. During a savage hand-to-hand struggle, Robert Carter disappeared, and several other men received critical wounds. Not until three days later did a search party find the scalped body of the slain Carter.[30]

Hunger, as well as the regiment's policy of aggressive pursuit, induced several Comanche bands to explore conditions for asylum at the Fort Cobb Reservation. Jess Marshal, the fort's adjutant, wrote to McCulloch that several bands of Comanches had sent representatives to the reservation to ascertain if it might be possible to negotiate a treaty with the whites, especially the hated Texans. Comanche women reported that several thousand Indians camped within seventy miles of Fort Cobb might come in under favorable conditions. According to the women, there was a severe drought in Texas, and their families were starving. Tribal leaders indicated that they wanted a treaty so they could receive the same rations of beef and corn as the native inhabitants of the reservation. Although the Indians indicated that they would come in ten to fifteen days, Marshal did not trust their "protestation of friendship." He warned McCulloch that a concentration of warriors might be headed for Texas.[31]

Through the end of summer and into the fall of 1861, the regiment continued to scout between the Red and the Concho rivers. Patrols occasionally ventured all the way south to the Rio Grande. During these extended reconnaissances, the troops glimpsed a few small parties of Indians, who prudently remained out of effective rifle range.[32]

Continued sightings of these small bands led McCulloch to order a regimental campaign against the persistent miscreants. An enlisted man described the planned fall operations: "And should old 'Abe' not send us 'work' from Kansas it is intended to make a grand campaign of the entire regiment against the red rascals in the autumn." McCulloch organized expeditions to leave Fort Chadbourne and Camps Concho and Colorado on September 1. Commanders of Fort Phantom Hill and Camp Cooper were to begin operations on September 12, with the Camp Jackson commander commencing operations three days later. The regimental commander instructed his subordinates to have every horse shod and everything in readiness for an extended operation. His arrangements included supply trains carrying at least sixty days' rations for each trooper. To transport necessary sustenance and ammunition, McCulloch allotted one wagon and ten pack mules for every fifty men. He advised that, if quarter-masters needed panniers (large baskets), they construct them from rawhide obtained from beef suppliers. He also reminded his officers to insure that every horse had two picket ropes and every mule a stake pin.[33]

The order included arrangements for arms and ammunition, as well as marching directives. McCulloch wanted every man to have one hundred rounds of ammunition and all weapons in serviceable condition. Because regimental members carried a variety of weapons, no standard issue of ammunition would suffice for an entire unit. In order that the regimental quartermaster could issue sufficient ammunition of proper types, McCulloch directed his commanders to report all classes of arms and ammunition on hand. Lastly, he assured each captain that marching orders, including further directives and explanations of rendezvous points, would reach them before operations commenced.[34]

Barry's orders included additional instructions from Burleson, along with supplies forwarded from regimental stores. Burleson mandated that seventy-five men be sent to maintain Barry's camp on the Brazos during the campaign. He reiterated the regimental commander's instructions concerning horses, arms, and rations. To bolster Company C's firepower, Barry received twenty-five percussion rifles, cartridge boxes, waist belts, and all other necessary accouterments. Since many of Barry's men carried shotguns, the arms issue included twenty-five pounds of buckshot, as well as fifty pounds of lead for casting bullets.[35]

Unfortunately, surviving records do not indicate the results of the September campaign, but an October outing proved eventful. On October 3, Burleson apprised Barry that Regimental Sergeant Major Wiggs recently had returned from Fort Cobb with reliable intelligence concerning a large party of Comanches. Wiggs's sources believed that the war party planned to cross into Texas and continue toward the headwaters of Beaver Creek. Barry's instructions included mounting a patrol of fifty picked men to sally up the Wichita to Beaver Creek and intercept the invading Comanches. Burleson bade Barry to remain on patrol for at least ten days and to cover 125 miles to the southwest of Camp Cooper if possible. All scouts and express riders were to be warned about the large war party. Burleson also cautioned Barry to keep his men "in close order" and to guard against surprise, as there "was no telling when the enemy might pounce upon you."[36]

Barry and Boggess assembled a sixty-one-man detachment to investigate the intelligence reports. The patrol evidently lasted longer than ten days. On November 1, along the Pease River, six troopers encountered twelve Indian scouts and held them at bay until the remainder of the patrol joined the fracas. The entire war party fled; in a long running battle, Barry's command killed ten of the Comanches. Several troopers believed that a large number of warriors had suffered mortal wounds, but others helped them escape. The Indians wounded two of Barry's men and downed several horses. The Texans made good the loss of the horses, however, by capturing several reliable Indian mounts. McCulloch cited the action in a circular that read: "Great credit to the men on this scout. The patience with which they bore privation and hardships, and gallantry displayed by them in the fight deserve commendation. Thanks from the regiment for chastising the ruthless savages and for the regiment's first decided victory."[37]

Shortly after leaving to seek out the raiding Comanches, Barry received a directive quite different from typical orders. A dispatch from regimental headquarters instructed him to provide an escort and rations of flour and salt meat for one hundred Seminoles passing from Camp Colorado to Fort Cobb. According to his instructions, the Indians, under the direction of Charles L. Neebken[?], were to be treated kindly and care taken to protect their rights and feelings. Barry was admonished to insure that the Indians did not bother citizens or their property during their journey across North Texas. Barry had to provide rations and escorts because the regiment was moving into winter quarters and the troops at Camp Jackson were leaving that post.[38]

In October, the companies moved into winter quarters. The horses, mostly in very poor shape, needed a long rest. The regimental officers hoped that the Indians would follow their usual practice and "hole up" for the winter. Captain Boggess's Company H moved from Phantom Hill into Camp Cooper, along with Barry's Company C, which also was wintering there. McCulloch's regimental headquarters and staff moved to Fort Mason, while Pitts's Company B remained at Camp Colorado and soon was joined for the winter by Homsley's Company G. Nelson's Company E initially remained at Camp Concho, while both Tobin's Company D and Robert A. Myers's Company F stayed at Fort Chadbourne until the spring of 1862. Myers had replaced the slain Davidson the previous August. By the end of March, 1862, Company F occupied Fort Inge and had a detachment of twenty-three men commanded by Lt. James S. Bigham at Camp Verde. Ashby's Company I and Webb's Company K occupied Fort Belknap. Fry's Company A moved into Fort McKavett during October and on to Camp Verde the following month. Company E transferred from Concho to Fort McKavett sometime in late October or early November. McCulloch attempted to lay in stores for the winter at his camps, but little was forthcoming in the way of forage and ammunition. The regiment did receive small amounts of medicines and quartermaster stores in late fall and winter.[39]

During the winter months, elections, along with daily drilling and routine patrols, occupied most of the men's time. Restrictions prevented undue use of horses and so spared the fatigued animals, unless in hot pursuit of Indians. Some abuses occurred, nevertheless, and will be discussed in later chapters. Yearning to "see fighting with the Yankees," Burleson tendered his resignation in October. He gave McCulloch two months' notice to fill the vacancy, but delays caused the postponement of any elections until February 1, 1862. Tobin and Barry contested for major, with Barry winning in a come-from-behind victory. To replace Barry, George E. Bushong defeated F. H. Combs for the captaincy of Company C.[40]

In November, 1861, the Department of Texas gave the regiment an assignment that none of the men relished. A large number of Union prisoners of war, many of whom the regiment had captured earlier at San Lucas Springs, came under control of the 1st Mounted Rifles. General Hebert ordered the prisoners moved from Camp Verde near San Antonio to Camps Colorado and Cooper and Forts Chadbourne and Belknap. A wagon train from San Antonio delivered fifty POWs to each of the posts. Several family members accompanied each group of prisoners, making the assignment even more loathsome to the Texans. Stephan Schwartz, one of the prisoners, remembered that at least ten wives of 8th U.S. Infantry band members worked as laundresses at Camp Verde. At least once each day, at roll calls conducted at reveille and retreat, a commissioned officer supervised the accounting of prisoners and their families.[41]

Along with the prisoners came orders governing their confinement and treatment. All prisoners and family members had to remain within one quarter-mile of the center of camp. If any prisoners escaped, the post commander was to take all measures necessary to recover them. Upon recapture, all returned prisoners were to be put into close confinement. McCulloch believed that this policy toward the prisoners would deter escape attempts. Men at posts that housed prisoners were to wear their sidearms at all times during the day and keep all firearms close to them at night. Men guarding prisoners were to follow all regulations regarding safekeeping and good order of prisoners. Commanders stressed humane treatment, proper rations, and protection of prisoners at all times. In April, 1862, to the immense relief of the cavalrymen, the departmental commander transferred all regimental POWs to Fort Mason to be guarded by state troops.[42]

In December, 1861, McCulloch assumed command of the Western Military Sub-District of Texas, which included all posts west, northwest, and south of San Antonio, including Victoria and Saluria, on the eastern end of

Matagorda Island in Calhoun County. McCulloch's headquarters were in San Antonio, and he remained away from his regiment in its final months of service. McCulloch elevated Frost to regimental commander until the companies' one-year enlistments expired in April, 1862.[43]

In mid-winter, several citizens complained to recently elected Gov. Francis R. Lubbock that their livestock was being stolen by small bands of marauding Indians. These settlers entreated the governor to provide increased vigilance to protect their lives and property. In response to the appeals and to keep pressure on the Indians during the winter months of 1862, Frost ordered expeditions out from most regimental posts. In a January circular, he instructed the commander of Fort Belknap to send out a patrol of fifty men and two officers on February 2 to scout to the headwaters of the Pease River. From Camp Cooper he dispatched a similar patrol about February 15 to scout up the Wichita River and then to the headwaters of the Main and North forks of the Brazos and back to Cooper. The commander at Camp Colorado was to depart on February 12 with as many men as the condition of his garrison allowed. Frost advised him to investigate the plains near the head of the Double Mountain Fork of the Brazos. The poor condition of horses and mules limited the size of the unit from Fort Chadbourne, but the circular directed the fort commander to march on February 10 and to scout the country to the plains at the head of the Colorado River. Fort McKavett's commander was to depart on the 5th with a detachment of unspecified size and move northwest along the streams that ran into the Concho River.[44]

Frost authorized all commanders to use their discretion in fitting out the patrols and selecting the routes to be followed to and from designated patrol points. He realized the possibility of sudden storms during this time of year and warned his officers to use good judgment in preventing unnecessary suffering and exposure of troops. Commanders were to keep constant pressure, as much as the condition of men and horses would allow, on the Indians' winter camps, but they were to place the lives and welfare of their men above all other considerations. He explained in the circular that he wanted to "establish a feeling of security in every house" on the frontier. He urged his men to "hardy and rigorous service," for their duty of frontier protection could be accomplished only by "labor, endurance, patience, . . . perseverance, and earnest effort to fulfill trusts."[45]

Existing correspondence indicates that the regiment had only two further clashes with hostile Indians. One occurred during the expeditions ordered by Frost. On patrol, four of Ashby's men found seven Indians along the Wichita River. One of the men rode for help, while the others engaged the enemy. In a running battle that lasted four hours and covered twelve miles, the determined cavalrymen "wounded two Indians for sure" and thought they might have hit others. Darkness fell before reinforcements could ride to the scene of the action. In his report on the skirmish, Ashby added that, despite vigorous efforts to keep the Indians at bay, most of his patrols found abundant Indian signs throughout his area of responsibility. In a second letter to Barry, he wrote that, during the period of full moon, some raiding parties penetrated down the Brazos Valley as far as Weatherford.[46]

The 1st Texas Mounted Rifles concluded its Indian campaigns in April, 1862. As their one-year enlistments had expired, the companies reported to Fort Mason to be mustered out of Confederate service. One company on its way to the fort ran head-on into a band of Comanches on the San Saba River. In a short, bitter fight, these warriors wounded four men and killed as many horses, while the troopers rode down and killed four of the war party. Although this was the last of the regiment's Indian campaigns, other incidents forged the regiment's character and reputation during its service on the desolate Texas plains.[47]

CHAPTER 4

Frontier Life, "We Must Endure It"

Pursuing and battling the elusive renegade Comanches and Kiowas did not occupy every moment of the regiment's time. McCulloch's soldiers expended considerable amounts of time and labor hunting horses, tracking down deserters, and herding beef cattle, as well as improving their living quarters and post facilities. The men learned to live in a regimented environment, explore a country alien to many Texans, and attend to the military minutiae that pervade any soldier's life. Each man had to confront the separation from family, loneliness, boredom, military drill, and resistance to authority that faced newly enlisted soldiers and their officers in isolated outposts. Varied descriptions of, and reactions to, life on a hostile frontier appear in both soldiers' correspondence and official reports. Even in a unit known for its discipline, some reactions of new recruits led to infractions of regulations and violent conflicts between individual soldiers.[1]

Initially, terrain, climate, available amenities, and location of their posting shaped volunteers' perspectives on frontier army life. Before active patrolling began, Capt. Sidney Green Davidson described Fort Chadbourne as a "large pretty post" with comfortable quarters for the men, but he also called it the "dullest place in the world." No Texas newspapers arrived at the fort; all that was available to read was the *St. Louis Republican,* for the overland mail carried few letters to the post. The veteran captain had seen no ladies since leaving home, he said, and this aggravated his sense of loneliness.[2]

Those troops who garrisoned Fort Mason enjoyed well-built headquarters and barracks buildings constructed of the abundant native limestone. Only a few smoke-blackened chimneys greeted those destined to occupy Phantom Hill—Comanches, or disgruntled departing Federal soldiers, burned the fort immediately after U.S. troops abandoned the post in 1854. In contrast, Camps

Colorado and Cooper had officers' quarters and a sutler's store but no permanent structures to house enlisted men. Camp Jackson provided the men with
a source of water and little else in the summer of 1861. Company commanders
had to erect temporary shelters or tents to protect their men from the elements.[3]

These posts epitomized the wide diversity of quarters available at the dis-
parate camps. The older U.S. Army installations generally boasted structures
that could be enlarged or modified for troop billets. With the limited amount
of lumber and shingles available, the men constructed temporary quarters for
themselves. Each company's quartermaster equipment included Sibley tents,
wall tents, and servants' tents, which provided shelter in the camps that had
no permanent structures. Tents provided only minimum protection, and winter weather forced McCulloch to consolidate his companies at posts where
adequate lodging existed or could be constructed.[4]

Employing tools and stocks of building material left behind by Federal forces,
the soldiers of the regiment made their living quarters more comfortable. They
built bunks, tables, and chairs for the permanent barracks and probably fabri-
cated frames for their beds in temporary barracks. Unit quartermasters issued
each man a bedsack, which he filled with his monthly allocation of twelve
pounds of fresh bedding straw. These mattresses, covered by a soldier's blankets, along with firewood hauled in for the barracks, furnished the only warmth
the men could expect during the winter. Officers and men received a monthly
allotment of firewood for heating and cooking purposes. During the winter
months, a company of seventy-five received about twenty-one cords of wood
per month. Firewood caused additional burdens on the regimental supply system; the Texas plains offered little firewood, and it had to be brought in from
wooded regions farther south and east.[5]

Although posts were near water sources, the dry Texas summer and cold,
windy winter played havoc with the health of both men and horses. U.S. Army
records of the frontier posts chronicle several instances in which men, horses,
and mules froze in the furious blizzards that rampage across the Texas plains.
In March, 1861, Davidson complained to his wife that the grass near
Chadbourne would not support a campaign against Indians. His horses remained weak and could not keep up with the Indians' ponies. He also indicated that there was some sickness at Chadbourne. Stagnant water in the pools
along the Brazos River and the broiling summer heat, as high as 112 degrees
Fahrenheit inside tents, resulted in ill health for troops stationed on the plains.
In both summer and winter, outbreaks of disease and fever frequently swept
through the camps. U.S. Army surgeons regularly mentioned soldiers incapacitated by "intermittent fever." Modern medical authorities believe that these

fig. 5. When available, tipi-shaped Sibley tents and wall tents served as shelter for the cavalrymen throughout the Civil War. The trooper with the carbine appears to be wasting ammunition in target practice. Colonel McCulloch constantly called attention to the scarcity of ammunition and warned his men not to waste precious cartridges. Courtesy Gene Swinson, Baird, Texas

fevers were combinations of malaria, typhoid, and typhus, spread by fleas and ticks. During their frontier service, these "fevers" certainly affected McCulloch's troops and reduced the present-for-duty strength of the regiment—rosters list several men who died of typhoid fever. In 1856, while campaigning with the 2d U.S. Cavalry, Robert E. Lee wrote of the area, "The sun was fiery hot. The atmosphere like the blast from a hot-air furnace, the water salt. . . . We must bear it. The worst is that the Clear Fork [of the Brazos] no longer deserves its title, but is converted into fetid stagnant pools."[6]

Wild creatures inhabiting the plains imposed additional hazards and miseries in the environment confronting the 1st Mounted Rifles. In *A Journey Through Texas,* Frederick Law Olmsted described some of the animal perils found on the prairies. Rattlesnakes longer than five and a half feet were not uncommon; these reptiles sometimes slithered into men's beds. Scorpions and centipedes also abounded in the region. These creatures squirmed into the dark hiding places afforded by men's boots and clothing. The frontier antidote for snakebite was whiskey, administered a pint at a time. To combat the pain and swelling of a scorpion or centipede sting, the men used ammonia. Modern medical expertise does not affirm the utility of these remedies; but, in the case of snakebite, men probably felt less pain after drinking copious amounts of medicinal whiskey.[7]

Diet and availability of provisions also affected the soldiers' morale and health. Requisitions for rations indicate that the men ate a varied diet of beef and pork—fresh, salted, or pickled. Troops surely followed the practice of frontiersmen and augmented their diet with fresh meat that roamed the countryside. Olmsted wrote that wild game such as buffalo, antelope, deer, and rabbit formed part of the diet of plains dwellers. He added that wild turkeys and prairie chickens expanded the bill of fare. George R. Gautier, a cowboy in the area patrolled by McCulloch's companies, confirmed that cowboys on the plains shot wild animals for food, even eating prairie dogs when necessary. Acquiring meat, then, created few obstacles for unit commissaries. Bread came in the form of hardbread (hardtack) or bread baked from the flour or cornmeal provided from regimental stores. Certainly cornbread remained a fixture of the Texans' meals. When available, beans, rice, potatoes, and desiccated vegetables complemented daily rations. Coffee, tea, sugar, salt, soap, and candles completed a soldier's issue of provisions. To deter the effects of scurvy, ration issues included a substantial amount of vinegar. Company commissary receipts also included pickles, purchased by both officers and enlisted men to combat the disease. During the Civil War, surgeons also used vinegar to cleanse wounds and, without knowing why, saved many wounded soldiers with its disinfectant power. Regimental surgeons or contract doctors inspected food supplies to protect the men from the intestinal maladies caused by spoiled victuals.[8]

To bring the regiment up to peak efficiency and occupy the idle time endemic in any unit, Col. Henry E. McCulloch inaugurated a vigorous regimen of drill and training. Commanders received instructions that all able-bodied men should drill and exercise daily. Since the regiment was engaged in fighting Indians, this drill undoubtedly consisted of training comparable to that conducted during the regimental officers' ranger service. The soldiers learned the requisite skills of firing a revolver and rifle accurately from a running horse, riding on the side of their mounts (as Capt. William A. Pitts said, "like a Comanche"), and dismounting quickly to fight from a defensive position. To demonstrate their competence as horsemen, many men could spur their horses from a standing start into a full gallop and easily reach down to pick up a small article from the ground. According to Pitts, proficiency in these skills allowed the Texans to overcome superior numbers of Indians in many engagements. Shortages of ammunition, unfortunately, curtailed honing the troopers' abilities as marksmen. Some may have resisted the daily routine, but Davidson, in a letter to his wife, indicated that the men at Fort Chadbourne enjoyed drilling and remained in high spirits.[9]

Separation from family caused most men to yearn for remembered lifestyles and to search for some means of returning home, at least for short visits. In their letters, men wrote of concern for loved ones and for the condition of crops upon which frontier families depended. From Chadbourne, Davidson wrote to his wife that the daughter of a U.S. Army officer, a "sweet girl" whom Davidson would miss when she left, made him long for his wife and children. He added that "he loved the service and wild life" that he lived but would be much more content if he could visit his family. In her letters, Davidson's wife Mary sought to assure him that his family was fine. She wrote that "the children are romping in the yard" and that son George "would grow up to be a Ranger like his father." She also described the good quality of the family's wheat and corn crops. Davidson, anticipating a leave, caught a pair of ground squirrels to take to a young girl staying with his family. The young girl never received the pet squirrels, however. Although homesick, he "knew his duty," and the responsibilities of command ruled out any leave for the captain. Before his death at the hand of raiding Comanches, Davidson conceived a plan to move his family to Fort Chadbourne, but his plan never came to fruition. Seemingly with a premonition, Davidson closed his last letter with "Goodbye." Of his existing letters, this was the only time he ended in such a manner.[10]

Departmental and Confederate army regulations, intended to guarantee that maximum numbers of troops were available for duty, prevented liberal leave policies in the regiment. In July, 1861, departmental orders restricted officer leaves and enlisted furloughs to only seven days, and these had to be approved by a field-grade officer. The departmental commander retained the authority to approve absences for any longer periods. Subsequent Confederate army regulations further delineated leave policies, allowing officers commanding posts to grant seven days' leave and an army commander thirty days in unusual circumstances. All requests for leave had to be processed through the chain of command, and officers were required to report their addresses for recall if necessary. Regulations restricted officers' leaves to insure that each company had at least one commissioned officer present for duty at all times. Each garrison or post was required to have at least two commissioned officers available for duty and "competent Medical attention" available to the troops at all times. Regulations prevented commanders of posts from being away from their place of duty for more than seven days during a one-month period.[11]

Additional requirements governed permission for and conduct of leaves for both enlisted men and officers. All soldiers granted leave or furlough for wounds or sickness received a certification of medical disability from the senior surgeon present at his duty station. Without a medical certification or valid leave form, men absent from their units were considered deserters. Enlisted men could not take government-owned arms or accouterments home on leave; all equipment was needed for troops on active duty. After January, 1862, commanders granted leaves only in cases of absolute necessity. Orders reminded officers that "time and services belong to their country, . . . energy and zeal as well as promptness [was] expected of them."[12]

Commanders who established a leave policy considered too liberal by higher command provoked an official upbraiding; thus, commanders resorted to various methods to secure leaves for themselves and their soldiers. In September, Maj. Edward Burleson heard rumors that many members of Capt. James B. "Buck" Barry's Company C were home on leave instead of at Camp Cooper. Burleson admonished his negligent captain that "this going home business has got to stop." Burleson reiterated to the erring captain that men should be out on patrol, not visiting family and friends. To allow short visits home, some commanders conspired to send troops on recruiting duty or led patrols near the men's homes. In February, 1862, Lt. Col. Thomas C. Frost authorized Barry to conduct an extended patrol from Camp Cooper to Barry's home county, Bosque. To circumvent directives, several unit leaders granted leaves of absence for more than seven days by authorizing their men to take the last seven days of one month and the first seven of the next month for an extended leave.[13]

Failure to secure a hoped-for furlough sometimes induced individuals to act rashly and disregard regulations, which usually led to disciplinary action against them. On December 7, 1861, Charles A. Williams, a blacksmith who was restricted to post awaiting the results of a court-martial for murder, left Fort Belknap without authorization. Under the influence of liquor, he asked

Burleson for an escort to Jacksboro but was refused. Williams left the post anyway, and a detail under Lt. Solomon C. Geron rode to the small town and arrested Williams. During his return ride to Belknap, Williams allegedly threatened Lt. Joseph S. Stewart of Company K by commenting that he "would not be surprised if Lieutenant Stewart was killed or hurt before he got home after he [Stewart] was mustered out." Williams then remarked, "I do not mean by this to say that I will kill or hurt him for I dont intend to do it," but he intimated that someone would do it before Stewart arrived home. At his court-martial in April, 1862, Williams claimed that he thought he could be absent for "two or three days" without being considered a deserter. Officers comprising the court-martial board found Williams guilty of desertion and sentenced him to thirty days' hard labor and forfeiture of all pay and allowances for two months. Of the charge of threatening a commissioned officer, the board found Williams not guilty.[14]

Personal business and financial affairs prompted many soldiers to request extended absences. On December 1, 1862, Pvt. Ezekiel J. Cody petitioned McCulloch for an extended leave to attend to "some very important business" in Kerns County. Cody's guardian in Alabama had requested that the private return to that state to settle Cody's father's estate. Cody knew that, as a soldier, he could not return to Alabama and requested a leave to travel to Kern County in order to make arrangements for his uncle to handle his father's estate. "Having business at Austin that requires my attention about Christmas" enabled Lt. Robert Cotter to receive a thirty-day leave in mid-December, 1861. On Christmas Eve, Pvt. William H. Day, Company B, "respectfully begged" a twenty-five-day furlough because, as administrator of his father's estate, his interests "are now and have already been greatly suffering for want of my immediate attention." The day after Christmas, 1861, Pvt. W. L. Chaudoin received a twenty-day furlough from Camp Verde to attend to matters which he described as "business of a financial character which will cause me to sustain a considerable loss if not attended to immediately." Still another trooper, Cpl. R. L. Cook, requested and received a thirty-day leave to conclude "Business of importance [*sic*], caused by the severe illness of my father [which] requires my attention at home." Interestingly, the majority of these requests occurred at Christmastime. All soldiers pined for their families during the Yule season, and it appeared that "business" afforded a justification for a trip home during the holidays.[15]

During the regiment's frontier service, troopers for various reasons absented themselves from their units without authorization and were arrested and tried by court-martial. Pvt. Willis Condra of Company F left his unit and returned home to Goliad, where he remained until a detail of five men and a noncommissioned officer brought him back to his unit. George A. Ferguson, also of Company F, left the company on May 20, 1861, on an approved visit to San Antonio. Ferguson failed to return as ordered, and a detachment arrested him and brought him back to his company. In court-martial proceedings, Condra proved himself innocent, but Ferguson spent eight days in the guardhouse for his indiscretion.[16]

In December, 1839, Ruben Ross, a noted drunkard and duelist, forced McCulloch, in a conflict over some ladies, to shoot and kill his intoxicated former friend. Himself well acquainted with the perils of whiskey and gambling, McCulloch, as regimental and departmental commander, issued orders restricting both whiskey drinking and gambling among his men. He required his officers to sustain the good reputation of his command and to demand "good order, good conduct, and gentlemanly deportment" of all men in the regiment. Eventually, official orders forbade whiskey drinking, "horse racing and gambling of every description." McCulloch's actions were in accord with most frontier Texans' belief that proper conduct was required, especially around women. Gautier wrote that men in social situations had to "be on Ps and Qs, or you would be turned out. This was first class, pure politeness. Good behavior was the order then."[17]

An order issued by Maj. Gen. Braxton Bragg and later published by the Confederate War Department echoed McCulloch's attitude concerning the menace of alcohol. This order required commanders of all grades to suppress drunkenness among soldiers: "It is the cause of nearly all evil of which we suffer." The order asserted that a large part of the sickness in the army resulted from overindulgence in alcohol. According to the order, drinking caused inefficiency among the troops, led to numerous courts-martial, and filled the guardhouses. Only a "miserable wretch" drinks, while "gallant soldiers would not fall [prey] to such temptations." Moreover, "intelligent and honorable" officers should set high moral examples for their troops. The order urged officers to encourage troops to send their pay home instead of spending it on sprees.[18]

McCulloch grudgingly allowed some whiskey in his commands but with certain exacting stipulations. Sutlers or others authorized to conduct business with the regiment could sell medicinal whiskey to members of the regiment if the purchaser possessed a certificate signed by a regimental surgeon or physician. Commanders received strict instructions to prohibit "temporary drinking establishments" or "peddling" of whiskey in their camps. All unauthorized liquor and spirits should be confiscated and destroyed.[19]

As a regimental commander, McCulloch regarded card playing and other forms of gambling as a breakdown in discipline, as well as a means by which unscrupulous individuals could take advantage of his troops. He demanded that any gamblers who came on post to "filch" the earnings of his men be removed without delay. McCulloch refused to allow gamblers to "hang about and rob men of their money." Because card games played for entertainment turned into gambling sessions, he prohibited all card playing "at any regimental post, camp, or station." To enforce these regulations, McCulloch banned sutlers from selling cards to his officers and men.[20]

No matter how vigilant McCulloch remained, some of his boisterous Texans disagreed with his curtailing their vices and violated regimental directives. Despite two orders to the contrary, at least two post commanders permitted their men to drink and gamble. Capt. Travis Hill Ashby complained that, while he strictly enforced regulations, men stationed at other posts enjoyed the amusement of playing poker and the taste of whiskey. William O. Yager, regimental adjutant, admitted that, through his omission, all orders prohibiting gambling for amusement had not arrived at every regimental post; he promised to reissue McCulloch's missives on the subject.[21]

The condition of his horses and the scarcity of winter feed concerned McCulloch. In addition, the Texans' fondness for horse racing sapped the dwindling stamina of the regimental mounts. In October, either civilians or regimental members reported to Burleson that some men of Barry's Company C were engaged in horse racing. Burleson warned Barry that the accounts would be investigated by proper authorities. In a letter the same month, McCulloch expressed his distress over indications that Company C, especially Lieutenant Price, was racing horses "against express orders to that effect." McCulloch continued that he did not want to believe the reports, but they had come from reliable sources. He warned Barry that, if the company commander did not have a satisfactory explanation, the matter would be investigated by court-martial.[22]

In the same letters, both McCulloch and Burleson questioned Barry about violations of orders that required soldiers to respect citizens' property and private rights at all times and not to "commit any trespass on them [the citizens] of any kind." Previously published orders clearly stated that "no depredations on stock, fields, fruits, gardens, etc.[,] of any of the citizens of the country" would be permitted. Any offenders "must be at once punished by their commanders in [the] most rigid manner in which their offenses merit." Officers failing to "comply strictly and reasonably will be held in neglect of duty." Company C's transgressions concerned alleged killing of privately owned free-ranging hogs near Camp Cooper. Local stock raisers had complained that mounted soldiers were killing their hogs, and McCulloch demanded an acceptable resolution of their grievances.[23]

No fool, Barry answered the accusations in a report also recounting the events of his successful Indian fight along Pease River. Barry implied that the hogs had no owners and that his camp should not be annoyed by animals that no one claimed. McCulloch gratefully accepted the explanation and offered no restrictions on shooting the balance of the hogs if necessary.[24]

Lieutenant Price took the blame for the horse racing. In a letter to Barry, McCulloch expressed his regret that one of his officers would construct a racetrack and conduct horse races when it was expressly forbidden. The excuse that the track was used to exercise the horses was unacceptable. McCulloch reiterated that all officers must realize that their mounts "had enough to do with drilling and scouting"—they needed rest, not exercise. The regimental commander accepted Barry's explanation but added, "Things must change in [the] way of horse racing."[25]

In all segments of society, there are those who resort to dishonesty to further their own ends. A few individuals in the 1st Mounted Rifles fell into this category. In February, 1862, Capt. Travis Hill Ashby wrote to Barry that he was trying to stop a series of thefts in Company K. Ashby related his version of how a "Colt patent Six-shooter" and some blankets had been stolen from his command and sold to troops in Barry's or Capt. Milton Boggess's companies. All the stolen items were government-issued equipment, and Ashby knew that a Mr. Hancock and a Mr. Grubbs could identify the pilfered Colt and blankets. Ashby believed that he had uncovered the culprit and would punish the guilty party if Barry would send someone to identify the person who sold the pistol and blankets to the soldiers at Camp Cooper. Whether or not he caught the thief is a mystery—existing records failed to mention any court-martial for thievery.[26]

Breaches of regulations and unsoldierly conduct resulted in courts-martial and punishments for those caught and found guilty of offenses. On June 26, 1861, Pvt. A. C. Hill refused to stand guard while Company F scouted for Indians. He continued with his rebellious conduct when he refused to surrender his arms to the company's first sergeant when ordered to do so, and when he told Capt. Governor H. Nelson that "he would not spend another day in this company." Found guilty of disobeying orders, insubordination, and mutinous conduct, Hill received a dishonorable discharge and forfeited all pay and allowances. Pvt. John C. Kirwin, Company C, and Pvt. B. W. Brazelle, Company B, both were found sleeping while on guard, Kirwin at Camp Cooper and Brazelle while on an Indian scout. Kirwin received thirty days' hard labor and then was drummed out of the service. Brazelle spent thirty days under guard subsisting on bread and water but was not dismissed from service. On May 15, 1861, Pvt. John McClure, Company F, "whilst in a state of intoxication, [did] strike a commissioned officer of his Company." For this offense, a court-martial sentenced McClure "to march for twenty days on foot, whilst the troops are on the march, and be kept in charge of the Guard until this sentence is fulfilled."[27]

In Hill's case, mitigating circumstances led to a reversal of his conviction and restoration of his reputation as a Texas patriot. After his conviction, Hill's brother James and a number of politically influential friends began a campaign to rectify a wrong done to the soldier. In letters to Brig. Gen. Paul O. Hebert, Hill's brother explained that, while Hill served with Nelson's company as a scout, he never officially had mustered into the unit because of a debilitating illness contracted while he was a teenager. Because of this "white swelling," the bone in one of Hill's legs fragmented from knee to ankle. In one of his letters, James Hill wrote, "Even though a cripple," he has "ever been one of the foremost to rush to the rescue when his country has needed his services."[28]

Hill's brother's letters continued with a long and detailed explanation of his brother's service that led to his predicament. If Hill's defenders could be believed, he had ridden with William Walker in Central America, commanded a "spy company" during the Cortina Wars, aided in the capture of the Federal troops in San Antonio, and then joined McCulloch's regiment as a volunteer scout, where he "marched Immediately to the Northwest frontier of Texas." James Hill explained how A. C. Hill attached himself to Nelson's company as a volunteer scout, with the understanding that Hill could not stand guard because of his infirmity.[29]

According to Hill's supporters, officers in the regiment treated him "very unjustly and cruelly." While on an Indian scout, Hill had been ordered on guard; because of his handicap, he refused to perform "foot service." When the patrol returned to Camp Concho, the officer commanding the patrol ordered Hill arrested. Hill protested that he previously had explained his infirmity to Nelson, who said he was "perfectly satisfied" that Hill could not stand guard but requested that he procure a certificate from a surgeon. Hill complained that, although he obtained such a certificate, Nelson still ordered him disarmed and arrested. Hill also accused Nelson of being drunk at the time but later, when sober, relenting and wanting to release Hill. According to James Hill's letters, Capt. James Fry insisted on preferring charges, and Hill was kept under arrest. James Hill pleaded for Hebert's intervention, describing his brother as a "high minded, honorable man, a gentleman & a christian who has ever been noted for his rectitude, sober habits, patriotism & energy. Ever ready to serve his country, even beyond his ability."[30]

Official records contradict Hill's protestations and his brother's letters; but, whatever the truth, A. C. Hill's conviction was rescinded, and he returned to duty with the 1st Texas Cavalry in 1863. Unit reports and muster rolls indicate that Asa C. Hill mustered into service for twelve months on April 20, 1861, at Bastrop. The same rolls, ironically, list G. H. Nelson as the enrolling officer. Hill claimed throughout his trial that he never officially mustered into regimental service; he must have forgotten the events of April 20. On May 1, 1863, after several months of deliberation, the Department of Texas issued Special Orders No. 165. It "remitted" Hill's dismissal and restored him to duty. It seems odd that departmental officers, after agreeing that Hill had some claim to mistreatment in his trial, restored him to active duty in a unit that he maintained he never joined.[31]

Additional court-martial records suggest the volatility of men accustomed to living in a turbulent era; sometimes they resorted to violent means of settling disagreements. During early July, 1861, Charles A. Williams, defendant in the court-martial mentioned above, committed two offenses that resulted in a charge of murder. On July 2, while on a patrol led by Pvt. David L. Bratton, Williams endangered the "lives and property of [the] detachment." Sometime "between 2 and 5 A.M.," he lay down and went to sleep while on guard duty. Three days later, at their semi-permanent camp on Halladay's Creek near the Big Wichita River, probably in an argument over endangering the patrol, Williams "did without cause or provocation raise his weapon and shoot Private Erasmus E. Freeman, of [the] same party, causing death." Williams claimed that the court-martial had no jurisdiction because the formal charges were not signed. The court-martial board overruled him, and he pled not guilty. For reasons unclear in the trial records (possibly self-defense), the court found Williams not guilty and returned him to duty.[32]

Arguments among armed men resulted in more powder smoke and another court-martial. On June 22, while Company I camped on Willow Creek, Pvt. Samuel Young, "without just cause or provocation, with a drawn pistol and in a violent manner approached Private William Riley" of the same company. Capt. Travis H. Ashby ordered Young not to shoot and to holster his pistol. Young replied, "I'll be damned if I don't shoot him" and fired at Riley. Evidently Young missed—he faced charges of positive and willful disobedience of orders, not murder. Found guilty of all charges and specifications, Young spent sixty days at hard labor and forfeited all pay and allowances during the period.[33]

In their actions and correspondence, officers and men of the 1st Mounted Rifles exhibited the full panoply of human emotions during their first year of service. Men who would have preferred to be at home with wife and family fought and died to protect their beloved state from the outrages of Indians whom they considered savages. Although desperately lonely and desirous of a leave, the vast majority remained at their posts under the most trying circumstances. Less than 1 percent of the Mounted Riflemen—far fewer than in most other units—deserted or shirked their duties. The pressure of frontier duty and inevitable conflicts among hard-bitten frontiersmen caused some to act in a manner contrary to regulations and beyond the bounds of normal behavior, but only a few resorted to such drastic actions. From capturing ground squirrels for a child to shooting a comrade, the Mounted Riflemen exposed their humanity, their virtues as well as their flaws.[34]

As the regiment's one-year term of service came to a close, its officers asked the men to reenlist, while preparing to muster the regiment out of service. Frost offered the standard sixty-day furlough for reenlistees but reiterated that the men had to reenlist by companies, for there was no provision for them to reorganize as they pleased. Concurrently, Frost ordered his commanders to assemble their companies near Fredericksburg or at or near Fort Mason for mustering-out procedures. He authorized them to hire local wagons and teams if regimental wagons were unavailable in sufficient quantity to effect the relocation of troops and supplies.

Barry received orders to remain in command of George E. Bushong's, James M. Homsley's, and Milton Webb's companies until they completed their twelve-month obligation. Since quartermaster stores and fodder were in short supply, Frost recommended that Barry encamp Webb's company on good pasture; he hoped that requisitioned rations and grain for the horses would arrive for the few companies left to protect public property. Frost emphasized regimental orders and policies concerning respect for private rights and property, and he admonished officers to prevent the sale of liquor to the troops.[35]

McCulloch attempted to convince at least a portion of his regiment that their duty lay with continued service to Texas and the Confederacy. In early April, 1862, he sent a handbill appealing to the men of the 1st Mounted Rifles to reenlist. The new term of service would be two years upon termination of their first twelve-month enlistment. Men would remain in the same unit, retain their arms, and receive a fifty-dollar reenlistment bounty. He also offered a furlough not to exceed sixty days. If enough men reenlisted, they had the right to form companies or battalions and elect their own officers. He could not guarantee, however, that the regiment would not remain on the Texas frontier. This diminished reenlistment zeal, for the men wished to be sent as a unit to fight in the East, "where there was a real enemy to be conquered."[36]

About half the regiment wanted to remain on active service; but, since the government offered no guarantees and many of the men felt the pull of home and family, Companies A, B, D, E, H, and I disbanded as their twelve-month obligations expired in the spring of 1862. The remaining companies concluded that their duty lay with continued service to Texas and the Confederacy; accordingly, they reorganized into a separate battalion and moved on to other assignments.[37]

CHAPTER 5

"They Are Permanently Located in the Soil of the Country"

In December, 1861, Henry E. McCulloch became commander of the Western Sub-District of Texas. His new command included responsibility for all posts west, northwest, and south of San Antonio, including Victoria and Saluria along the vulnerable Texas coast. His new duties required him to relinquish command of the 1st Texas Mounted Rifles, newly designated the 1st Texas Cavalry by the Confederate secretary of war. In his place, Lt. Col. Thomas C. Frost assumed leadership of the regiment. Like most western Confederate commands, McCulloch's was short of money, supplies, and men. His district lacked sufficient cavalry to patrol the frontier properly, guard the long Texas coastline, and guarantee that the vital cotton trade through Mexico remained uninterrupted. To alleviate the deficiency in mounted forces, he secured special orders for his adjutant, German-born Capt. William O. Yager, to raise a battalion of cavalry consisting of six companies. With an additional battalion of cavalry stationed in southern Texas, McCulloch could avoid stretching his meager forces to the breaking point.[1]

After the war, and possibly before, Yager resided at Seguin in Guadalupe County, as did McCulloch. Yager knew McCulloch, and quite possibly they were close friends. Yager apparently had had professional military training in Europe before emigrating to Texas. By appointing him regimental training officer and adjutant, McCulloch certainly recognized Yager's superior talents. The method popular at the time called for a commander to appoint an adjutant personally known to him, to insure that he had a loyal and intelligent aide.

fig. 6. William Kuykendall joined Yager's battalion and later wrote a memoir of his Civil War service. Courtesy Marshal Kuykendall, Austin

Yager's ability to write and his skilled penmanship indicated extensive education. He joined McCulloch's staff as a first lieutenant and soon garnered a promotion to captain. Pvt. William Kuykendall, of Company D of Yager's new command, described his commanding officer as being about thirty years of age, "sociable and devoid in the remarkable degree of the arogant [*sic*] manner that Characterized many of the officers of the even subordinate grade." On December 18, 1861, Yager moved up to the Western Sub-District adjutant's job under McCulloch.[2]

On December 24, Brig. Gen. Paul O. Hebert, with McCulloch's enthusiastic recommendation, offered Yager a major's commission to raise and command a mounted battalion for service along the Rio Grande. In a letter of December 28 from San Antonio, Yager accepted the appointment. A month later, on January 29, 1862, he and a portion of his 3rd Battalion of Texas Cavalry reported to Col. P. N. Luckett at Fort Brown near the mouth of the Rio Grande.[3]

In late February, Yager moved to Camp Aransas on the Texas coast and began to organize his new command. The camp actually was divided between two locations—one on the northeastern tip of Mustang Island and another on the

fig. 7. Wyley Kuykendall,
William's cousin, enlisted at
the same time and served
the entire war with Com-
pany D. Courtesy Marshal
Kuykendall, Austin

nearby shoreline at the junction of Aransas and Corpus Christi bays. The unfinished fortifications consisted of sand embankments and some wooden platforms upon which to mount artillery. Traveling with a small party, Yager arrived before the bulk of his men. On February 24, he reported the arrival of the first two companies of his battalion. They had traveled overland from Fort Brown, owing to the unavailability of water transportation and the danger imposed by Union blockaders.[4]

Union blockaders sailed freely along the Texas coast, and their armed launches halted all Confederate trade in the area. Yager immediately took steps to counter the blockaders' activities. When Yager arrived, soldiers manning the bulwarks pointed out the mastheads of blockading Union schooners protruding above the horizon. From the crow's nests of these vessels, lookouts observed everything in the Confederate camp. Prior to Yager's arrival, two infantry companies of Luckett's regiment had occupied the camp and exchanged shots with several Federal foraging parties. The Yankee ships landed parties of up to 130 men, who scoured the countryside for beef, pork, fresh water, and wood. The Union troops also had burned several homes and barns in the area. To conceal the activities of his troops, Yager established his cavalry camp four miles from the beach. He also sent details to round up all the beeves they could locate and drive them inland, away from enemy foragers and raiders. Yager's measures to protect the coast had some small, early effect. One of his patrols captured a Yankee, Captain Kittredge, when the latter's fondness for buttermilk motivated him to wander too far from his landing party.[5]

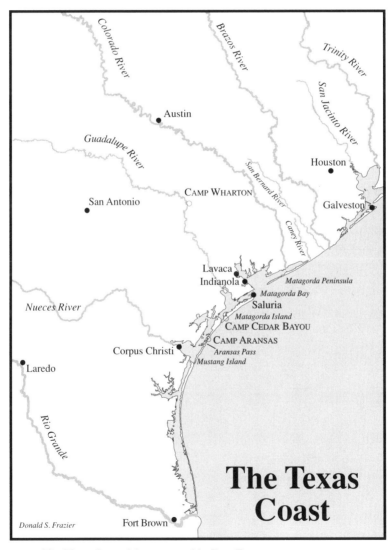

map 3. The Texas Coast. Map prepared by Don Frazier

Yager's 3rd Battalion of Texas Cavalry consisted of a combination of previously organized and newly mustered companies from several areas of the Texas coastal plain. In his diary, Kuykendall described the men who joined the unit and their daily routines at Camp Aransas. Of the troops, Kuykendall wrote, "Almost every existing condition of existing society was represented upon our muster rolls the moral and the immoral the Christian Deist the scholar and the illiterate, shoulder to shoulder without distinction of nationality or creed bound together by a tie of mutual interest and patriotism." His portrayal of daily events was less flattering: "Our duties were monotonous. Drilling in both cavalry and infantry drill from two to four hours per day was the usual routine which to a civilian soon becomes exceeding irksome." In addition to training and drilling his recruits, Yager established small patrol bases garrisoned by about twenty-five men armed with a miscellany of shotguns, pistols, and "civilian rifles." From these modest posts, he hoped to picket the coast and protect the countryside from foraging parties landed from the blockading ships.[6]

In his reports to headquarters, Yager detailed his estimate of the situation at Camp Aransas. He concluded that, with some additional aid in arms, improved fortifications, a few more men, and some bridging, the position could be held against attack and local trade resumed. Previously, a brisk trade in cotton, salt, corn, lead, and lumber had provided supplies to both the Confederate and the Texas troops. Yager asserted that his men, aided by a few trained carpenters and mechanics, could make all essential improvements at Camp Aransas. He wrote that a high priority must be to hasten urgently needed cannon to him. To be able to defend the redoubt against attack, he requested, at a minimum, two eighteen-pounders, one twelve-pounder, and two six-pounders, along with ammunition and the equipment required to service the guns. He added that, in his opinion, an armed schooner supported by a few armed launches could drive off the blockading ships. He reminded McCulloch that such a schooner lay at anchor at Galveston; it needed only to be fitted with cannon. To bolster his garrison, he requested that the remainder of his battalion be sent to him as soon as possible. Yager's letters also included petitions for the requisite funds and authority to charter local vessels and purchase the necessary materials to initiate his planned fortification improvements and the disposition of troops.[7]

By and large, Yager's requests went unfulfilled. The Confederacy lacked sufficient money, supplies, and equipment to send him all that he deemed essential. The Department of Texas provided some light artillery, small-arms ammunition, and a modest amount of building supplies, but not enough lumber to construct a bridge linking the mainland and island sections of the camp.

Transportation and communication between the shore and the island persisted as one of Yager's major problems. All dispatches and supplies had to be carried over water, and the link could be broken at any time by enemy action or inclement weather. Yager managed to charter a sloop, the *Rebecca,* but the single small vessel could not cope with the larger, more numerous Federal ships.[8]

During the spring of 1862, Yager's success in combating destructive Union raiding parties enhanced his reputation as a fighting commander. On April 22, a force of Union sailors and soldiers, under cover of darkness and with muffled oars, stealthily rowed up Cedar Bayou, toward today's Sweeny, in several launches. The Federal raiding party surprised the crews of three Confederate sloops anchored in the waterway. They quickly overpowered the crews and seized control of the *Swan* and the *Mustang.* They left the other sloop, the *Democrat,* without sails and sent the captain and crew off in small boats. The Union raiding party, pretending to be Rebels, intended to sail the sloops, along with their captured crews, down the bayou past the fort at Shell Bank and into Matagorda Bay to rejoin the Union fleet.[9]

Confederate scouts informed Yager of the ships' capture, and he swiftly ordered his men into action. Leading a hurriedly organized thirty-two-man detachment, he saddled and rode to Cedar Bayou. Yager's small command, bent on reprisal, procured a few small boats and intercepted the Federal force as it made slow headway down the bayou. With cocked pistols and drawn sabers, the Texans, like swashbuckling pirates, vaulted over the gunwales of the captured craft. In a short, heated firefight, Yager's troops recaptured the ships, as well as several enemy launches. During the brief action, the Confederate cavalrymen captured several Federal prisoners while liberating their compatriots. Yager estimated that twenty-two of the Union sailors, including their commander, escaped in the darkness and made their way to the coast, where they were rescued by other launches from the blockading ships. In addition to the raiding party's cutters and launches, Yager's prizes included "a fine mariner's compass, a pennant, two pairs of handcuffs, and two guns ... sails of the *Democrat,* some rations, one boarding pistol, and other trifles." Yager sent the compass to be presented, "from the officers engaged in the expedition," to Commodore William Hunter, chief naval commander of the Department of Texas. After this foray misfired, the Union blockaders were less bold; and Yager's battalion spent the majority of its efforts on routine patrols along the coast until late May, 1862.[10]

On May 27, Yager received orders to relocate his battalion to Ringgold Barracks, a few miles up the Rio Grande from Brownsville. Kuykendall penned the men's mood: "Though we should have greatly preferred to being ordered east to the seat of war, we cheerfully began preparations for immediate departure." On the morning of May 29, three companies fell into line and, with the command of "twos from the right, forward march," the horsemen rode toward their new post. Yager had managed to raise only four companies, numbering 404 men, of the six companies authorized for his battalion. Company B, originally assigned as a mounted unit with the 6th Texas Infantry, temporarily remained near Camp Aransas, while the bulk of the battalion occupied Ringgold Barracks. A detachment of Company B, under 2d Lt. Isaac A. Patton, had received complimentary mention in previous reports for their "coolness and soldierly behavior under heavy fire of shells" during a Federal raid on Aransas Pass.[11]

Fragmentary surviving records of the time reveal little about the unit except that, for a few brief interludes, Yager's cavalry patrolled the Rio Grande up as far as Laredo and north along the coast toward Corpus Christi, a distance of almost three hundred straight-line miles. Kuykendall described his company's frontier duties as "scouting between the mouth of [the] river [Rio Grande] and Ringgold Barracks." Charged with protecting the crucial cotton trade routes into Mexico from Mexican bandits and marauding Texas Unionists (the latter anticipated but in fact not prevalent), the troopers spent most of their time in dry, dusty patrolling. According to Kuykendall, many travelers had a "mortal terror of Mexican robbers who were constantly committing crimes along the border." He continued, "Lawless elements of both countries found a comparatively safe asylum in the vicinity of this river from which they could depredate upon the unoffending citizens . . . of either border with little fear of Chastisement." The dense chaparral "rendered their apprehension very difficult."[12]

Kuykendall scribbled several tales of his unit's escapades along the border. On June 17, he accompanied a detachment escorting supply wagons from Ringgold Barracks. Bivouacked for the night on Resaca de la Palma, several men took the opportunity to explore the Mexican War battlefield. Kuykendall reported that the trees still bore the scars of cannon fire, and grapeshot littered the chaparral. Several rifle pits also were in evidence. On December 26, 1862, a messenger notified Capt. James C. Borden of Company D that a "band of marauders" had ambushed and captured a government train of four wagons "laden with supplies" at Salado Ranch. Reports indicated that several soldiers died defending the wagons. Borden rapidly organized a detail of thirty-three men and within an hour led this pursuit force toward the scene of fighting, eighteen miles below Ringgold Barracks. Arriving at the ranch, Borden's horsemen found seven or eight bodies of the supply train's escort, including McDonald of Company D. The robbers had looted the wagons and made good their escape through the thick *brasada,* or brush country, toward the Rio Grande. Borden's detachment followed the raiders to a small ranch where the Texans, believing that the occupants had assisted the robbers, burned several *jacales* (small dwellings constructed of posts and mud, usually with a thatched roof). Kuykendall related that the command remained overnight "feasting on chickens and honey."[13]

Because they lived and worked along the coast, a large contingent of Yager's troops were highly proficient in sailing and volunteered for marine service. While at Fort Brown, seven of these men from Company A executed a daring feat, carrying out a brazen daylight raid right under the noses of the Federal blockaders. Disguising themselves in "sailor's costumes," the impertinent Texans rowed out in a small boat and "boldly approached and boarded a Yankee merchantman" lying at anchor outside the bar. Leaping over the gunwales and dashing along the ship's deck, the Texas cavalrymen, as Kuykendall explained, quickly "secured the officers and crew, hoisted sail, weighed anchor, and beached the vessel on the Texas beach." So quickly did the Texans act that the crews of other Yankee ships were so astonished they only "fired a few shots at the retreating merchantman but without effect." Yager's command secured the cargo of general merchandise that contained a large assortment of hoop skirts. Kuykendall opined that "these skirts no doubt was greatly appreciated by the ladies into whose hands they possibly fell."[14]

In March, 1863, according to J. I. Campbell of the 3rd Cavalry Battalion, Yager's men generated more excitement along the Rio Grande. Union Col. Edmund J. Davis had accompanied Federal troops into Mexico and established a headquarters in Matamoros. Davis was uniquely qualified to accomplish his mission of monitoring Confederate activities and gathering volunteers among the Texas Unionists who had fled into Mexico. Before the war, he had been a resident of southern Texas, serving as a judge. Davis spent much of his time around Matamoros openly recruiting and training volunteers for his 1st Regiment of Texas Cavalry (Union). Kuykendall described Davis as "the most prominent of these renegades."[15]

The excitement came, as Campbell and later newspaper articles asserted, when, on or about March 15, 1863, a body of Yager's men, in a clandestine operation, crossed into Mexico and captured Davis and his aide, Capt. William W. Montgomery. Kuykendall recounted that the raiding "party [was] composed principally of our [Yager's] command." Yager's men knew both officers as despised Texans who had left the state to fight for the Union. Accusing Montgomery as both a traitor and the murderer of a Texas citizen, the Confederate cavalrymen hanged him from a tall mesquite tree. They planned to

fig. 8. Edmund J. Davis. A Texas Unionist who left the state to form the 1st Texas Cavalry Regiment (Union). He fought against the men who attempted to hang him in the Red River Campaign in Louisiana in 1864. After the Civil War, he returned to Texas and became one of the most controversial governors of the state. Courtesy Massachusetts Commandery, Military Order of the Loyal Legion, and U.S. Army Military History Institute, Carlisle Barracks, Pennsylvania

spirit Davis back into Texas and use him as a bargaining tool with the Union blockaders, but Mexican authorities, probably alerted by Davis's wife, quickly ordered out their troops and forced his release. After the war, Davis became the controversial "radical Republican" Reconstruction governor of Texas. The Confederate commander of the area, Brig. Gen. Hamilton P. Bee, and all of his officers denied any knowledge of Davis's kidnapping. British Lt. Col. James Arthur Fremantle, touring the border at that time, offered information contradicting the Confederate officers. James M. Duff, commanding another regiment, introduced Fremantle to the soldier allegedly responsible for Montgomery's hanging. Fremantle described him as "a rather sinister looking party, with long yellow hair down to his shoulders." In their correspondence, Confederate officials also indicated that they were aware of Montgomery's hanging. The Confederate commissioner in Monterrey wrote, in reference to Montgomery and other Texas Unionists, "I have reason to believe that they will not commit treason again in this world. They are permanently located in the soil of the country."[16]

In Louisiana a year later, Yager's command, the 1st Regiment of Texas Cavalry, met Davis's Unionists for a second time. Kuykendall recorded his version of the encounter with Davis's "renegades" in his diary. The opposing forces fought in the bayou country south of Alexandria, and the Confederates "had the pleasure of chastising them driving them before us for the greater part of one day." Kuykendall scorned the caliber of those who left Texas to fight for the Union: "As might have been expected of the character of the material of which this [Davis] regiment was composed, they displayed none of the usual courage that characterized Texas troops." Concerning Texans who left the state to fight for the Union, Kuykendall certainly cannot be considered an impartial observer.[17]

CHAPTER 6

"The Blackest Crime in Texas Warfare"

  William O. Yager's battalion was not the only direct military descendant of the 1st Texas Mounted Rifles. When the regiment disbanded in April, 1862, members of Companies C, F, G, and K elected to remain on active duty. These companies, after some minor changes in personnel, reorganized to become Companies A, B, D, and E of the 8th Battalion, Texas Cavalry. By popular election the men selected Dr. Joseph Taylor as their commander, and he received his commission as major on June 1, 1862.[1]

  Taylor, a doctor prominent in Harrison County before the war, had made a name for himself in both local and state politics. He stood for election to the state senate in the late 1850s but lost by a narrow margin in a runoff election. Taylor's political views as a southern Democrat naturally aligned him with the Confederacy. He initially served as a surgeon with the 1st Texas Mounted Rifles on the frontier. Evidently ambition convinced him that he could serve his state better by leading men in combat than by practicing the healing arts. A Tyler newspaper later reported that the company commanders of Taylor's battalion were Capts. Harold Combs, Garvion [actually Solomon C. Geron], James Neery, [Leonidas] Mark Price, and Frank van der Stucken. All these men were veterans, and many had been on the frontier with the 1st Texas Mounted Rifles.[2]

  To complete the 8th Battalion's complement of five companies, Department of Texas headquarters joined the four remaining companies of the 1st Mounted Rifles with an unusual independent mounted unit recruited among the German immigrants residing in the hill country region around Fredericksburg and New Braunfels. In March, 1862, Frank van der Stucken began to assemble this company of seventy-five men and was elected its captain. Contrary to popular belief, many German settlers volunteered for service in Confederate units recruited in Texas. These settlers joined for sundry reasons. Although most did not support slavery, they believed that, with the Federal soldiers gone, their homes and families were in danger from Indian raids. Thus they signed up in companies formed for frontier defense. According to scattered, unconfirmed claims, some immigrants mustered into Confederate service just to protect their families from reprisals by a venal Confederate government. Whatever the reasons, the 1st Texas Cavalry, like numerous other Texas units, had more than a sprinkling of German immigrants among its members.[3]

Jean François "Frank" van der Stucken, born in Antwerp, Belgium, in 1830, came to Texas with Henri Castro in 1846. French-born Castro became a U.S. citizen and a noted impresario in Texas, bringing over 485 families and 457 single men into the state. Intelligent and fluent in Flemish, German, French, and English, the sixteen-year-old van der Stucken gained a laudable reputation among early Texas pioneers. About 1852, van der Stucken moved to Fredericksburg, where he married Barbara Sophie Schoenewolf on December 23, 1852. Van der Stucken made lucrative contacts with local U.S. Army officers, signing contracts to freight government supplies and to assist in construction of army posts in the region. In 1859, he formed a very successful partnership with Henry Runge in a freighting business and joined with his brother Felix in building a steam-powered flour mill in Fredericksburg. As a prosperous businessmen and noted citizen of Fredericksburg, he was elected chief magistrate (now county judge) of Gillespie County in 1860.[4]

As the war progressed during the summer of 1861, van der Stucken initially attempted to join a frontier defense company being formed by Jacob Kuechler at Fredericksburg; but, because of local conflicts, he ended up mustering his own company, which served in various assignments before becoming part of Taylor's battalion. In letters to Gov. Francis R. Lubbock, prominent citizens like van der Stucken and Charles Nimitz reported that Kuechler restricted his roster to known Union sympathizers, preventing anyone who supported the Confederacy from enlisting. After Lubbock discovered that Kuechler planned military action against the government, he dissolved Kuechler's company. Following considerable local turmoil, Lubbock commissioned van der Stucken to enlist his own Home Guard company.[5]

On May 7, 1862, van der Stucken mustered in his independent unit and moved it to Fort Mason, where it reinforced the remnants of the 1st Mounted Rifles in patrolling the frontier. Van der Stucken's company's major duty, however, seems to have been guarding Federal prisoners and "apprehending disloyal persons." One of the prisoners, German-born Stephan Schwartz, referred to Major Taylor as a "brutal beast and tyrant." He quoted Taylor's son as call-ing his father a "crazy old fool" and commented that the boy was afraid of Taylor. One must remember, however, that Schwartz's opinion undoubtedly reflected his status as a captive. He acknowledged that a majority of Taylor's officers "were gentlemen, not only in word, but in deeds." He described van der Stucken as especially considerate of the prisoners' welfare.[6]

On January 1, 1863, van der Stucken's company left San Antonio Springs escorting 370 Union prisoners to Louisiana for exchange. The caravan trav-eled overland to Shreveport and then downriver by steamboat. Near Baton Rouge, van der Stucken exchanged his prisoners for Confederate soldiers cap-tured near New Orleans and returned to Houston with twenty wagons loaded with arms and ammunition. Schwartz complimented his Texas guards: "Any-thing those men could do for us, they did it with the greatest of pleasure." On July 25, 1863, van der Stucken's company completed its assignment and joined the 1st Texas Cavalry. Prior to the safe delivery of the prisoners of war, dubious rumors had alleged that van der Stucken planned to allow the Union prison-ers to escape and aid them in joining Federal forces assembling in Mexico. According to the unverified suppositions, van der Stucken, initially a Union-ist, had had a change of loyalties and foiled the escape. If such rumors were true, how did van der Stucken maintain the loyalty of his men when he changed sides? And what kept them from overpowering or killing their commander and freeing the prisoners on their own? Events proved this hearsay to be only figments of revisionists' imagination. The early schism between Unionists and Secessionists (or *abzusonderners,* as the German immigrants called them) did, however, portend several fatal incidents in the German communities within a few months.[7]

When Taylor's 8th Texas Cavalry Battalion formed in June, 1862, it initially remained in Texas as a separate unit under the Department of Texas. The battalion's assignment required it to assume either of two main missions. First, it stood ready to supplement state troops in protecting the frontier settlements and posts. A very important part of this assignment included keeping the over-land trade route open to Matamoros. Because of the coastal blockade, that route became the only one via which cotton could be transported and sold to pur-chase war materials and consumer goods. Second, Taylor maintained his men and horses on constant alert, prepared to move rapidly to the Texas coast and repel any invasion by U.S. forces.[8]

In order to be centrally located for these missions, Taylor headquartered his 407 men at San Antonio Springs, just outside the city of San Antonio. With its shade trees and abundant water, the location was ideally suited for a cavalry

fig. 9. Jacob and Elizabeth Gold (probably at their marriage), circa 1869. Gold joined van der Stucken's company in 1862 and served with it during the entire war. After the Civil War, Gold became a successful farmer and freighter near Fredericksburg. Courtesy Betty S. Foy, Bryan, Texas

encampment. The thirsty horsemen probably enjoyed the beer garden also located at the springs. Taylor, as the situation dictated, commanded the San Antonio garrison, as well as the 8th Battalion of cavalry. He held these commands except while he was on furlough during July and August, 1862, and from February through April, 1863. Taylor's political influence must have been great and his duty not too demanding; other officers and men did not receive such liberal time on furlough.[9]

One of the most lamentable acts perpetrated by Texans during the war was committed by a mixed unit of Partisan Rangers, state troops, and a detachment of Taylor's battalion. While Taylor was absent on leave, these acts were carried out against German settlers sympathetic to the Union. Most Texans considered these settlers traitors. Some Germans did not show great support for secession but initially were not active Unionists. In late 1860 or early 1861, however, German immigrants around Fredericksburg and New Braunfels sensed *"politische schwierigkeiten am horizont"* (political troubles on the horizon) and organized the Union Loyal League (ULL).[10]

Eighteen German communities began to enlist militias, and each member took an oath that he would "never betray the United States of America." In March, 1862, Col. Henry E. McCulloch, commander of the Western Sub-District of Texas, reported that German Unionists were openly celebrating Federal victories and organizing military companies "well armed with shotguns, rifles, and pistols, with plenty of ammunition." He declared that martial law "would soon be necessary" and began to organize a force to crush "the malignant acts of these cowardly traitors." Before he could act, however, he was relieved as commander of the sub-district by Brig. Gen. Hamilton P. Bee. By July 4, 1862, three companies of armed militia had been organized and an estimated five hundred members mustered, some more fervent Unionists than others. Organizers of the ULL included Frederick "Fritz" Tegener, who was made major and commander of the newly organized battalion. Supporters of the league proclaimed that they had formed the military organization only to protect the German settlements against marauding Indians and outlaws.[11]

Because of information received from reliable citizens and the league's activities, the Confederate government in Austin doubted the league's professed purpose and considered it an internal threat, if not an open rebellion. The state sent a combined force of state militia and Confederate cavalry under Capt. James M. Duff to control the situation. Taylor directed small detachments from companies A through E to cooperate with Duff's operations around Fredericksburg. The detachments from the 8th Battalion established Camp "Perdenalis" [*sic*] about ten miles west of Fredericksburg and began scouting "the mountain districts" for "camps and depots" located there by "men in arms against the government."[12]

In May, 1862, Duff, having been appointed provost marshal for the area, proclaimed martial law in Gillespie and sections of surrounding counties. Revisionists claim that reports of Unionist activities around Fredericksburg were unfounded. Nimitz, in trials concerning the disturbances, however, testified that a young man, whose name has not survived, was beaten to death by drunken German Unionists for his Confederate sympathies. On July 5, 1862, Basil Stewart, a former member of the ULL and an informant to Duff, was executed from ambush as a traitor by a member of the military arm of the ULL. Pvt. Levi Lamoni Wight of van der Stucken's company divulged a Unionist plot to assassinate van der Stucken because of his support for the Confederacy. According to Wight, the Unionist "conspird to kill" his company commander as he returned to San Antonio from a trip to Fredericksburg. Someone betrayed the plan to van der Stucken and, although the Unionist "way laid" the main road to San Antonio, van der Stucken and his escort "sliped out through another rout and pasd unmolested."[13]

Following these and other incidents, armed bands of German Unionists began gathering in the rough, cedar-choked ravines and valleys near Fredericksburg, their leaders contemplating attacking Duff's units. The ULL was moving into the second phase of an insurgent war—military action against an established government. Duff deemed the situation quite serious and executed several German immigrants whom he considered to be troublemakers. Many of Duff's men, however, disagreed with his actions and believed him unfit to command the state's troops. As a result of Duff's harassment, several citizens of Edwards, Gillespie, Kendall, Kerr, and Kimble counties met and decided that it might be best, for political and safety reasons, to leave the state.[14]

On August 1, 1862, approximately eighty men assembled on Turtle Creek, eighteen miles west of Kerrville, and an estimated sixty-one of these decided to flee to Mexico. With Tegener in charge, the men left the German settlements between August 1 and 3. Charles Burgmann (or Bergmann) and, probably, Charles Nimitz reported their departure to Duff. At least one of them reported that the departing settlers were well armed. The fleeing German immigrants planned to ride to the Devil's River and follow it until they could cross into Mexico. When informed of the planned exodus, Duff dispatched a detachment of ninety-six men in pursuit. He did not accompany the force of mixed units himself but placed 1st Lt. Colin D. McRae, 2nd Texas Mounted Rifles, in command of a unit formed from Duff's Partisan Rangers, state militia, and detachments from Taylor's cavalry. From Taylor's 8th Battalion, 1st Lt. James M. Homsley commanded the men from Company A; 1st Lt. James S. Bigham led the squad from Company B; and 2d Lt. John S. Williams led a party from companies C, D, and E. Taylor's officers' performance sustained their men's confidence, but several state troopers later reported that they considered their officers worse than Duff, without a doubt unfit to lead men.[15]

For several days, beginning on August 3, the detachment tracked the Germans from the Pedernales River down the Guadalupe. Along the route, a party of four or five men joined the fleeing Unionists. At one abandoned camp, using signs left by horses and mules, the tracking party estimated the Unionists to number between sixty and one hundred. The trail continued to the Medina and the Frio rivers, then finally to a bend in the Nueces. Following a very plain trail, scouts located the Germans on the afternoon of August 9. Near sunset, after returning hunting parties reported unidentified riders on their backtrail, a few of the Germans became concerned about being followed or attacked. Tegener scoffed at these reports and directed the immigrants to camp on a small, grass-covered prairie encircled by a scattering of cedar trees. He posted only two guards.[16]

At 11 P.M., the Texans removed their hats, tied on white headbands for identification, and organized for an attack. Leaving his horses with a guard at a rendezvous point and thereby reducing his assault force, McRae ordered his command across the Nueces River toward the unsuspecting Unionists. Two detachments, one under McRae and the other under Homsley of Taylor's battalion, separated to strike the sleeping Unionists from two sides. The Texans agreed that a single pistol shot would signal the attack, and by one o'clock in the morning the men were moving through the moonlit jumble of rocks and cedars toward the camp. Both squads crept as silently as possible to within fifty yards of the German perimeter. McRae deployed his men to the southwest of the camp, while Homsley quietly maneuvered his troops into position northeast of the undisturbed enemy.[17]

Two Germans wandering from their camp in the darkness stumbled upon Homsley's concealed force. The roar of a single rifle shot shattered the night's stillness and silenced the chirping insects. Without orders, a Confederate had fired, instantly killing one of the unsuspecting men and prematurely signaling the attack. The other Unionist fired his rifle into the darkness, then scurried back toward his companions. The Germans leapt from their blankets and took what cover was available. A member of McRae's party, R. H. Williams, recalled, "Instantly the camp was in a buzz, like a swarm of bees." The camp's occupants opened fire, and firing became general between them and Homsley's men. At least one German caught outside the camp perimeter died in the crossfire. For some unknown reason, perhaps poor planning, the Confederates failed to mount an organized two-pronged assault on the unprepared enemy camp. Williams believed that an immediate charge would have "carried the camp with little loss." Evidently Homsley thought the same and led an abortive attempt to overwhelm enemy opposition on his side of the fray. John W. Sansom, a survivor of the battle and one of the men first fired upon, reported that the Confederates made a brief charge, which was "gallantly repulsed." The Germans then tried to force their way through Homsley's troops but themselves were thrown back. While McRae's men lay quiet, never firing a shot in support of their compatriots, sporadic muzzle flashes lit up the space between Homsley's line and the camp until daylight. During the initial stage of combat, two Unionists died and as many as four were wounded, with Tegener hit twice. Surviving evidence of the encounter indicates no Confederate casualties up to this point.[18]

Tegener's party took advantage of the darkness and their opponents' disarray to fortify their position as best they could, but the shock of a surprise attack by what the Germans perceived to be a superior force caused a major

fig. 10. Colin D. McRae commanded the detachment of mixed Texas troops who pursued the German Unionists to the banks of the Nueces River. Courtesy Douglas Travers, San Antonio

change in their situation. Consulting with one another, they shifted their positions and piled their saddles and some logs into hasty breastworks for an all-around defense. Although they believed they faced up to two hundred assailants, about half were prepared, as one survivor later wrote, "to stay and die at my post if need be." Others were not so determined, however, and twenty-three to twenty-eight decided to abandon the fight. Sometime between the first volleys and dawn, these men stealthily gathered their horses and slipped through the porous Confederate cordon. In small groups they sneaked past McRae's troops and, at a distance great enough to muffle their egress, stepped into their stirrups and rode off, attempting to return home by several circuitous routes, many surviving only on prickly pear fruit and bear grass. With the departure of these men and their rifles, the odds shifted in favor of the Texas troops. About ninety Confederates faced between thirty and thirty-five unwounded defenders.[19]

As the first rays of sunlight filtered through the cedars and the wafting powder smoke, an increase in action signaled the unfolding of the decisive phase of the battle. Two men ran from the camp chasing a group of frightened horses, and a volley of rifle fire from McRae's line dropped one of them. McRae then ordered a slow advance across the open area toward the camp. Both his and Homsley's detachments assaulted the camp, "firing as we advanced until within about 30 paces of their line, when I ordered a charge of both divisions, which was executed in fine style, resulting in the complete rout and flight of the enemy."[20]

When the Texans charged toward the camp, the defenders made a determined stand and, amid the confusion of bellowing rifles, yelling men, barking pistols, and choking powder smoke, killed two and wounded nineteen more of their attackers. Williams's account of the fighting states that some of the Confederates were hit while "foolishly exposing themselves." He characterized a determined defense from the camp: "They showed a bold front and dared us to come up." He continued, "Bullets were whistling pretty thickly over the heads of six or seven of us who were fighting together, and from our then position—it was difficult to return the fire with much effect." One of Duff's men fell dead with a bullet through the head, and four or five others were wounded; McRae tumbled to the ground with two wounds. Twice, intense fire from the camp forced the Confederates to fall back, but a renewed charge dispersed the settlers. Henry Schwethelm, one of the defenders, described the final attack. He heard the Confederate leader exclaim, "Charge them, boys! Charge them! Give them hell!" With what Williams remembered as a "galling fire," the cavalrymen rushed the camp. Sansom recalled that the Confederate "soldiers charged in with pistols blazing." This intense volume of fire and escalating casualties broke any final resistance, and McRae's remaining troops swept through the camp. Realizing they were in an untenable position, the remnants of Tegener's party, including the commander and five other wounded, succeeded in escaping through the thick cedar brakes.[21]

Unfortunately, after the shooting quieted, some of McRae's troops acted despicably and committed heinous atrocities upon the fallen German settlers. Nineteen dead and wounded immigrants lay scattered through the cedars. Several Confederates attempted to care for the wounded prisoners and bring them water. Despite their efforts, a group from Duff's battalion, later described as "cowardly wretches," carried or dragged nine to eleven of the wounded Germans into the thick cedar trees, where Lt. Edwin (or Edward) Lilly and his Partisan Rangers shot them in the head. Williams called Lilly "the remorseless, treacherous villain!" He later cited what he believed to be the motivation for the executions. "[Lilly's] chief motive, I believe, was to prove his zeal and devotion to the Southern cause, and by these base murders make himself popular with the authorities in San Antonio." McRae sent to Fort Clark, near Brackettville, about twenty miles away, for medical help for the wounded. The

fig. 11. John W. Sansom survived the "Battle of the Nueces" and went on to join the 1st Texas Cavalry Regiment (Union). He fought in the Red River Campaign of 1864 and after the war became a respected Texas Ranger. Courtesy Frankie Davis Glenn, Boerne, Texas

Confederates buried their dead in a long trench but left the Germans to the buzzards and wolves. Not until 1865 did a party recover the remains and bury them permanently in the soil near Comfort, Texas.[22]

In the aftermath of the battle, no one officially reported the murder of the wounded prisoners. McRae, wounded in the initial attack, either ignored Lilly's actions or, inexplicably, remained unaware of the executions. Sometime during the trip to Fort Clark, Lilly and his men, who claimed to be lost during a search for water, abandoned the column with the Confederate wounded. Four of the injured men died, either en route or after the procession finally straggled into Fort Clark. Although members of Taylor's battalion did not participate in the prisoners' executions, the event remained a blot on the history of the 1st Texas Cavalry, because guilt by association linked the regiment with what the *Dallas Morning News* in 1929 termed "the blackest crime in Texas warfare." Ironically, a few of the German survivors served with the 1st Texas Cavalry (Union), organized later in New Orleans, and fought against the 1st Texas Cavalry along the Red River in Louisiana.[23]

Revisionists such as Ella Lonn (*Foreigners in the Confederacy*), Don H. Biggers (*German Pioneers in Texas*), and descendants of the Unionists fervently attempt to portray the Germans as "poorly armed" farmers who were surprised and massacred by bloodthirsty Confederate soldiers. People die in war, but killing prisoners cannot be condoned or pardoned under any circumstances. Lilly's reprehensible murders must be condemned in the most forceful terms possible. Still, sources not cited by most writers disclose that the fleeing immigrants, contrary to popular belief, possessed a large quantity of weapons, including Colt revolvers; and their Jäger rifles were more than a match for the Confederate long arms. A few of Taylor's troops carried breech-loading Sharps carbines issued when they served with the 1st Texas Mounted Rifles, but the majority of McRae's force shouldered as their primary weapons a miscellany of percussion rifles and shotguns. Unionists who left camp before the fighting and those who escaped afterward carried away between forty and forty-five weapons. McRae listed thirty-three small arms and thirteen pistols captured at the site. Tegener's party then possessed between eighty-five and ninety weapons, proving they were not "poorly armed." Henry Schwethelm, one of the Unionists, stated that the settlers were "fully equipped with rifles and six-shooters (the rifles mostly of German make) and mounted on good horses with pack animals." At one camp along the trail, the settlers cut human figures into large trees and used them for rifle practice—an indication that they were not poor, defenseless farmers.[24]

Despite their unpreparedness, the defenders fought bravely and well, inflicting over 22 percent casualties on their attackers—losses large enough that, by modern standards, McRae's unit would be considered combat ineffective. Sansom later wrote, "We put up a fight of which not one of us needs be or is ashamed . . . Major Tegener and the brave men he commanded fought as heroes . . . and sustained themselves manfully." Williams supported Sansom's statement by commenting on "the gallant fight the enemy had made." The wounded immigrants were not "trampled to death" by McRae's horsemen, as T. R. Fehrenbach claimed; or dragged to nearby trees and hanged, as Ella Lonn alleged in *Foreigners in the Confederacy*. Unfortunately, most writers have based their versions of the battle on these flawed accounts.[25]

Of the casualties inflicted on Taylor's battalion, W. E. Poe (Company E) died on the scene, John K. Morris (Company B) fell mortally wounded, and Henry W. Barker (Company E) also was hit. The detachment from Company A sustained the highest proportion of casualties. Defending marksmen brought down five of these men with well-aimed shots: Latimore Edmundson, Stephen L. Erwin, Thomas J. Singleton, John Welch, and Wiley Williams. Taylor had had the prudence not to send any of the Germans of van der Stucken's company along with the Fredericksburg contingent.[26]

At the conclusion of the engagement, the pro-Union German casualties totaled twenty-five to twenty-seven, and the pursuing cavalrymen controlled the battlefield. The results, nonetheless, might have been quite different. As the Texans charged toward the camp, the defenders had made a determined stand, downing at least eleven of McRae's men and ten more of Homsley's. McRae's report stated that the Germans "offered the most determined resistance and fought with desperation." During the final throes of combat, Amil [or Amrey] Schreiner, who assumed leadership when Tegener fell wounded, endeavored to rally the Unionists by shouting, "*Laszt uns unser Leben so teuer wie moglich verkaufen*" ["Let us sell our lives as dearly as we can"]. Even so, the Germans had been surprised and were in a poor defensive posture. If Tegener had been more wary and the twenty-eight men who left had stayed to fight, McRae's troops might well have lost the battle. As events transpired, however, after the battle McRae was able to write, "My officers and men all behaved with the greatest coolness and gallantry, seeming to vie with each other in deeds of daring chivalry. It would be invidious to draw any distinction when all did their part nobly and gloriously." Bee, on October 21, 1862, also praised the Confederates and their actions: "Lieutenant McRae and his command behaved with admirable coolness and bravery, and did their work most effectually."[27]

From Fort Clark and Fredericksburg, Taylor's remaining contingents rode directly to their headquarters near San Antonio, while the battalion commander returned to find the situation quieted but with an undercurrent of unrest. Taylor's official records show him to be commander of a camp at San Antonio Springs from September through November, 1862. Evidently he decided that he needed to be present for duty after the uproar caused by the engagement on the Nueces. After that skirmish, the sparse records available offer little evidence that the battalion undertook anything other than routine patrols for several months.[28]

According to Sansom, on October 18, 1862, a patrol led by Homsley clashed with another group leaving the state, and eight more German Unionists were killed. No other accounts of this encounter were discovered, so this fray cannot be corroborated in extant sources. A medical furlough, however, issued on February 1, 1863, may be significant. Surgeon Henry P. Howard certified Pvt. Edwin J. Rancier, Company B, 8th (Taylor's) Cavalry Battalion, unfit for duty because of a gunshot wound to the arm incurred several weeks earlier, proving that some type of confrontation had occurred. Between December, 1862, and April, 1863, the battalion relocated several times. From San Antonio Springs the unit moved to Ringgold Barracks, where some kind of altercation occurred between Taylor and one of his company commanders.[29]

On February 22, 1863, Capt. James N. Harris sent a letter of resignation to Bee. Harris was a long-time member of both the 1st Mounted Rifles and the 8th Battalion of Cavalry. He had served previously as company clerk of Company K and hospital steward of McCulloch's Regiment. Elected captain of Company D, 8th Battalion Texas Cavalry, he commanded that unit until his verbal altercation with Taylor. Harris's letter described how, "In an unguarded moment I used offensive language to Maj. Jas. [*sic*] Taylor for which I have apologized and he has very kindly forgiven me." Taylor's forgiveness, however, was incomplete. Harris added that Taylor advised him to resign because "I know my nature is such I cannot control a body of men in such a manner as to make them as useful to our country as they should be in our present important struggle." He hoped his resignation would be accepted and "afford me an opportunity of serving my country as I can better do than by performing the duties either of an officer or soldier." Maj. Robert A. Myers approved the resignation, and Bee concurred when the letter reached his headquarters.[30]

Leaving Ringgold Barracks, the battalion relocated to Carricitas Lake in Cameron County on the Rio Grande, about twenty-five miles above Fort Brown. From this post, Taylor's cavalrymen continued the bone-wearying patrols necessary to safeguard the indispensable cotton trade. To prevent Mexican bandits or those few Unionists in Texas bold enough to strike out against the Confederacy from molesting isolated supply trains, the Texans spent endless hours in the saddle under the blistering South Texas sun. The unit's essential mission did not change significantly when, on May 2, 1863, it combined with Yager's 3rd Battalion of Cavalry and Capt. James A. Ware's company of Partisan Rangers to reconstitute the 1st Regiment of Texas Cavalry.[31]

CHAPTER 7

Bullets, Beans, Stalwart Men, and Sturdy Steeds

The 1st Regiment Mounted Rifles and the 1st Texas Cavalry faced numerous problems in recruiting men and procuring adequate supplies. Examining these difficulties illuminates the wider problems involved in creating new fighting units in Texas and the Confederacy. The ability to recruit troops in Texas varied considerably over time. "War fever" usually kept recruiting officers busy filling new Confederate army units. At times, however, the recruiting officers found few men willing to enlist. Numerous reasons lay behind the great variation in enlistment cycles. Col. Henry E. McCulloch faced problems on the frontier because settlers only reluctantly left their families and property at the mercy of the Plains Indians. Men had no desire to leave their families defenseless on the sparsely populated frontier.[1]

Initial Confederate victories at Oak Hill, Missouri, and Bull Run, Virginia, also slowed recruiting. Why volunteer to go fight back east when the Confederacy would win without further volunteers? Many men were unwilling to enlist for three years or the duration of the war. Texans clung to the American citizen-soldier tradition of enlisting for only a short term. A one-year obligation seemed quite adequate to most Texas volunteers. To counter this reluctance, Brig. Gen. Paul O. Hebert, Texas Departmental Commander, issued a general order stating that, after November 6, 1861, troops must enlist for no less than three years or the duration of the war. The fact remained that some men hesitated to enlist simply because they, for diverse reasons, were reluctant to confront the United States.[2]

On April 16, 1862, to alleviate recruiting problems, the Confederate government passed the Conscription Act. This law contained sundry provisions governing recruiting and exemptions to mandatory service. All enlisted men between eighteen and thirty-five who were in service before April 16, 1862, suddenly realized that their commitment had increased to three years. This held true even if soldiers originally had enlisted for only twelve months. Supposedly, all men from eighteen to thirty-five years of age, if healthy, were subject to conscription. A lengthy list of exemptions, however, allowed loopholes for many eligible men. Exemptions from the law caused another slowdown in volunteers. A significant number of men subject to mandatory service saw the exemptions as unfair and declared that this was "a rich man's war and a poor man's fight."[3]

The Conscription Act, nevertheless, had a positive impact on recruiting. Often pride took over and Texans volunteered instead of being conscripted, which was considered dishonorable. Some men volunteered in order to choose the type of unit in which they would serve. Continued rumors of Federal invasions of the state also stimulated cavalry recruiting until the end of the war. Other than the usual difficulty in recruiting men from the frontier settlements, cavalry recruiting officers generally had few problems filling their enlistment quotas.[4]

Recruiting a company was never a smooth operation, but Texans answered the call much more willingly if they knew that they were joining a cavalry unit. A vast majority of Texans wished to fight only on horseback and shunned the infantry. Some sources asserted that Texans volunteered for the cavalry at a rate of 27 to 1 over the infantry. Actual figures of regiments raised gave Texas cavalry a numerical superiority of 2.4 to 1 over the infantry. In any case, cavalry units formed rapidly. Recruiters also offered a fifty-dollar enlistment bounty to men enlisting for three years or the war. Bounty money often encouraged men to "jine the cavalry."[5]

Texas contributed such a large number of cavalry units to the Confederate army that many of them had to be dismounted to provide essential infantry. Texans did not gracefully accept being without horses and insisted upon calling themselves "dismounted cavalry" instead of admitting to being infantry. While garrisoned at Sabine Pass, the 1st Texas Cavalry operated without a portion of its mounts for about two months. The government pastured the horses inland at Camp Bernard, but the regiment never officially dismounted.[6]

Little difference existed between the men who enrolled in the companies of the 1st Regiment of Texas Cavalry and other Texas units. Regimental membership included some native Texans, but the majority of the troops were born

fig. 12. Augustus Buchel, a European-trained professional soldier, commanded the 1st Texas Cavalry from May, 1863, until his death at Pleasant Hill, Louisiana, on April 12, 1864. Courtesy Archives Division, Texas State Library, Austin

elsewhere. Although almost every state in the Union was represented, most came from the southern and border states. Germany, Ireland, Scotland, England, and France also contributed individuals to the unit. The regiment represented the entire spectrum of the state's population. Companies rode out of Marshall, Tyler, and the counties of East Texas. Indianola, Victoria, and the coastal counties sent their best officers and men to the regiment. Certainly the counties around San Antonio and Austin gave of the best "gentlemen" in the state. Surprisingly, the Germans from the settlements surrounding Fredericksburg and New Braunfels enlisted in numbers sufficient as to be quite noticeable. Muster rolls of the regiment truly exemplified a cross-section of the population of Texas. Several Mexican nationals also served with the companies. Both Col. Augustus Buchel, a military professional from Germany who commanded both the 3rd Texas Infantry and 1st Texas Cavalry, and Maj. William O. Yager made disparaging remarks about the Mexican soldiers, however. Both considered them virtually useless. In dispatches, Buchel wrote that he thought them more of a detriment than any aid. They deserted freely and could be enticed away from their posts with a "few dollars and some whiskey." He felt the same about the Federal deserters who entered Confederate service.[7]

Men who joined the regiment had held a variety of jobs or professional positions before becoming soldiers. Muster rolls verified that physicians, surgeons, and members of the bar signed up to serve. Others formerly had occupied positions with the U.S. government—as U.S. marshals, judges, customs agents, and inspectors, for example. The regimental rosters also contained farmers, stock raisers, *rancheros* (cowboys), sailors, store clerks, and at least one buffalo hunter. Since the troops enlisted from all sections of Texas, their occupations reflected those of the entire state.[8]

Reasons for enlisting also varied greatly. Enthusiasm for states' rights stood high on the list, as it did throughout the secessionist states. Inflammatory speeches concerning southern rights stirred the sectionalist pride of the men, and they joined up. A circular written by McCulloch stated, "Every ablebodied freeman should contribute his might and life if necessary to uphold southern liberties." Pride in state and nation brought some to volunteer, but the romantic vision of glory in war and fifty dollars in promised bounty money could not be discounted as motivators.[9]

Like other southerners, many Texans considered northern society a "godless and grasping thing intent on destroying their way of life," and guilty for years of tramping on southern rights. Northern politicians had "been totally unreasonable," almost thwarting Missouri's entry into the Union as a slave state, barring the South from southwestward expansion after the Mexican War, and threatening the South's economy with high protective tariffs. Moreover, hypocritical northerners kept white factory workers "in a condition far worse than slavery," while denouncing black slavery in the South. Northern Radicals also gave liberal financial support to "vile monsters" such as the fanatical abolitionist William Lloyd Garrison. To many Texans, these actions struck at their concepts of personal and states' rights, which, for some, were inextricably linked to slavery. Especially in cotton-producing East Texas, slavery was so interwoven with the cause of states' rights that the two became indistinguishable. If they were not already slave owners, numerous young Texans probably sought the opportunity to invest in land and slaves, hoping thereby to reap the economic benefits of "the peculiar institution." While many Texans may not have said outright that protection of slavery was their motive for volunteering, slavery likely figured in their notion of what constituted states' rights.[10]

Correspondence among the German settlers reveals no one explicit reason why they left their farms to join the regiment. German immigrants typically rejected the institution of slavery and supported the Union. Most German settlers wanted to remain in the Union, but with the "full rights of the people respected." Most of the German representatives to the Texas Secessionist

Convention voted to leave the Union, but counties with large German populations voted against secession. Comal County was a noted exception.[11]

German immigrants held a great variety of views about leaving the Union. Some in Gillespie County favored a convention of slave states. Apparently the Germans took the responsibilities of citizenship earnestly and contributed to the defense of their adopted country and of a state's right to solve its own problems without federal interference. Also influencing the German settlers' opinions was the governmental oppression they had witnessed in Europe during the 1840s and 1850s.[12]

Similar concern for individual and independent action manifested itself in the manner in which officers were selected in the regiment. The men elected their officers by popular vote, and these elections promoted men by popularity, not by ability. In contrast to many Confederate organizations, Texans elected officers hardened by years of fighting Indians and bandits along an advancing frontier. Most Texas officers had fought in the Mexican War or campaigned with ranging companies and knew each other personally or by reputation. Although few had formal military training, they displayed the mandatory traits of personal courage and ability to lead men. As a result, few inept officers impaired the 1st Texas Cavalry's performance of its duties. Civilians generally lacked the training or skills to lead or control unruly men in stressful situations. Most Texans despised discipline and drill, and it required an uncommon commander to demand discipline and keep the unruly Texans in line. Fortunately for its members, the 1st Texas Cavalry's commanders were unwavering, forceful men who exacted the very best performance from their subordinates. Either the men elected their noncommissioned officers or the captain appointed them, depending on the company. After elections, the men took an oath to the state and the Confederacy and mustered into the Confederate army. More than a few Texas cavalrymen took their oath seriously but reported for duty more than a little drunk.[13]

Texas furnished the Confederacy many more cavalrymen than in any other branch of service. In the Trans-Mississippi alone in 1861–62, the state provided thirty-nine regiments and ten separate battalions. Average regimental strength totaled 947 officers and men, while the battalions averaged 440, bringing the total strength of Texas cavalrymen to 41,333. In 1863–65, Texas had in service eighteen cavalry regiments and five battalions, with average strengths of 800 and 400 respectively, for a total of 16,400. The 1st Texas Mounted Rifles mustered 1,009 initially. In the spring of 1863, Yager's battalion listed 404 troopers fit for duty and Taylor's 407. The 1st Texas Cavalry's muster rolls in December, 1863, listed 72 officers and 1,273 men present for duty. By the end of the war, the number of men on the rolls had decreased to less than 500 officers and men present and fit for duty. As the conflict dragged on, the regiment shrank, as casualties due to combat, disease, and desertion took their toll. To exacerbate the problem, fewer recruits volunteered to fill vacancies. By the end of 1862, recruiting of new units had slowed considerably, and in 1864 it stopped altogether. New recruits were sent to organized regiments in an attempt to maintain them at their required strength. Judging from the number of troops fit for duty at the war's end, the attempt obviously failed.[14]

Supplying the cavalry proved much more difficult than inducting volunteers. Texas lacked the means to provide the vast amounts of arms, ammunition, food, clothing, medicines, and various incidentals required by an army campaigning in the field. After 1845 and statehood, most Texas citizens came to rely upon imported goods for their daily needs. Large numbers of Texas residents drifted away from self-manufacturing and looked to merchants and traders for life's necessities. After a few months, Union blockades cut off imports of essential manufactured products, inaugurating years of hardships. Texas possessed little in the way of iron or steel manufacturing. Although thousands of bales of cotton were raised in the state, the clothing and textile industry advanced little prior to the war. Because of other priorities, the state did little to improve or advance the textile industry during the Civil War. The scarcity of manufacturing and textile production directly affected the 1st Texas Cavalry; the state could not adequately supply the men with required clothing and equipment.[15]

Cotton became the most important commodity in Texas. Europeans, especially the English, bought large quantities of cotton, and the money received financed the war effort. In addition to currency, some dealers exchanged cotton directly for arms, ammunition, and other military goods. To guarantee a constant flow of war materiel, the Confederate military appropriated control of the cotton trade and appointed army officers as examining agents for contracts on cotton shipments. The officers had the responsibility of conducting the exchange of cotton for receipts and specie, which the quartermasters then used to purchase arms, ammunition, and other supplies. Buchel served as an examining agent until late 1863. The military considered the trade so important that, in late 1863, Brig. Gen. Hamilton P. Bee delayed his departure from the Rio Grande when ordered to East Texas to counter a threatened Federal invasion. Bee remained to insure that a consignment of Enfield rifles and ammunition passed rapidly from Matamoros, Mexico, to Brownsville. The cotton trade remained the only means of sustaining the war effort. Maintaining open trade routes required stationing several units of Confederate cavalry between San Antonio and Fort Brown.[16]

Texas boasted one enormous, reliable resource not dependent on the cotton trade: the Texas plains provided a steady supply of sturdy horses. On the Llano Estacado, or staked plains, alone, more than fifty thousand wild horses roamed over the rich prairie grass. Before the war, "mustangers" chasing wild horses easily corralled one hundred to four hundred mustangs in a single roundup. Because of the state's poor roads and vast distances, Texans relied upon large numbers of horses for transportation.[17]

Immigrants brought blooded horses to Texas, and some of them escaped, mixing with the Spanish Andalusian strain of horses already roaming the plains. This mixing of bloodlines produced a breed of rugged but agile mustangs that provided a ready supply of mounts for the cavalry. Referring to the mixed-blooded horses, a Jackson County settler wrote to the *Austin City Gazette* on July 25, 1840, "The result is that the crosses, or half-breeds, are the best horses that we have ever had. They are said to combine more of action, hardiness, and kindness of disposition than any other kind."[18]

This "Texas horse" aptly proved itself equal or superior to "American horses." In 1848 Viktor Bracht wrote, "This breed has great endurance, is of medium size, strongly built, and is considerably less expensive to keep than is the fine American horse." Except for a few months toward the end of the conflict, Texas units never suffered any shortage of horses. In the fall of 1862, Bee reported that his Western Sub-District of Texas had more than 1,100 horses for about a thousand cavalrymen. The state even offered to ship Gen. Robert E. Lee 1,000 horses, but the plan never came to fruition. Only a faulty supply system in the Confederate Trans-Mississippi Department resulted in a lack of remounts on the battlefield.[19]

Under a Congressional Act of March 6, 1861, the Confederate army required cavalry volunteers to provide their own mounts and accouterments. Soldiers received forty cents per day for providing their own horses and equipment. The government also promised reimbursement for an individual's horse if the animal was killed in action. When recruits mustered in, boards of officers appraised the value of their horses and equipment. Values of horses in the 1st Texas Cavalry ran from $15 to $195 early in the war to more than $600 after Confederate currency became almost worthless late in the conflict. Estimates of the value of saddles and equipment ranged from $10 to $100. Confederate officials concluded that individuals could provide better mounts by private purchase than the government could buy. They also reasoned that a soldier would be more likely to take care of his own property than of the government's. Regulations required that the horses be branded "CS" to identify them as military mounts. Unit quartermasters were responsible for providing grain, hay, and veterinary supplies for the animals.[20]

Most Texans who owned horses simply mounted and rode their private saddle horses in to volunteer. For those who lacked horses, the army rounded up wild mustangs and herded them in to be purchased by the prospective cavalrymen. Sometimes private individuals and organizations donated horses to local cavalry units. The wild horses brought in had to be broken to saddle and bridle; some exhibited such frenzied behavior that they had to be roped and thrown just to be shod. For excitement, the Texans frequently trained unbroken horses on a town's main street near the camp, "just to liven up the citizenry a little."[21]

Confederates confiscated several hundred U.S. cavalry horses and mules when Federal troops departed from Texas. A majority of the horses were fine eastern mounts, much larger than the saddle horses common in Texas. Officers who had been trained back east were accustomed to horses fifteen hands high and taller; they considered the mustangs too small and frail to carry the large loads required for cavalrymen. As events unfolded, however, the eastern-bred horses failed to stand up to the long, dry marches essential to campaigning in Texas. To maintain their stamina, the large horses required considerable amounts of grain. Even then, they quickly broke down, especially after a few days pursuing Indians or Mexican bandits across Texas' sun-scorched plains and *brasada*. During peak summer heat and bleak winters on the plains, even the wiry mustangs, accustomed to surviving on little water and scant grass, could not long endure extended campaigning without supplemental grain and hay.[22]

Controversy still exists over which horses were best; but the short, stocky mustang proved that it was better than the bigger horses at surviving long scouts on the plains and carrying the fight to the Yankees in Louisiana. Army officers familiar with the little horses often expressed their admiration. In 1833, Col. H. C. Brish penned an opinion that he had "never met with anything of the horse kind that possessed the strength, action, and wind equal to the 'mustang' horse . . . or that could endure fatigue and hunger equal to them." He believed the mustang "superior to any others on the face of the earth for cavalry purposes." Another officer described one of his "prairie studs," saying the animal had "fine hard hoofs, pretty good legs and muscle, his color is white and he is about 14-1/2 hands high." In 1846, Marcellus Bell Edwards, accompanying U.S. troops during the Mexican War, described the mustangs as "small, vicious, and fiery, and generally well-trained." Touring the Texas-Mexican border in April, 1863, English Lt. Col. James Arthur Fremantle described the mustangs as "rather rawboned animals, but hardy and fast." Faced with constant shortages of grain, the sturdy little mustang remained in better condition than the saddlebreds and jumpers of Missouri and Louisiana. The ability of their horses to graze off the local grasses and stay healthy with little care gave the Texans an advantage over their enemies in terms of mobility.[23]

Frequently quartermasters failed to secure enough grain for unit animals, or companies operated at some distance from their source of supply. Early in the war, if feed was available, cavalrymen paid the owner for the feed and then requested reimbursement from the government. Later, quartermaster officers and individual soldiers commandeered feed for the animals and, sometimes, paid with a government voucher. The daily allowance for each horse and mule was nine pounds of oats or barley or six pounds of corn in the summer months. During the winter, when the animals needed more energy, they were allocated nine pounds of corn and thirteen pounds of hay or other fodder.[24]

Providing the necessary amount of feed for the animals required large expenditures of time and money. For example, a company of eighty-five men with thirty mules and pack horses required 31,050 pounds of grain for thirty days and an additional 44,850 pounds of hay in winter. Multiply the amount by ten companies, and the large burden placed on the supply system, just to provide feed for regimental animals, becomes readily obvious.[25]

Paying for large amounts of horse feed and provisions for the men placed added stress on the 1st Texas Cavalry. McCulloch owned three horses and his men at least one each; some officers had two or more. Providing food for these animals placed a financial burden on men who did not receive any pay for several months. State officials declined to appropriate money to reimburse the regiment for expenses until some months after the unit entered service. Letters from L. B. Northrop, head of the Confederate Department of Subsistence, to Capt. John R. King, regimental commissary, indicated that the Confederate government sent between $9,500 and $10,000 per quarter to fund regimental expenses, but this money seldom arrived on a timely basis. Once McCulloch wrote to inform King that $10,000 in Confederate notes were en route "by Private George Munson, if he lives to reach your post." The government rushed into the war so unprepared that McCulloch's staff and commanders utilized U.S. Army forms to request payment for their disbursements. Regimental quartermaster and commissary officers crossed out the "U.S." and entered "C.S." on requisition forms.[26]

In addition to horses, Confederate cavalrymen provided their own tack and other equipment. Individual equipment normally consisted of at least one bridle, picket rope, saddle blanket, and saddle (usually Texas-style, with a horn and two cinches). Fremantle described the Texans' saddles as "nearly like [those of] the Mexicans." If a trooper rode a government-supplied saddle, it was usually a McClellan or similar military style, with no horn. Government equipment issues routinely included one or more pairs of spurs, a saddle, bridle, blanket, curry combs and brushes, a picket pin, a lariat (more than likely called a rope by the Texans), and other incidentals the trooper might find necessary to care for his mount.[27]

Losing a horse and associated accouterments was a virtual calamity for a mounted soldier. Army regulations dictated that he replace his mount and equipment at his own expense and then request reimbursement. Low pay and continued devaluation of Confederate currency made any purchase seem exorbitant. In his reminiscences, Pvt. Levi Lamoni Wight, who enlisted in the company of Capt. Frank van der Stucken in 1862, recalled that "at the time Confedret money was good"; during the ensuing years, however, the money became "worthles," and "we served out our time with out pay." Cavalry privates earned $12 per month, corporals $24, and sergeants $29. They were paid only every three to six months. Their officers fared better, with captains receiving $140 per month, second lieutenants $90, and first lieutenants $100. Field officers collected even better pay; colonels received $210 per month and majors $162. Even so, by 1864 a good horse sometimes cost over $600 in Confederate currency. Early in the war, the army allowed soldiers to leave on furlough to procure another horse, but later such large numbers of men left the fighting that the Trans-Mississippi Department began to hold a pool of horses from which individuals could purchase remounts. After June, 1864, the army allowed a soldier forty days to secure a new mount or be transferred to an infantry unit from his state.[28]

Saddles and other equipment also grew scarce and escalated in value. One Texas cavalryman who was captured and returned to his unit vowed to kill the Yankee who had his saddle or "if not that one then another one." By the end of the war, newly established saddle manufacturers near Tyler provided saddles and other leather goods to the Trans-Mississippi Department. Texas horsemen then had an opportunity to purchase replacement saddles and equipment, but these new sources never completely alleviated shortages of saddles, harness, and other tack.[29]

Wild horses may have been recalcitrant and saddles difficult to replace, but neither presented the multiplicity of problems encountered in outfitting the regiment with arms and ammunition. From beginning to end, the 1st Texas Mounted Rifles and 1st Texas Cavalry were short of both. McCulloch issued a substantial number of carbines, rifles, pistols, and sabers from the captured Federal arsenals, but he could not afford to distribute all the captured weapons to his regiment. Texas had formed several regiments, and these new units demanded their share of available weapons and ammunition. An additional one thousand Colt revolvers purchased for the state in late 1861 did not relieve the shortage of serviceable firearms for the military. Many old flintlocks had to be converted to percussion-cap mechanisms to be of any great value in warfare. Gov. Edward Clark estimated that civilians owned over forty thousand weapons, and the state government attempted to buy these firearms, but with little success. Clark may have forgotten that most of these rifles and pistols were desperately needed to defend frontier settlers against Indian attacks. Eventually, when men began to volunteer, large numbers of privately owned weapons found their way into army service.[30]

Because procuring large numbers of military weapons required time and money, the Confederate government made several attempts to induce volunteers to provide their own arms. On May 17, 1862, the Department of Texas issued General Orders No. 40, which included several provisions regulating compensation to individuals who supplied their own arms and equipment. For soldiers who provided their own arms, the government offered two options. Recruits might either sell their weapons to the Confederate States at full price, or collect one dollar per month for their use. Texas endeavored to supply cartridge boxes, holsters, belts, screwdrivers, and other equipment required by a soldier but, because of shortages, many volunteers brought their own accouterments along with their firearms. Men bore a variety of cartridge boxes, pouches, cap boxes, belts, and knapsacks. Types of material mattered little. If a board of evaluating officers judged the gear durable and serviceable, the government reimbursed enlistees for providing their individual equipment. The order also stipulated that each soldier must provide, or be provided, one hundred rounds of ammunition suitable for his weapon. Ordnance officers, upon requisitions approved by regimental commanders, furnished fixed ammunition, lead, powder, buckshot, caps, and flints as required. The military stamped all private firearms consigned to army service with some type of Confederate identification. Stamping provided a means of tracking the weapons and prevented them from being sold to the government repeatedly.[31]

Men who brought their own weapons when they enlisted eased one problem but intensified another set of difficulties. Requirements for varied types of ammunition plagued the 1st Texas Cavalry throughout the war. Civilians owned a great conglomeration of rifles, shotguns, and pistols, requiring an assortment of ammunition. In May, 1861, McCulloch directed King that, in addition to his commissary duties, he was to secure one hundred thousand rounds of ammunition. Because new recruits carried a variety of weapons, McCulloch instructed King to procure a mixture of munitions, one-fourth to one-third rifle powder, shot (buckshot), and caps, with the "balance for Sharps carbine, percussion rifle, and Colt's six shooters of both sizes." McCulloch expressed his concern that much of the ammunition available to the regiment was "damaged and unusable." Because of shortages, Texas horsemen often cast their own bullets and used bulk powder and blank cartridges to prepare their own fixed ammunition. Buck and ball (a cartridge containing both a round ball and buckshot) was extremely popular with the cavalrymen. Captured Union weapons provided the troops with quality arms, but ammunition remained a burden for the Ordnance Department. Providing myriad types of ammunition to the regiment only aggravated supply hardships.[32]

Obviously no standard weapons existed in the regiment. The 1st Texas Cavalry carried a variety of firearms: percussion rifles, Sharps carbines, shotguns, and both Army and Navy Colt pistols. Pvt. William Kuykendall, Company D, wrote that his company was "armed mainly with shotguns and civilian rifles." In September, 1862, ammunition requests indicated that Taylor's battalion still carried the same miscellany of weapons. A tri-monthly report from the 1st Texas Cavalry, dated December 20, 1863, listed 54 muskets, 253 Enfield rifles, 53 carbines and musketoons, 100 Mississippi Rifles, 47 Minié muskets, 16 shotguns, 28 Sharps rifles, 51 revolvers, 28 sporting rifles, 3 pairs of holster pistols, and 13 Harper's Ferry rifles. Pvt. Pleasant S. Hagy wrote that, during the Matagorda campaign in the winter of 1863–64, Company F carried Enfield rifles exclusively. The Enfields could have been one of two types, either the British Enfield imported through Mexico in exchange for cotton, or a rifle manufactured in Tyler called the "Enfield Rifle" or "Texas Rifle." Since the 1st Texas Cavalry initially operated near Mexico, regimental rifles probably were English Enfields.[33]

In addition to arms manufactured both in the U.S. and abroad, the 1st Texas Cavalry bore weapons supplied by Texas manufacturers, but lack of raw materials slowed production. In Lancaster, Dallas County, Labon E. Tucker, A. W. Tucker, J. H. Sherrard, W. L. Killen, and Pleasant Taylor formed a manufacturing firm chartered under the name of Tucker, Sherrard, and Company. On January 11, 1862, the Texas Military Board passed an article "to manufacture quality arms for military defense of the state." Tucker and Sherrard received a contract to produce 1,500 "army type 44 caliber pistols" and 1,500 "36 caliber navy type pistols." Because of production delays and inflated currency, the company produced only 400 revolvers; these were sold to private individuals, not the state government. Tucker, Sherrard, and Company manufactured revolvers patterned after the famous and dependable .44-caliber Army and .36-caliber Navy Colt handguns. Some of the revolvers sported a fancy German-silver star in the grips and were prized by Texas cavalrymen. Those Texans who owned one of the pistols considered them equal in quality and dependability to any Colt firearm.[34]

Colt revolvers certainly were the pistols of choice for the Texans. When forming the regiment, McCulloch instructed his men to obtain a Colt revolver, mentioning Colt by name. Abundant references to Colts and "six shooters" appeared in service records and letters of the period. Most concern the 1851 .36-caliber Navy model and the 1860 .44-caliber Army Colt, but .36- and .44-caliber Remington revolvers must have filled several holsters. The larger Walker Colt and "Dragoon Model," also .44-caliber, undoubtedly rode along with many Texas cavalrymen. References to "five shooters" presumably alluded to one of three main types of Colt pistols: the 1849 Pocket Model, the 1862 Police Model, or the venerable Patterson Colt that the Texas Rangers had brought to Texas in the late 1830s. Members of the 1st Texas Cavalry strapped on a variety of pistols; late in the war, many carried two or three different models.[35]

A substantial number of volunteers mustered in without any firearms at all. The Confederate government attempted to supply acceptable arms to these men, but a dearth of suitable weapons persisted. A very small number of enlistees received a short, double-barreled shotgun and two single-shot saddle-holster pistols, which were virtually useless when fighting on horseback. Soldiers who were issued these obsolete pistols soon traded them for more practical revolvers. Shortages of modern weapons and the variety of ammunition required by the regiment resulted in the Texans' being outgunned by Union cavalry, who carried more sophisticated breech-loading Sharps or Maynard carbines.[36]

Extracts from 1863 ordnance receipts of several companies of the 1st Texas Cavalry exemplify the myriad types of ammunition required by the regiment:

2 kegs powder
6000 caps
3000 pistol cartridges
2000 Miss. Rifle Ball Cartridges
1000 Holster Pistol Ball
5000 B[uck] & ball cartridges
6000 percussion musket caps
600 pounds powder rifle
300 pounds lead
38 bullet molds pistols
11 bullet molds rifle
3000 colts pistol cartridges (N S [Navy size])

3000 colts pistol cartridges (A.S. [Army size])
4000 perc[ussio]n. rifle cartridges, good condition
50 pounds buck shot
960 blank cartridges, good[37]

The regiment overwhelmed the Yankees in one area, however. Almost to a man, the Texans sported heavy-bladed "Bowie" knives. Most frontiersmen considered a good knife a necessity for eating, mess duties, and general camp life. Jim Bowie's reputation proved that a stout, long-bladed knife could be deadly in close-quarter fights, and most young men believed that such a knife was a mandatory item of equipment. To enhance their soldierly appearance, many young volunteers purchased specially made, and sometimes gaudy, knives before they left home for the army. Many troopers found these long, heavy knives quite cumbersome, however, and discarded them in a few months.[38]

Differing from other cavalry units, the 1st Texas Cavalry employed sabers even though most Texans considered the saber an unfamiliar, long, unwieldy knife. Some "gentlemen" had experience with fencing and sword duels, but dueling called for a much lighter blade than the heavy cavalry saber; experience with smaller-bladed weapons could be discounted in most instances. In a mounted saber charge, the trooper carried the weapon at shoulder height, with the point forward. Upon reaching the enemy, the trooper rammed the point home, followed by a backhand slash across the enemy body. The saber could be devastating in a close-quarter cavalry fight, but most Texans preferred a brace of revolvers. Records and receipts confirm that the 1st Mounted Rifles were issued sabers during their frontier service. Because of McCulloch's misgivings concerning sabers, the regiment may have stored them away, preferring to carry more ammunition rather than a saber. Supply records indicate that several men paid seven dollars for lost sabers; whether they lost the weapons on patrol or misplaced them in camp remains unclear. By 1863, the 1st Texas Cavalry not only carried sabers but trained to use them as cavalry, not just as mounted infantry. Several instances of the regiment's brandishing sabers and wielding them in charges against the Yankees appear in accounts of the regiment's exploits along the coast and in the Red River Expedition.[39]

Army regulations established exact amounts of foodstuffs parceled out in soldiers' rations. Provisions issued included beef (fresh or salted), bacon or pork, flour, cornmeal, beans, rice, vinegar, salt, and desiccated vegetables. The soldiers also received molasses, soap, and candles when available. Normal issue included one pound of fresh beef or one-half pound of pork or bacon. Commissaries allocated twelve ounces of baked bread per ration, but if no bread or hardtack (called hardbread by the Texans) was available, they distributed one and a half pounds of corn meal or flour to each man per day. Regulations allowed six pounds of coffee and twelve pounds of sugar per one hundred men.[40]

Providing adequate food and sustenance for the regiment posed complicated logistical and monetary issues almost immediately after the regiment's activation. On April 20, 1861, McCulloch reported that bread and flour rations at Camps Cooper and Colorado and at Fort Chadbourne were almost exhausted and that other posts had no bread at all. He ordered King to contract immediately for ten thousand pounds of flour "from the wheat producing portions of Texas." McCulloch imagined that the flour would be cheaper and more quickly delivered by local contractors than by New Orleans merchants. On May 24, King reported signing contracts to deliver sixty thousand pounds of flour to the regiment; in June he signed a receipt for ten thousand more, shipped to Camps Cooper and Colorado. In August, 1861, Texas Departmental Headquarters directed King to secure civilian contracts guaranteeing flour and beef deliveries to meet regimental requirements until June, 1862. Deliveries were sporadic, however, and company commissary officers often complained about lack of bread and flour. Much of the flour came from mills at the German community of Fredericksburg. When the regiment ran short of flour in December, 1861, the German immigrants in that vicinity donated several hundred pounds of flour, along with corn and two hundred live beeves to feed the soldiers who protected them and their property from Indian raids.[41]

Texas cavalrymen prepared flour, when available, using a variety of cooking methods. When time and ovens were convenient, unit cooks mixed flour into dough and baked bread in loaves, but cornbread predominated in the men's menu. On extended patrols and campaigns, the men seldom received flour. If they received such a luxury, they usually made it into flapjacks fried in bacon fat and eaten with equally scarce molasses, if available. At times troops mixed flour, salt, and water into a thick dough which they wrapped around a rifle ramrod or long stick. Placing the dough where it would bake over a campfire, the Texans called this concoction "snake bread." Ramrods also served as hangers upon which soldiers suspended bacon over a fire. Another method of preparing bread involved wrapping the dough in cornshucks and baking it in the hot coals of a campfire. As the war progressed, flour became so scarce that Texans considered it a luxury.[42]

Securing adequate amounts of beef and pork frustrated the best efforts of regimental commissary officers. King arranged contracts with William O.

Burnam, Arver Crownover, and I. T. Ward to deliver fresh beef to the frontier posts garrisoned by the 1st Mounted Rifles. Although fresh beef arrived on the hoof, companies periodically ran short of meat rations. For the first few months of the war, the Department of Texas lacked sufficient salted beef, pork, and bacon to provide the growing number of regiments the requisite amounts of cured meat; fresh beef and pork could not be delivered fast enough to compensate for these shortages. King received instructions to issue live beef at least five times a week and more often if beef cattle were available. His instructions included issuing salt meat "as sparingly as possible." Shortages of meat continued throughout the war, and regimental records are full of letters referring to the need for promptly securing meat contracts. In November, 1861, for example, McCulloch, citing scarcity of bacon, directed King to "search for [a] contract at ten cents per pound for hog-round or twelve cents per pound per side of good quality bacon." The regiment operated on less than the required meat rations for most of the war. Sometimes the men jerked or smoked beef to retard spoilage and to make it lighter to carry. When patrolling along the Rio Grande, the regiment lived on Mexican beef. Sometimes they issued the owners of the beeves they butchered a voucher for payment, but generally they just roped an animal and dragged it off to camp. Lacking adequate meat supplies, commissaries issued mutton during the Red River Campaign. Texans, raised in cattle country, did not readily accept eating snotty-nosed sheep![43]

Receipts signed in October, 1862, by Lt. Hugo O. Hefter, commissary officer for Taylor's 8th Battalion, afford an excellent picture of "subsistence stores" supplied to troops from the Department of Texas:

7 barrels of pork
1300 pounds of bacon
5087 pounds of flour
5754 pounds of meal
30 bushels of hominy
370 pounds of coffee
203 pounds of wheat
1310 pounds of sugar
83 pounds of molasses
15 bushels of salt
700 pounds of desct. [desiccated] vegetables
500 pounds of desct. [desiccated] potatoes
846 pounds of sugar
361 pounds of soft soap[44]

Families remaining at home planted gardens and extra food crops to feed the soldiers away at the front. Civilians donated food supplies to the units camped near their homes and sent wagonloads of provisions to the army in the field. Winter, money, and transportation difficulties presented major impediments to soldiers' receiving sufficient rations. Winter was problematical because of the lack of fruit and vegetables in the orchards and fields for foraging parties. When food became scarce, the cavalry sent out parties to scour the countryside for provisions. Foragers scrounged anything edible growing in fields and orchards. Of course, pigs, chickens, cattle, and any other livestock became fair game for both campaigning armies. Civilians sold provisions to the army, but many were mercenary in their business arrangements. In Louisiana, for example, farmers sold corn and grain to Federal troops for $3.00 a barrel when Confederates offered only $1.50 in almost worthless Confederate notes. Cavalrymen ate reasonably well when supply trains reached them; frequently, however, especially in Louisiana, they suffered from food shortages. When rations were scarce, a Texas soldier's daily ration sometimes consisted of only a few handfuls of parched corn.[45]

Transportation of food and other supplies became a major concern of Confederate officers. Ordnance, commissary, and quartermaster departments lacked wagons and carts adequate to supply the troops, especially when units relocated in rapidly shifting combat situations. Texas lacked sufficient government rolling stock to gather and distribute crucial supplies. The quartermaster depot in San Antonio asked private citizens to bring their corn and taxes in kind to San Antonio, because the depot lacked the facilities to collect the corn. The depot also entreated citizens to sell hay and fodder to the army. Again, private citizens provided their own wagons to carry the fodder to San Antonio. The depot quartermaster promised to pay transportation fees and not to impress private wagons hauling grain to San Antonio. Wagon-yards built wagons and ambulances in East Texas during the war, but a critical shortage of rolling stock continued to plague the cavalry throughout the war. During campaigns in Louisiana, lack of wagons limited the combat effectiveness of the cavalry, because many soldiers had to be detached from fighting duties to comb the countryside for scarce supplies. Company commanders appointed ordnance, commissary, and quartermaster sergeants to gather supplies for their units, but they could not alleviate the supply shortages, especially of coffee, which the Texans deemed essential to daily life. Soldiers boiled parched Indian corn and okra seeds to make mock coffee.[46]

Periodically the 1st Texas Cavalry enjoyed a fine repast, but service from South and West Texas to the bayou country of Louisiana frequently subjected troopers to paltry meals. Texans living along the frontier habitually survived with little food for long intervals, and many excelled at augmenting their diet with wild game. Hardy frontiersmen taught these skills to less skillful townsmen who were untutored in foraging and living off the land. While beef and cornmeal generally constituted the major portion of rations, the horsemen were able to supplement their issued rations with deer, rabbits, turkey, quail, and other game. Pvt. H. C. Medford, a member of another regiment accompanying the 1st Texas Cavalry on its 1864 march to Louisiana, described his daily fare. He breakfasted on "fried bacon, beefsteaks, cornbread, hardbread, and coffee." For supper, he ate "boiled beef, boiled pork, [and] cornbread." Generally he described the same diet, except for a meal eaten at a hotel near Sabine Pass, which included "biscuits, fried ham, butter, cornbread, mock coffee, and milk," which the hotel owner provided at no charge. Fresh potatoes and yams became available in Louisiana and East Texas, but boiled bacon and cold cornbread usually greeted the Texans at mealtime.[47]

Early in the war, the Confederate government admitted that it could not properly supply the army, and obtaining proper clothing and uniforms persisted as an obstacle difficult to overcome. The task of providing uniforms and clothing to the military fell to the individual states. Anything made of cloth—tents, blankets, and wagon sheets, for example—had to be supplied at the state level. Governor Clark directed that all cloth manufactured by the state penitentiary be utilized only for military purposes. As Texas controlled no other manufacturing resources to provide uniforms for its troops, the burden of clothing newly formed regiments fell upon private citizens. In March, 1861, for instance, Capt. Sidney G. Davidson wrote to his wife, asking for a pair of pants, one white shirt, and two pairs of cotton socks, because his quartermaster had no clothing to provide to his men. Initially some local companies outfitted themselves with a variety of uniforms, but shortages of material prevented most soldiers from donning regulation attire. In September, 1861, the 1st Mounted Rifles received a large issue of uniforms, but the 779 uniforms allocated failed to clothe the 1,009 members of the regiment. The definitive yellow gilt braid and brass buttons of fancy cavalry uniforms were seldom seen on Texas horsemen. Sometimes officers acquired uniforms trimmed with braid, but the common soldier seldom had fancy, yellow-striped cavalry pants.[48]

Troops in the 1st Texas Cavalry wore a miscellany of mixed uniforms and civilian clothing. Typical attire included cotton, wool, and sometimes linen pants. The men usually donned shirts of the same material. Flannel shirts were also popular and appeared as part of army clothing issues. Invoices of clothing revealed a multiplicity of colors in both shirts and pants: blue, red, black, brown, checked, undyed, and hickory all were issued. Materials varied, too, with cotton, linen, and flannel being most prevalent. Quartermasters also distributed cotton and woolen drawers and stockings when they were available. Cavalrymen preferred the tough, homespun "butternut" clothing over the gray flannel material produced at the penitentiary at Huntsville. The "butternut" material outlasted the flannel, especially in jackets and pants. Riding through trees and brush quickly ripped the soft flannel cloth to shreds. Wight wrote that, late in the war, the men had "scant clothing"; "as for me my wife spun and wove the most part of my clothes and sent them to me."[49]

The army issued hats and shoes, but widespread shortages left the choice of both up to the individual. Issued hats came in many types and colors, but most Texans wore a wide-brimmed hat of fur felt or cloth. Colors varied from black to brown and light gray. Virtually no one in the 1st Texas Cavalry complied with General Orders No. 4 from the Confederate War Department, which defined the type of forage cap authorized for wear by Confederate soldiers. Texans disdained the little round "French style Kepi" with yellow sides and crown denoting the cavalry branch. Kepis, even with a "duck or linen 'havelock' apron falling behind to protect ears and neck," failed to shield the wearer from the intense Texas sun or a cold driving rain; therefore, Texans opted for more familiar and functional wide-brimmed hats. Shoes and "bootees" were distributed infrequently, so troopers donned all types of footwear. Tall and short boots, shoes of all kinds, and moccasins protected the cavalrymen's feet.[50]

By 1863, the regiment was uniform only in its nonconformity. The Texas cavalrymen were adorned with what they normally had worn or used prior to joining the army. Fremantle described a group of Texas cavalrymen as dressed in "flannel shirts, very ancient trousers, jackboots with enormous spurs, and black felt hats ornamented with the 'Lone Star of Texas'." Upon meeting two of Joseph Taylor's men, he remarked that "these Rangers all wear the most enormous spurs I ever saw." He also commented that most Texas horsemen "looked rough and dirty." Every Texan Fremantle met "carried a six shooter."[51]

Tents, blankets, and cold-weather clothing never reached the regiment in sufficient quantities to prevent misery during inclement weather. As early as September, 1861, McCulloch, as departmental commander, wrote to Maj. Edward Burleson that enough Sibley tents for the 1st Mounted Rifles were not available, for "everything in San Antonio is exhausted and we still have an army to be supplied from the department." Tentage remained a luxury during the entire war. Troops employed carpets and curtains partially to compensate for the shortage of blankets. Texas citizens collected winter coats, vests, heavy drawers, and blankets and shipped them to Texas soldiers in the field. These clothing articles, like agricultural produce, usually arrived at military camps in privately owned wagons. The cotton trade demanded most of Texas' rolling stock, and Confederate logistical concerns required utilizing available military wagons farther north and east.[52]

As with all other supplies, medical stocks for Texas army units deteriorated and became scarcer during the war. The state possessed little in the way of supplies to succor its troops. The majority of medicinal stores arrived from foreign ports and entered Texas via the cotton trade. Texans erected a distillery at Tyler to produce medicines and alcohol for medical purposes, but it came into being too late in the war to offset deficiencies in medicinal supplies. The army contracted physicians and surgeons to certify volunteers fit for duty and deliver timely, competent medical care for wounded and ailing men in the regiments. Lacking sufficient volunteer physicians, Texas relied on contract doctors to fill the void in medical personnel. Contract doctors received one hundred dollars per month, provided their own horses, and accompanied the regiment on all campaigns. To guarantee competency of both volunteer and contract medical staff, Trans-Mississippi Departmental Headquarters established a medical examining board. Physicians and surgeons failing examinations were eliminated from the service and their contracts voided. Maj. James A. White had this experience when he refused to submit to the required examination and the 1st Texas Cavalry dropped him from its rolls in February, 1864.[53]

The daily life of the regimental trooper varied, depending on whether his unit remained in bivouac or was engaged in combat operations. Drills and training occupied time in camp, while combat activities meant long, miserable, bone-weary hours in the saddle combating Indians, bandits, or Yankees. Camp life offered the opportunity to maintain or repair equipment, pay some attention to personal necessities, and in general live a more orderly life. Usually the camps served better food in greater abundance. Guard duty, picket duty, and caring for the horses came daily, whether in camp or not. Long nights on guard gave the men time to think about home and family and to wonder why they were fighting those who once had been their friends. During idle hours, thoughts drifted to the war and the future. Medford exemplified a Texan's attitude when, on the 1864 march to Louisiana, he wrote that Texans will "fight to [the] bitter end." He continued, "We are fighting for matters real and tangible, they [the Yankees] for matters abstract and intangible."[54]

Throughout their military service, the veterans of the 1st Texas Cavalry experienced the vagaries of both climate and terrain in two very distinct regions. When on patrol in Texas, time crawled slowly by, and the men and horses returned so covered with dust that they were unrecognizable. In such instances, the troopers craved only one thing: cool water to rinse their throats clear of the choking alkali dust and to wash off the filth that covered them. Along the Texas Gulf coast and in Louisiana, though, the soldiers saw more than enough water. The damp climate and fever-ridden swamps swept more men from the saddle than did Federal minié balls. Dysentery and other diseases caused by foul water and poorly cooked food posed far greater dangers than did the rifles of Union sharpshooters. Whether in camp or battling an enemy, troops generally slept on the ground, covered by a blanket and resting their heads on their saddles. The land in Texas, however, usually offered a dry bed, and the climate was healthier. Regimental service records contain abundant proof that present-for-duty strength decreased dramatically when, in 1863, the regiment began operations in more humid, lower-lying terrain. Muster rolls were replete with cases of unwell men sent to hospitals with miscellaneous diseases. Average regimental soldiers were only ordinary citizens serving their state, country, and a cause in which they believed; many made the ultimate sacrifice for their convictions long before they fired their first shot at an enemy.[55]

CHAPTER 8

"A Gallant, Efficient, and Meritorious Officer"

On December 10, 1861, the Confederate secretary of war redesignated the 1st Regiment of Texas Mounted Rifles the 1st Regiment of Texas Cavalry. Unit commanders and staff, however, insisted on using the old designation until well into 1863. Finally, Brig. Gen. Hamilton P. Bee, commander of the Western Sub-district of Texas, requested and received clarification on the issue. Maj. Gen. John B. Magruder, commander of the Department of Texas, New Mexico, and Arizona, directed that, according to Departmental Special Orders No. 127, which reformed the unit, the organization officially was titled the 1st Regiment of Texas Cavalry. Issued on May 2, 1863, this order combined Maj. William O. Yager's 3rd Battalion, Maj. Joseph Taylor's 8th Battalion of Texas Cavalry, and Capt. James A. Ware's company of Partisan Rangers to form a regimental command of ten companies. The order named the newly promoted Col. Augustus Buchel as regimental commander; Yager as lieutenant colonel; Robert A. Myers as major; and both James A. White and John L. White as surgeons. On August 13, Buchel appointed W. R. D. Stockton as regimental chaplain.[1]

Initially the 1st Texas Cavalry established its headquarters near Carricitas Lake on the Rio Grande, twenty-five miles above Fort Brown, and prepared to assume the missions previously discharged by its component units. Primarily, these duties included protecting the indispensable cotton trade and defending the southern Texas coast against Federal invasion. Executing these critical missions required rugged, dedicated men; sturdy horses; and depend-

fig. 13. John B. Magruder, commander of the Department of Texas, defended the coast of Texas and ordered most of his cavalry to fight off a Union offensive in Louisiana in early 1864. Courtesy Archives Division, Texas State Archives, Austin

able arms and ammunition; along with all the other equipment and supplies essential for a cavalry unit facing extended campaigns. Because available grazing land could not support all of the regiment's mounts, a fifty-man detail—five from each company—under Lt. George R. Kuykendall, Company K, drove a large number of the horses to the ranch of Don Chene Cavasas, where better grass was available. Lack of mounts forced many of the soldiers to participate in infantry training, which irked Texans accustomed to duty on horseback.[2]

Buchel came to the 1st Regiment of Texas Cavalry by appointment, and some troopers resented the short man who spoke with a strange accent. Several men hatched a plot to dunk him in Carricitas Lake until he agreed to resign. Regimental members then would be free to elect their own commander. No reckless individual willing to lead such an audacious enterprise came forward, however, and the plotters abandoned the scheme. Regimental soldiers later expressed gratitude that they had not forced Buchel to resign. Pvt. J. I. Campbell, Company B, wrote, "Buchel proved a leader skilled in arms, he was a soldier and gentleman. He was an ideal commander, the peer of anyone his rank in the entire [Confederate] Army."[3]

Born on October 7, 1813, in Gunthersblum, Province of Hesse, Buchel spent his early life in the countryside near the present city of Mainz, Germany. He was the last of six children of Frederick Charles Buchel and Christine Philippine Laun. His father made a comfortable living as a minor official of the local government. Buchel received a normal education until, at age fourteen, he passed the rigorous examinations that gained him admission to the military academy at nearby Darmstadt. Although two years under age for enrollment, he excelled at his studies and at eighteen received a commission as second lieutenant in the 1st Infantry Regiment of Hesse-Darmstadt. He served in this regiment until 1835, when his service obligation ended. He then obtained admission to the Ecole Militaire in Paris, where he continued his military training. Upon graduation, he was made a lieutenant in the Foreign Legion of France.[4]

Buchel's entry into the Foreign Legion led him to another country and to another of the six flags under which he would serve. In 1836, King Louis Phillipe of France sent a corps of the Foreign Legion to Spain to support the regency of Queen María Cristina against the revolutionaries of Don Carlos. As a lieutenant of the legion, Buchel experienced the forced marches, starvation, and fierce combat that brought the size of the corps down to that of a "corporal's guard." Hardships, however, did not deter Buchel in the performance of his duty. On May 24, 1837, at the Battle of Huesca, he distinguished himself by conspicuous gallantry and leadership. On February 1, 1838, in reward for his heroism, Queen María Cristina awarded Buchel the Cross of San Fernando and a knighthood. When the Foreign Legion received its discharge, the medal was all that Buchel had to show for his service in Spain. The war had emptied the Spanish treasury, and the government could not pay the French soldiers when their unit disbanded in December, 1838.[5]

Broke and relying on his family for support, Buchel traveled to Austria in search of employment. In Vienna he met a representative of the Ottoman Empire and secured a position as a military instructor in the empire's army. For several years he served as senior cavalry instructor to the Ottoman Empire. He rose to the rank of colonel and may have received the honored title of "Pasha." Because he refused to renounce his Christian religion and convert to Islam, however, he could rise no higher in the empire's army. Resigning his commission, Buchel returned to Europe.[6]

Buchel's activities in Europe remain something of an enigma. By many accounts, he killed a man in a duel in Germany, and family honor demanded that he leave the country. English Lt. Col. James Arthur Fremantle wrote that Buchel had been involved in "several affairs of honor." In the spring of 1845, Buchel resided in Paris, attempting to secure his back pay from the Spanish government. Perhaps he succeeded in obtaining the pay, for, in 1845, he sailed from Antwerp, Belgium, with his brother Karl and other members of the *Adelsverein,* a German colonial organization. In October, 1845, he arrived at Karlshafen, located on Matagorda Bay in Calhoun County. The town soon became known as Indianola.[7]

Buchel's brother began farming in DeWitt County, but that life seemed too staid for the adventurous Buchel. Answering the call for volunteers for the Mexican War, he raised a company of eighty-eight German immigrants from Indianola and marched them south to join Gen. Zachary Taylor near the Rio Grande. Buchel's small component formed Company H, 1st Brigade of Texas Volunteer Footriflemen under the command of Col. Albert Sidney Johnston, who called them "the best drilled unit in the army." Buchel's men had enlisted for only ninety days, and the company disbanded without seeing any action. Because of Buchel's prior military experience and fluency in Spanish, Taylor appointed him to his staff as an interpreter and plans officer. For his expertise in planning and his bravery in the Battle of Buena Vista, Buchel earned Taylor's respect, a commendation, and promotion to the rank of major. Buchel remained on Taylor's staff until the end of the war.[8]

After the Mexican War, Buchel returned to Indianola. Several of his friends indicated that Zachary Taylor, as president of the United States, intended to appoint Buchel ambassador to Brazil, but Taylor's untimely death prevented the appointment. President Franklin Pierce later appointed him customs inspector for the port of La Vaca and the District of Saluria. Buchel also formed a partnership with M. T. Huck in a lumber and building material business. He remained active in that enterprise until the beginning of the Civil War.[9]

Before Texas entered the Civil War, another opportunity to serve his adopted state stirred the soldier of fortune in Buchel. In 1859, the Mexican bandit Juan Cortina led his men in a series of raids along the Rio Grande into Texas. These depredations became known as the "Cortina Wars." Several Texas volunteer units attempted to capture the bandits. Buchel organized a force of twenty men and again rode south as captain of the volunteers. In this endeavor, he used his own funds to finance most of his men's expenses. He led the "Indianola Volunteers" in an aggressive campaign to capture Cortina, but the bandit eluded Buchel in the *brasada,* or brush country, of South Texas and northern Mexico.

State Sen. Fletcher S. Stockdale expressed regret to Buchel that his volunteers had been unable to capture Cortina, and he introduced a bill in the Texas Senate to insure that Buchel and his men received financial compensation for their time and services.[10]

The restless Buchel briefly returned to civilian life until Texas joined the Confederacy. He did not actively petition the Confederate government for a commission; as a result, men less qualified than he received appointments as generals. Only his friends in Texas recognized his many military talents and sought a position for him. As a result of their efforts, Gov. Edward Clark appointed Buchel to a series of posts. The governor first appointed Buchel as his aide-de-camp to act as a recruiting officer for Texas. Clark divided the state into six military districts; and Buchel, with five other prominent Texans, each received a gubernatorial appointment to head one of these districts. Along with this appointment came a commission to recruit five hundred men from his district surrounding Indianola and Saluria. Buchel armed his new recruits with rifles previously sent to him from the state's store of weapons. Interestingly, Henry Runge, Frank van der Stucken's partner, shipped these firearms to Buchel.[11]

As the year 1861 passed, Buchel moved into several new positions. On April 18, Governor Clark appointed him aide-de-camp to the commander-in-chief of the 13th Division of Texas Militia. Additionally, he continued to function as a recruiting officer until appointed as the training officer for state troops on July 11, 1861, where he quickly organized training facilities for the growing numbers of volunteers.[12]

Buchel's competency in dealing with difficult situations finally earned him recognition by the Confederate army. On September 1, 1861, he received a commission as lieutenant colonel from Brig. Gen. Earl Van Dorn, commander of the Department of Texas. Buchel's orders sent him to Ringgold Barracks, near Brownsville, as second in command of Col. Phillip N. Luckett's 3rd Regiment of Texas Infantry. Buchel soon moved to Fort Brown and became commander of the post, as well as the regiment, during Luckett's many absences.[13]

As commander of Fort Brown, Buchel faced myriad problems. His primary mission required him to prevent Union forces from invading the Rio Grande Valley and interrupting the valuable cotton trade into Mexico. With a tight Union blockade of Confederate ports, the cotton trade through Texas and Mexico became the main source of war materiel for the Trans-Mississippi. Thus Buchel accepted additional responsibilities as an examining officer for Confederate cotton contracts. As examining officer, Buchel controlled shipment and receipt of cotton and coordinated delivery of supplies to quartermaster officers. This duty only further complicated his harried life at Fort Brown.[14]

Two other problems occupied much of Buchel's time as commander of the fort. The shortage of quality volunteers and the number of desertions resulted in low morale and lack of adequately trained men for the post. Many of Buchel's soldiers were Mexican conscripts or Federal deserters who had joined the Confederate army. According to Buchel, many of the 3rd Regiment's companies mustered only half their required strength because the low-class soldiers could be lured into Mexico "for a few dollars and some whiskey." He suggested to the Department of Texas that any future companies recruited for his command be of "higher class and intelligence."[15]

Lack of arms, ammunition, and means of subsistence for his seven hundred men and four hundred horses also plagued Buchel. Many merchants in Brownsville would not accept Confederate money or credit, and those who did added thirty percent to the price of merchandise. Traders in Mexico accepted only gold or silver and sometimes failed to deliver supplies already purchased. The governor of the Mexican state of Tamaulipas confiscated one shipment of corn destined for Fort Brown. Buchel offered to march into Mexico and seize the needed supplies if permitted by Confederate authorities. Cooler heads prevailed and denied him permission for such an adventure. A shipment of gold from the Confederate assistant treasurer in New Orleans only partially solved Buchel's problems. His ability to accomplish his assignments in spite of difficulties, however, led to Buchel's recognition and promotion to colonel of the 1st Regiment of Texas Cavalry.[16]

The regiment had been patrolling the *brasada* of the Rio Grande country and lower Texas coast for only about a month when it departed from the temporary headquarters at Carricitas Lake. Reports of a large Federal force crossing the Mississippi River prompted Lt. Gen. Edmund Kirby Smith, commander of the Trans-Mississippi Department, to order troops to march from Texas to oppose the rumored Federal movements in Louisiana. During the relocation toward the coast, the regiment converged with its horses, which had been driven to pasture on the King Ranch near the coast.[17]

On June 17, Magruder received substantiated intelligence verifying that the rumors were false, and he countermanded orders moving his units away from South and West Texas. He ordered Luckett to form a cavalry brigade composed of Peter Cavanaugh Woods's and Buchel's regiments. Magruder selected Buchel as second in command and directed him to make camp as near the western frontier as possible. Buchel's instructions included ensuring "continuous subsistence," as well as the camp's "integrity and efficiency." Magruder directed the district commissary and quartermaster to gather necessary supplies and send them to support the troops in their new camp. The 1st Texas Cavalry located its headquarters about ten miles below Goliad on the San Antonio River and made ready to resume another march on short notice. Buchel recognized that enemy movements along the coast might necessitate his cavalry's moving swiftly to defend that vital region. Events were to prove him correct.[18]

Pvt. William Kuykendall, Company D, conveyed the Texans' general emotions regarding the movements east:

> When we enlisted in the service we expected to be sent to the seat of war where we would at once see active service and thus be able to prove ourselves worthy of the cause we espoused. One year had now expired and our ambition to meet the enemy and annihilate him had not been gratified. Instead we had been kept against our earnest protest on our Southwestern frontier where no enemy had polluted our soil and we were greatly chagrined lest the war should terminate before we should have an opportunity to prove our valor. Subsequent events proved however that scouting on the Rio Grande with full haversacks was not the most trying ordeal of a soldiers life. But in the words of Sir John Falstaff "honor pricked on us" and we were enthused with the prospect of realizing our ardent wish to be ordered to the front.[19]

On August 13, Magruder directed Bee, commander of the Western Subdistrict of Texas, to keep Buchel's and Woods's regiments within supporting distance of Corpus Christi and Saluria. The Confederate commander expected a Union attack on one or both of these places or up the Brazos River toward the hinterland. Magruder concluded that all his coastal defenses would crumble if the Federals gained control of these three vital areas. Only 486 of Buchel's 823 men were present for duty in this camp. One of his battalions probably remained nearer the Rio Grande. Maintaining this portion of the regiment in constant readiness for an immediate march proved farsighted.[20]

Kuykendall's experiences may explain why some of Buchel's soldiers were not in camp. Kuykendall's horse wandered off and could not be located. He bought a Mexican pony for two hundred dollars in Confederate money, but the animal proved too frail for cavalry service. To buy a suitable mount, he secured a leave to journey to his home near Victoria. On his trip, he paused at a house for a drink, and a farmer offered him a pitcher of buttermilk, to "which I did ample justice." The milk proved rancid, however, and Kuykendall "vomited for three days." Happily, he discovered his errant mount with several other horses at a ranch and bought a breakfast of "black coffee, tasso beef, and cornbread" for fifty cents. After a short visit with family, he returned to his regiment, which bivouacked on Martínez Creek a few miles from Goliad.[21]

fig. 14. Hamilton P. Bee. The 1st Texas Cavalry came under Bee's command in both Texas and Louisiana. His military competence was called into question during the Red River Campaign in Louisiana in 1864. Courtesy Archives Division, Texas State Library, Austin

Additional rumors and Union military operations caused the regiment to pack up and move again. In September and October, the Union navy increased its activities along the upper Texas coast from Galveston Island all the way to Sabine Pass at the Louisiana border. Acting on orders from Washington, Maj. Gen. Nathaniel Prentice Banks, commander of the Department of the Gulf, planned an invasion into Texas along the poorly defended marshes at Sabine Pass. He boasted that he would "plant the flag in Texas" inside a week. Federal ships increased their bombardment of Confederate installations and sent more substantial landing parties ashore along the entire coast. On September 8, the Federals attempted a strong invasion at Sabine Pass. The Confederates, commanded by Irish-born entrepreneur 1st Lt. Richard W. "Dick" Dowling, with only forty-seven cannoneers of Company F, 1st Texas Heavy Artillery, and six guns, repulsed the Federal invasion fleet.[22]

Less than a week after the embarrassment at Sabine Pass, Banks launched an overland expedition through southwestern Louisiana, believing that he easily could march into the Lone Star State across the open grassy prairies from New Iberia, Vermillionville, or Opelousas. Some thirty thousand Union troops under

Banks marched out of New Orleans and advanced toward the Texas border, with the leading elements reaching Bayou Courtableau near Opelousas. Maj. Gen. Richard Taylor, commanding the Confederate army in West Louisiana, sent Magruder intelligence accounts stating that Federal troops from New Iberia were moving toward Abbeville, Louisiana, with a force of over two hundred cavalry, escorting a long train of pontoon bridges. These escalating enemy actions led Magruder to conclude that the Federals intended to invade Texas along the lower coast of Louisiana, or at least supply a sea-landed invading force along the lower coastal roads of Louisiana and Texas. The fact that the enemy needed bridges and pontoons to cross all the rivers and streams confirmed, at least to Magruder, their intentions. In late August, to counter the increasing threat of invasion from Louisiana, he had ordered Buchel to move advance units of his regiment toward Sabine Pass.[23]

Commotion of some type followed the 1st Texas Cavalry almost constantly along its path toward Louisiana. The line of march crossed the Guadalupe River above Victoria and passed through the little town of Hallettsville, where an apparently volatile Dr. John L. White, regimental assistant surgeon, "shot and instantly killed" a citizen named Smoothers. According to Kuykendall, "A gambling spree the night before led to the killing." The local sheriff and a posse followed the command and attempted to arrest White. Buchel, however, refused to acquiesce to civilian authority and surrender his surgeon.[24]

Other incidents suggest the jocular disposition of the men, regardless of their serious duties. While the regiment camped on Skull Creek, a few miles from its juncture with the Colorado River, Lt. Landon C. Preston led a fifteen-man detail through the surrounding brush country searching for Confederate deserters. Kuykendall's description of the thick brush indicates that it "offered every facility for secretion and made captures not only difficult but exciting." In the end, "with much diligence we succeeded in capturing several [deserters] and witnessed a good many amusing incidents." A German lived on a small, brush-lined stream and generally remained hidden among the thickets during the day, but occasionally at night returned home "to replenish the larder." One morning when he was leaving the house, he spied Kuykendall's detail carefully guiding their horses toward the deserter's house. He immediately dropped the sack of meal he carried, bolted into the house, and "took to his virtuous couch and feigned great illness." When Preston entered the house, he found "this exemplary citizen in great distress" and called for "Doctor Kuykendall" to come in and examine the patient. Kuykendall assumed a "professional attitude" and with "much dignity" made "thorough diagnosis of the case," recommending ipecac as a cure. None could be found, "otherwise my patient would have been minus his supper in short order." The fake physician determined that the fake patient "might be removed without further delay," and the detail marched the prisoner to camp where "it is needless to say that his recovery was as sudden as his attack."[25]

During the first week of September, the 1st Texas Cavalry continued its journey toward Sabine Pass. Buchel's horsemen rode to the railway depot at East Bernard, where most of the men were dismounted. A guard herded their horses to pasture. Officers ordered the men to board a train of flatcars destined for Beaumont. Although the soldiers grumbled at being unhorsed, Kuykendall explained that Buchel, "in whom the regiment collectively and individually reposed the greatest confidence," assured the men that their mounts would be returned in a short time. Without further complaint, the troops boarded the train. Not all of the companies, however, left their horses at the depot. One contingent of men and their mounts rode the train to Beaumont, where steamboats ferried them to Sabine Pass.[26]

Initial elements of the regiment arrived at Sabine Pass about two days after Dowling's stunning victory on September 8. Kuykendall wrote that many of the men saw their "first dead Yankees and had [a] glimpse of real war." He revealed that "a good many" bloated corpses of Federal troops killed a few days before continued to float ashore. On September 22, Magruder reported to Kirby Smith that he had sent a light brigade to Sabine Pass under Buchel, "a gallant, efficient, and meritorious officer." Buchel's new brigade included Companies A and F, 1st Texas Heavy Artillery; the 20th Texas Infantry; Reuben R. Brown's cavalry battalion; and Buchel's cavalry (commanded by Buchel until its arrival at Sabine Pass, where Maj. Robert A. Myers assumed command). The brigade also included Nicholas C. Gould's and James Griffin's cavalry battalions, Col. Philip N. Luckett's regiment of infantry (with Lt. Col. E. F. Gray commanding), and O. G. Jones's artillery battery. Buchel commanded this brigade until the spring of 1864, when he returned to the 1st Texas Cavalry to lead the regiment into Louisiana. Magruder informed Kirby Smith that he also expected more than one thousand state cavalrymen to be ready shortly to reinforce Sabine Pass.[27]

Buchel faced multitudinous problems as forces arrived piecemeal at Sabine Pass. Initially he sent mounted detachments into Louisiana to reconnoiter the waters at the mouth of the Calcasieu River to ascertain if passage from Niblett's Bluff to Lake Arthur was possible. If so, he might find it necessary to send a large force across the Calcasieu to oppose the approaching enemy troops. He dispatched his most competent scouts to "judge" the route and the enemy threat. Magruder had instructed Buchel to forward all reports "post haste" to Hous-

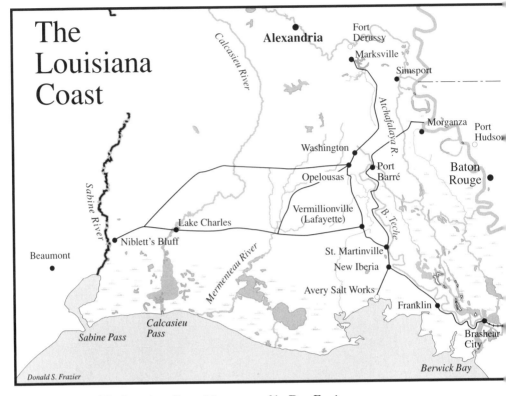

map. 4. The Louisiana Coast. Map prepared by Don Frazier

ton. The Confederate telegraph link ended at Beaumont. Buchel therefore established a regular courier service between Beaumont and Sabine Pass to guarantee timely communication with departmental headquarters in Houston. Buchel's cavalrymen ranged along the swamps and through the pine barrens to report road conditions from Sabine City through Lake Arthur and farther east.[28]

Buchel's command responsibilities necessarily included any and all measures relating to logistical support for the region surrounding Sabine Pass. He coordinated transportation of goods and supplies in the area, as well as reporting the weather, local shipping conditions, and processed Confederate cotton brought to Niblett's Bluff from both Texas and Louisiana for shipment into Mexico. When weather permitted, he planned for the steamer *Dime* to take Capt. Andrew Daley's company to reinforce Capt. Edward Beaumont's combined command of over a hundred men, who already were occupying the Louisiana side of the Sabine River. When building materials became available, he expected to build a bridge over the mud flat to ease transportation. To clarify his orders, Buchel requested telegraphic instructions from Magruder as to the disposition of steamers and boats on Lake Charles in the event that Union forces advanced toward Niblett's Bluff. In his reports to Magruder, he explained that two Federal gunboats and one schooner-of-war outside the bar complicated his problems by interrupting transportation of supplies. Kuykendall saw these Federal warships lying off the pass in plain view and commented that "in appearance [they] looked quite formidable."[29]

Inadequacy of manpower exacerbated Buchel's problems in both patrolling and defending a large area of Texas and Louisiana. The 1st Texas Cavalry arrived with only five of its assigned companies and one section of light artillery. In his reports to Departmental Headquarters in Houston, Buchel outlined his immediate need for the remainder of his cavalry. According to his estimates, he needed at least five hundred additional men and horses to cover the area from Niblett's Bluff to the Mermentau Bayou. Kuykendall confirmed Buchel's dearth of assets, estimating the command at Sabine Pass as no more than two thousand men "of all arms." Buchel advised Magruder that only a large, mobile force could properly protect all roads and ferries and also threaten the enemy line of communication toward Opelousas. If possible, with his meager strength, he intended "to inflict severe punishment" on any enemy force discovered. Buchel added that he expected more of his regiment and two sections of artillery to arrive by the third week of October. Until more guns arrived, Buchel possessed little in the way of cannon to defend the pass. He informed Magruder that, when he arrived at Niblett's Bluff, the artillery reported at the station was not to be found.[30]

Upon arriving at Niblett's Bluff, the 1st Texas Cavalry immediately launched operations to ascertain Union intentions in Louisiana. Regimental officers sent a detachment under Lt. C. E. Aiken across the Calcasieu and additional scouts along the roads toward the Mermentau Bayou. Buchel later augmented this force across the river by directing Capt. Matthew Nolan and his few men to join Aiken on the Calcasieu. To extend his reconnaissance capabilities, Buchel induced a small detachment of state troops to leave Texas and sent Captain Bland and a lieutenant with ten volunteers of state cavalry to reinforce Nolan in his forward positions. Buchel employed the balance of Bland's troops at Niblett's Bluff and used them as couriers on the road to Beaumont.[31]

Although no official documents survive confirming the incident, Kuykendall describes a tactical deception operation employed to discourage further Federal invasion attempts at Sabine Pass. He related that Magruder ordered, as he did in the Virginia peninsular campaign, units to march in patterns and formations suggesting greater troop strength than actually existed. The Texans formed into hollow squares and, Kuykendall explained, "our little army was paraded." After a while, "we were ordered to march in column of twos over the point of the ridge and to lowlands behind the ridge." According to Kuykendall's diary, Buchel's command continued marching and countermarching around the ridge "until we were well nigh brokendown." Confederate officers hoped that, from these diversionary tactics, the Yankees would "infer that we were many thousands strong . . . instead of a few hundred poorly armed dismounted cavalry—and one field battery."[32]

By October 20, the remainder of the 1st Texas Cavalry and its supporting artillery, along with a promised 32-pounder, arrived by steamer. Buchel, however, did not consider these reinforcements adequate to his requirements. He reiterated his request for more cavalry and infantry to observe the enemy and defend the position. He indicated that he needed an additional fifteen hundred troops to garrison the fort and surrounding defenses properly. Arriving at Sabine Post, Buchel found that the inadequate hospital contained little medicine and no bandages. He immediately requested a full supply of medical, commissary, and quartermaster stores for his command. His brigade was organized so haphazardly that shortages existed at every turn. He emphasized to Magruder that the only communication to Sabine City was by land through Beaumont and that the command needed steamers to transport forage for the horses and shuttle troops across the rivers and bayous. Lack of sufficient transportation prevented him from stockpiling forage and sustenance for his brigade. Buchel repeated that, with only one steamer available, his command could not transport enough supplies and forage to withstand a siege.[33]

The 1st Texas Cavalry arrived at Sabine Pass to find the defenses and breastworks in a deplorable, unfinished condition, having been abandoned by work parties. Buchel's engineering officer assessed the main defenses on the Louisiana side as nearly finished, calculating that, if they had tools, "seventy-five Negroes could complete the work in about a week." He suggested that Negroes, along with shovels and picks, might be brought from Sabine Pass by steamer. A critical shortage of axes existed. All eastern district axes had been lent to the Texas and New Orleans Railroad and had not been returned. The nearby pine forests offered readily accessible cover and concealment for an enemy approach. To complicate matters, brush covered the abatis. For a proper defense, the entire area needed to be clean-cut and the cut wood burned.[34]

Assessment of the defensive works on the Texas side were even more discouraging. Engineers projected that, to complete the defenses, "more than 100 Negroes would be required to work steadily for over two weeks." Buchel also considered the camp unhealthy and in a poor position, in a low, marshy, thickly

fig. 15. Nathaniel P. Banks, personally brave but tactically inept, in 1863–64 led three failed attempts to invade Texas. Courtesy U.S. Army Military History Institute, Carlisle Barracks, Pennsylvania

timbered section. Pvt. Levi Lamoni Wight, Company E, confirmed Buchel's assessment. In letters written to his wife in October and November, Wight apprised her of considerable sickness in the regiment and "mosquitoes is vry [*sic*] numerous and the largest I ever saw. Some of them has actual got feathers." He continued, "They rise in the evening in such swarms as to darken the earth." The fort contained only a small fraction of the materials and timber necessary to construct ammunition magazines and bombproofs for his men. Buchel's engineers submitted that "four or five carpenters and twenty-five Negroes could finish it in five or six days." In a letter to Magruder, Buchel illustrated the many weaknesses of his position and the strengths of the enemy's. He emphasized his need for reinforcements of weapons and personnel to hold Sabine Pass if attacked. Buchel said he would "stay and defend to the death if ordered" but warned the commanding general that the position could not be held without more men and completed fortifications.[35]

A report from Ben Allston, assistant inspector general from Kirby Smith's Trans-Mississippi headquarters, supported Buchel's judgments concerning the problems at Sabine Pass. Allston considered Buchel an "old and experienced officer, very conversant with his duties," but reported that the men lived in "barely tolerable conditions," even though many of them were quartered in abandoned civilian houses. Most soldiers lived in what Kuykendall described as "extemporized quarters" constructed with "palmetto for covering and siding." Wight wrote that he and a friend had constructed a two-man shelter covered with stone from the Sabine River. Allston considered Buchel's command overextended, as it covered the coastal plains from Liberty and Galveston east to Sabine and Niblett's Bluff. Buchel's responsibilities also entailed sending reconnaissance scouts as far as the Calcasieu in Louisiana.[36]

Allston reminded his commander that, although muster rolls listed over three thousand men in Buchel's brigade, only about fifteen hundred were present for duty. The great discrepancy arose from the number of men detached on various duties. Magruder had attempted to ease the problem by issuing an order recalling to Buchel's brigade all men who were on quartermaster and commissary duties. While the inspector general conducted his inspection tour, an order arrived from Kirby Smith's headquarters detailing two men for quartermaster duty at Shreveport. This was the second time the inspector general had seen orders from Kirby Smith's headquarters detailing Buchel's officers elsewhere. Allston's report reminded the departmental commander that he only compounded the manpower shortage by ordering officers and men away and depleting Buchel's ranks. In his letter to Kirby Smith, Allston bluntly told him that departmental edicts were "not conducive to the general good conduct of the men."[37]

Maj. Robert A. Myers commanded the 1st Texas Cavalry while Buchel led the brigade. Yager remained on detached duty with Bee at Brownsville. According to Allston's report, Myers did not appear to be a man of "much force or soldierly qualities." He added that Buchel claimed that Yager was "a good officer," but Yager had been absent for some time. Detachments of officers and troops caused a "lack of drill," and to the inspector general these sundry detachments appeared unnecessary.[38]

Allston discovered numerous other examples of men on detached duty that reduced unit efficiency. Buchel utilized a soldier as a cook. He explained to the inspector general that he could not hire servants locally or on the Rio Grande. Enlisted men served as cooks and performed other duties when officers were unable to hire servants. The brigade commander realized that making use of enlisted men as servants violated General Orders Number 20, but Buchel protested that he and his officers had no other choice. He also urged that his officers be granted an additional ration. Because of high food prices and "worthless

[Confederate] money," most of his officers' pay went to the commissary. Allston supported Buchel's recommendation to Kirby Smith that the ration be granted to officers and suggested overlooking the matter of employing soldiers as servants.[39]

The inspector general's letter continued with a description of the brigade's condition and combat readiness. Buchel's soldiers possessed a miscellany of arms in bad repair. All their accouterments, too, were in poor condition. Men exhibited a lack of military appearance. Expecting to be at Sabine Pass only a short time, the 1st Texas Cavalry had left most of the men's clothing with their horses at Camp Bernard. The department had created Buchel's command so hastily that he arrived without such brigade components as a regular adjutant's office and an inspector general. A post hospital, quartermaster, and commissary existed, but all lacked adequate stores and equipment.[40]

In late October, Federal troops in Louisiana commenced offensive maneuvering that added to Buchel's and the regiment's headaches. Union forces began advancing toward Texas along the roads to Vermillionville and Opelousas, in what appeared to be a prelude to invading Texas from southwestern Louisiana. Realizing the need for more cavalry, Banks had mounted several infantry regiments, giving the Union forces a vast numerical superiority in both foot and mounted troops. If the Federal advance continued to push westward, the hard-pressed Texans would be unable to counter these moves because most of their horses remained in pasture at Camp Bernard, near Columbus, and therefore were unavailable for immediate use. To compound the lack of Confederate cavalry, Texas state mounted troops refused to cross into Louisiana even for a few days to scout for Buchel. Magruder issued a stinging letter to the state troops and chided them for shirking their duty to the Confederacy. "Do not let it go forth that you decline to meet the enemy," he ranted. "Do not stain your noble state by withholding your duty. A poor example of weakness by a few companies should not be followed." Some companies of state cavalry finally agreed to fill the gap until the Confederate cavalry's horses and saddles arrived at the Sabine.[41]

To further complicate Buchel's discomfiture, his only steamer ran aground, resulting in a rapidly diminishing supply of corn and fodder at his headquarters. He had sent five cartloads of corn to his outposts on the Calcasieu, escorted by Beaumont and fifty-two men. The regiment stretched its meager mounted force to the limit. Cavalry pickets maintained constant observation on all the fords and ferries on the Mermentau and Calcasieu, and patrols scouted the roads leading into Texas. One company secured a cargo of powder and caps from the blockade runner *Antelope*, fast aground near the mouth of Lacacene

Bayou. Buchel feared that his command might be surrounded by the advancing Federal columns, but he promised to "cut his way through a superior force if necessary," provided that Magruder sent a relief column toward the Sabine.[42]

In letters and reports to Magruder, Buchel expressed his unreserved lack of confidence in state troops and requested that no more of them be sent to his command. He wanted only "regular Confederate soldiers" whom he knew he could depend on. He also pleaded for a "reliable officer" to be put in charge of the two marine department steamboats that carried supplies along the coast. He complained that the masters of the ships wasted too much time in voyages and repairs due to either carelessness or neglect. The captains also charged exorbitant rates for delivering small quantities of stores to his command. To ensure sufficient supplies for his men and horses, Buchel suggested a steady stream of wagons from Beaumont to the Sabine and on to the Calcasieu.[43]

Because he lacked enough reliable troops to execute all his assigned missions, Buchel continued to experience problems along the Sabine. He ordered all state cavalry, except Captain Montgomery's company, back to Beaumont. Fortunately, Montgomery agreed to remain on scouting duties for a few days in Louisiana to bolster the Texas troops there. Magruder promised Buchel more state cavalry, but they never arrived at the Sabine. Alleviating the situation somewhat, the balance of the 1st Texas Cavalry's horses arrived during the first week of November, and Myers mounted all his men present for duty. Kuykendall exulted in the return of the regimental steeds, saying, "A cavalry man is only half soldier without his horse."[44]

After a stay of only a few weeks, Magruder ordered Col. Xavier B. DeBray's regiment back to Galveston. Magruder previously had ordered DeBray up from Galveston to reinforce Buchel, but Federal activities along the lower Texas coast forced the harried Magruder to recall DeBray's regiment. Once again Buchel's brigade and the 1st Texas Cavalry had to protect an area that required many more horsemen than they had available. Because of detachments and the exigencies of extended patrolling, of 1,101 men listed on the 1st Texas Cavalry roster, only 627 mustered present for duty. Although the regiment experienced undue shortages of men and supplies, Magruder nevertheless ordered it to take the offensive.[45]

Magruder directed Buchel to remain at Niblett's Bluff himself and send as substantial a cavalry force as he could organize against the advancing enemy. Regimental orders included routing a cavalry force toward Opelousas to guarantee that communications remained open with General Taylor. Additionally, the few companies of cavalry available were ordered to fortify and defend the crossing at the Calcasieu. The Texans had little chance of stopping a determined Yankee advance. Well over 27,000 Federal troops, with large numbers of cavalry and dragoons, were prepared to push westward from Opelousas. Magruder authorized Buchel to use all wagons, mules, and drivers available at Orange and Sabine Pass to supply his brigade. The cargo of powder from the *Antelope* required additional wagons and an escort of mounted men to insure its safe evacuation to Niblett's Bluff and thence to departmental headquarters at Houston. Despite his reservations, Buchel employed some state cavalry as couriers and found them useful in rounding up beeves for the rest of the brigade. Luckily for Buchel and the regiment, given their shortages of men and materiel, the predicted Union advance never appeared.[46]

The Federals halted their advance near Opelousas, allowing Buchel some respite. He informed Departmental Headquarters at Houston that, regardless of enemy intentions, he lacked sufficient cavalry to screen all possible avenues of approach and simultaneously to defend crucial river crossings. For unknown reasons, artillery reinforcements promised to Buchel never arrived at Sabine Pass. Despite a paucity of assets and logistical support, however, Buchel sustained a productive scouting program against the Union forces in Louisiana. His patrols justified their sleepless nights and incessant hours in the saddle when Confederate horsemen discovered all Federal units withdrawing toward Berwick. In late October, Banks had gone to New Orleans to plan another Union invasion of the South Texas coast. He handed over command of his forces to Maj. Gen. William B. Franklin, without giving Franklin specific instructions concerning his plans. After a Confederate victory along the Bayou Bourbeux on November 3, 1863, Franklin began withdrawing his forces toward Vermillionville.[47]

The 1st Texas Cavalry continued to picket important crossing sites but reported little activity west of the Mermentau. An exception was the capture of four alleged Union spies captured while attempting to sneak across the bayou into Texas. Alert sentries noticed a suspicious party skulking around a small launch and detained them for questioning. The leader of the group, Joseph Rivhey, according to those who recognized him, "knew all the bays, bars, rivers, and inlets of Texas." Buchel considered him a "dangerous man and a valuable Union spy." Several Confederate officers correctly intuited that Rivhey's actions and the withdrawal of Union troops indicated an invasion of the Texas coast farther south.[48]

In messages to Magruder, Buchel protested that his brigade should be assigned more important duties if the enemy continued to withdraw, but Magruder vacillated as to a course of action. According to Buchel's tactical postulations, a small cavalry unit and the 20th Texas Infantry easily could picket the river and guard Sabine Pass against dwindling enemy pressure. Magruder initially disagreed. On November 15, 1863, he ordered Buchel to send a large cavalry force to drive the small Union garrison remaining in Vermillionville out of the city. He also instructed Buchel to strengthen the Calcasieu crossings to defend against any large Union force attempting to cross the bayou.[49]

Although he desired the work on the fortifications at Niblett's Bluff to continue, Magruder ordered still more of Buchel's command to relocate to Galveston. Union attempts to invade Texas had forced Magruder to reevaluate his plans for coastal defense. On November 2, 1863, the U.S. 13th Army Corps, commanded by Maj. Gen. C. C. Washburn and accompanied by Banks, commander of the Department of the Gulf, landed in southern Texas; seized Brazos Santiago; and, on November 6, forced Bee to evacuate Fort Brown. From his base at the mouth of the Rio Grande, Banks marched up the coast toward Corpus Christi and the Matagorda Peninsula, threatening Galveston and inland Texas.[50]

CHAPTER 9

"With Minnié Balls Flying"

On December 1, 1863, Maj. Gen. John B. Magruder responded to the incursion by U.S. forces under the command of Maj. Gen. Nathaniel P. Banks. Banks's corps-sized invasion of South Texas compelled Magruder to reorganize and redeploy his troops along the southern Texas coast. Col. Augustus Buchel received the order: "Rapidly concentrate your brigade at Indianola." The orders detached Maj. William Davidson's cavalry battalion, which remained at Niblett's Bluff, to screen any Federal movements near there. Magruder informed Buchel that part of his artillery, "the light batteries," were already moving and "may stop at Wharton." With Federal forces landing near Velasco, near the mouth of the Brazos River, Magruder needed all the forces he could rapidly concentrate to oppose them. Buchel sent a courier to overtake his light artillery and order his cannoneers to move rapidly to Indianola. Buchel's reorganized brigade included the 1st Texas Cavalry, Alexander W. Terrell's cavalry regiment, Reuben R. Brown's cavalry regiment, Davidson's cavalry battalion (detached), Robert J. Hughes's Texas Battery, and Capt. William G. Moseley's Texas Battery.[1]

On December 3, Buchel, along with other commanders, commenced a forced march of infantry, cavalry, and artillery toward the east bank of the San Bernard River to oppose any attempt by Union troops to cross. Pvt. William Kuykendall, Company D, described the march as "over almost impassable roads and during the coldest weather I had ever experienced." A bugle call woke the men at 3 A.M., and by first light the troops again were slogging down cold, muddy trails.[2]

Lack of winter clothing exacerbated the cavalrymen's plight. Kuykendall related, "We were thinly clad. I believe I would be in the bounds of truth to say there were not a dozen overcoats in the command." Only "a light blanket composed our bedding and [we had] no tents or other protection from cold and rain." Because the horsemen lacked proper gear, "our suffering was necessarily severe."[3]

On December 8, Magruder issued a bulletin reprimanding several Texas cavalry units for stealing food from civilians, shooting hogs, behaving badly, and burning fences for firewood. The well-disciplined 1st Texas Cavalry received no such official remonstrations. Maj. Robert A. Myers ordered company commanders of the 1st Texas Cavalry to dispatch squads of soldiers ahead to prepare corn and meal to avoid delaying the troops' rapid deployment.[4]

Buchel's and DeBray's brigades marched to La Vaca via Wharton and Texana and, following their orders, arrayed their commands east of the San Bernard River. Buchel established his headquarters near Churchill's Ferry, about six miles from the mouth of the river. The 1st Texas Cavalry, along with the rest of Buchel's brigade, found itself assigned to Brig. Gen. James E. Slaughter's division for about a week, and then it was transferred to Bee's 2d Cavalry Division, where Buchel's command constituted the division's 2d Brigade.[5]

The fluid situation along the coast caused Confederate units to be shifted repeatedly. On December 22, Buchel began a rapid movement to take his command to Cedar Lake in Brazoria County to join other units already encamped there. As early as November 22, Texas units skirmished with Union forces advancing along Cedar Bayou. On November 30, the Federals landed a force on Matagorda Island and captured Fort Esperanza, a few miles north of Aransas Pass.[6]

Magruder intended to halt Banks's advance up the coast and called his commanders together for a council of war. Buchel attended this council at Subdistrict Headquarters on McNeil's Plantation, while his unit marched toward its new encampment. Magruder and his commanders emerged from his headquarters with a plan to oppose the Union advance with slashing attacks all along the coast. The presence of determined Confederate forces deterred the indecisive Banks from moving inland, but not from capturing Port La Vaca and Indianola by the last week of December.[7]

Their new encampment at Cedar Lake placed the 1st Texas Cavalry in an advantageous position to attack and drive a large Federal landing party off Matagorda Peninsula, a narrow spit of land approximately one mile wide and fifty miles long, located about halfway between Galveston and Corpus Christi. On December 28, 1863, Col. Frank C. Hesseltine boarded a large detachment of his 13th Maine Infantry Regiment onto the Federal gunboat *Granite City*, in an attempt to capture an isolated Confederate unit and reconnoiter Confederate positions on the peninsula. The *Granite City* sailed from the head of the peninsula and, on the morning of the 29th, landed the infantry in small boats. Hesseltine had orders to reconnoiter the landing area and return to the gunboat, but rough surf made it impossible to return to the ship. He therefore formed his men into a line of skirmishers and moved down the peninsula toward friendly lines. The "down-easters" drove back the few Confederates who appeared to oppose their progression down the low-lying peninsula.[8]

Shortly after noon on December 29, mounted Confederate scouts reported the landing of Hesseltine's force to Buchel. The scouts described a landing by two to three hundred enemy troops seven miles below the mouth of the Caney River on the Gulf shore of Matagorda Peninsula. Buchel immediately ordered five companies of the 1st Texas Cavalry and a detachment of Brown's cavalry to saddle up and dash down the peninsula to capture or expel the landing party.[9]

At 2 P.M., the first Confederate cavalry approached the retreating enemy. The Federals called in their skirmishers and shortened their line to strengthen their position. Hesseltine later mistakenly reported that the Confederate cavalry numbered between eight hundred and one thousand men. The Texas cavalry threw out skirmishers and advanced under a "heavy fire" from the gunboat. Kuykendall wrote that, "though we urged our horses to a brisk gallop[,] the Yankee boat managed to keep abreast of us and to waste Uncle Sam's ammunition upon us." Ignoring the shot and shell, the cavalry rapidly advanced to push back the Federal line. Kuykendall noted some poor marksmanship by the Federal sailors: "Shells frequently passed overhead and fell into the bay." Pvt. Levi Lamoni Wight, Company E, also recounted his impression of the cannonading: "Fortunatly for us no harm was don. Only I got quite nervieous becaus we could not make better time down the penenecely . . . every boom of cannon seemed nearer to me."[10]

As Hesseltine's infantry retreated, a volley from the Union soldiers reportedly "emptied a few saddles," and the cavalry withdrew. Hesseltine organized his defense on a neck of the bay, and his men hastily constructed a barricade of the abundant driftwood. The mounted Texans swiftly skirted what Kuykendall described as "a very strong position" and crossed the bayou to the enemy's rear. This movement around their flanks forced the Federals to wheel onto the beach and erect barricades on three sides.[11]

Heedless of danger, Buchel's cavalrymen fearlessly approached to reconnoiter the Yankee position but, according to Hesseltine's report, drew back "with Minniè balls flying." Because of the favorable position held by the enemy, Buchel decided against a frontal attack upon the Union force. A small lake or lagoon protected the Federal left flank, with a bayou and morass fronting the infantry's line. Hesseltine's unit stood covered, behind the speedily raised breastwork of driftwood. The *Granite City* made the position even more formidable, because its gunners had clear fields of fire over the low, open ground around the beleaguered infantry. The gunboat made events "quite interesting," according to Kuykendall. Despite Union assertions of a large cavalry force, only about three hundred Texans faced the fortified Yankees. Many men exhausted their mounts galloping hurriedly over the soft, sandy ground to the landing site. Buchel's cavalry had pursued the fleeing enemy most of the day, until the Federal infantry faced about and built the protecting barricade. The supporting gunboat constantly shelled the Texans, and Buchel feared a heavy loss of his men if they charged against the prepared enemy positions. Terrain favored the enemy and provided little cover for his men if they attacked. Kuykendall supported his commander's decision, saying that, "[with] these natural advantages" and supporting warships, it was "not deemed advisable" to attack.[12]

Darkness came early with a heavy mist, and soon a torrential downpour made the night "intensely dark." Federal troops waited at the barricades all night and, despite the heavy rain, kept fires burning to mark their positions for the gunboat. Federal sailors also periodically swept the low-lying coast with searchlights, in an effort to ascertain the cavalry's intentions and locations. The Union infantry, as a ruse or threat, "gave out" several cheers during the night. Under cover of darkness, the *Skeeota* replaced the *Granite City*, which steamed down the coast for reinforcements. Pickets from both sides exchanged fire until midnight, when the Texans launched a dismounted assault and, by strong pressure on the Union left, forced in the infantry pickets. A sharp fire from the entrenched infantry and a broadside from the *Skeeota* obliged the Rebels to retreat. The remainder of the night passed quietly.[13]

The following morning, a dense fog covered the battleground until about 10 A.M., which induced a lull in the fighting. As the fog dissipated, a force of cavalry rode near the Union redoubt but attempted no assault on the entrenched enemy. During the day, Hesseltine's soldiers busied themselves improving their positions. They dug rifle pits with their bayonets and used their blankets as sandbags to fill holes in the barricades. At noon, the Confederate gunboat *John F. Carr* came down and shelled the Federals with its twenty-pounder Parrot rifle. (Relevant documents fail to indicate where the Confederate gunboat came from. Perhaps it had steamed down the bay side of the peninsula, while the Federal gunboats remained on the Gulf side, preventing any engagement between the opposing warships.)[14]

When no aid had come by 3 P.M., Hesseltine determined to abandon his position. Somehow he managed secretly to move his men out of their entrenchments and down the peninsula. The Rebel gunboat continued to shell the abandoned position, keeping the Texans at a distance from the deserted barricade. Fog and night hid the Yankees until the next day, when they moved to the beach and were taken aboard the *Skeeota*. The 1st Regiment of Texas Cavalry reported no casualties, but several men failed to answer muster the day after the battle. Some officers suggested that the horses the missing men rode had broken down, so they could not return to camp. Kuykendall upheld this theory when he wrote that he had ridden along the Gulf beach, traveling "many miles under fire from the 2 gunboats."[15]

On January 2, 1864, Buchel sent a letter to Bee's headquarters, explaining why he failed to mount a frontal assault on the entrenched enemy on the Matagorda Peninsula. Evidently someone higher in the chain of command had questioned why he refused to attack the Union infantry with the troops available.[16]

A secondary element of Buchel's mission had been to relieve a few state troops who unwisely had maneuvered themselves between two Union forces on Matagorda Peninsula. In his letter, Buchel explained why he thought sending troops down the peninsula to recover the horses lost by Capt. George Henderson to be a very unwise move. Buchel believed that, had Captain Henderson followed Buchel's and his scouts' instructions, men and horses would not have been lost in the first place. Twenty of Capt. E. S. Rugely's men froze to death after swamping their boat during an abortive attempt to relieve Henderson, who foolishly advanced down the peninsula toward DeCrow's Point. Several Confederate officers had arranged with civilians to recover the animals if possible. Buchel further criticized Henderson for not shooting the horses to keep them out of enemy hands in the first place.[17]

On January 6, 1864, Col. James B. Liken's regiment and Col. N. W. Towne's brigade moved to reinforce Buchel's command, while Union blockaders attempted to make the cavalry's mission as difficult and dangerous as possible. Buchel employed Towne's brigade as pickets on the coast from the mouth of Caney River to Velasco and some distance down toward Matagorda. Bee instructed Buchel to maintain "a complete line of communication," watch the movements of the enemy, and "make a correct and speedy report" to headquarters at Camp Wharton. As Buchel made these dispositions, Federal ships and gunboats continued to blast away at all Confederate forts along the Caney and San Bernard rivers. Federal vessels also shelled any cavalry patrols spied riding near the beaches. On January 8, Pvt. William Behrends, Company E, died from a shellburst salvo into the fortifications at the mouth of the Caney River. Buchel reported that the gunboat lay at anchor all night and "commenced shelling them again" at "first light" the next day. Firing "about 40 rounds" during the day, the Federal warship inflicted no further casualties and moved off. Wight remembered that "while on the cost we had some active servis. The gun boats would ocationly land troops and we would chase them back."[18]

Although few casualties appeared on existing reports for this period, regimental returns indicated a major reduction in personnel between December, 1863, and the end of January, 1864. The men listed present for duty dropped from 1,273 to 703 at Camp Cedar Bayou. Regimental morning reports listed total strength as 796 men present and absent. Illness, casualties, and desertions had reduced the ranks severely in only one month. Since the weather had been cold enough to freeze men to death, harsh weather and disease decimated the ranks more than other causes. Kuykendall's diary sustains this conclusion. He drafted a short chronicle depicting much illness in camp: "Tired and wet a few days after this adventure [the Matagorda fray] I was prostrated by a severe attack of typhoid pneumonia from which I only recovered after many weeks of suffering in the hospital." He also related that "about this time measles broke out in camp, resulting in many deaths." Wight affirmed an epidemic of measles, writing that "more than half of our regement was pro[s]trated with mesals. Quite a number died."[19]

Kuykendall exposed the poor state of medical facilities available to the Texas soldiers. Confederate army regulations prevented injured enlisted men or those stricken with some malady from going home on sick leave unless a general officer approved a furlough and a surgeon's certificate of disability accompanied the request for leave. Most soldiers suffering from an affliction therefore remained in camp and were nursed by friends. In more serious cases, they were transferred to a nearby hospital. Kuykendall alleges, "A strict enforcement of this order frequently entailed unnecessary hardship upon the afflicted as the means of the disposition of the hospital staff in the field was notoriously inadequate to give proper care to the sick," so that "many succumbed [who under] more favorable conditions would have recovered." Kuykendall, as a personal friend of Regimental Surgeon James A. White, accepted an invitation to "take his meals" with the physician, as "fare on his table was far better than that provided for the sick in the hospital." Kuykendall maintained that only better food and a furlough home, secured through friends in command positions, enabled him to survive his illness.[20]

In early January, 1864, Magruder ordered Bee to prevent at all costs enemy occupation or control of the region around the mouth of the Caney River. The departmental commander also directed Bee to dismount all his horsemen except the 1st Regiment of Texas Cavalry. The dismounted cavalry, along with regular infantry, held the line against the Federal corps that only occasionally

sallied forth from DeCrow's Point and northward along Matagorda Peninsula. The 1st Texas Cavalry patrolled the coast and scouted the beaches for
enemy landing parties. Incomplete construction of a pontoon bridge over the
Bernard River prevented any rapid movement of cavalry to the east. Bee instructed Buchel to "make the best use of forces available." Bee's directives included measures to insure that "not less than 100 men remained in the forts at
all times."[21]

Regularly scheduled cavalry patrols investigated the beach above and below the river mouth to prevent surprise attacks by Union landing parties. Patrols rotated every two hours so that the relieving men would meet the returning
patrol at a location halfway from the starting point. Each patrol covered about
ten miles toward the Caney River on one side and Velasco on the other. Buchel
allowed the cavalry detachments to camp "where wood and water was available." Scouting parties established recognition signals to be used day or night
between their camps and the Confederate forts. They utilized signal fires until
a requisition of more visible rockets arrived. While on the coast, the regiment
received more abundant supplies, and the quartermaster managed to stockpile
more than a three-week supply of corn and fodder for his men and horses. To
relieve the necessity of using the stored animal feed, the regiment pastured its
mounts inland on the abundant coastal prairie grass.[22]

As the only mounted cavalry regiment in the area, the 1st Texas continued
to monitor enemy activities during January and February, 1864. Through intelligence gathered by the cavalry, Bee discerned that Banks's Union corps
intended to depart from the coast. Bee planned an attack on the weakened
garrison at Indianola, to be spearheaded by Buchel's cavalry. Bee's letters informed Magruder that the men's morale was low. Disease, poor camp conditions, and the furlough of state troops disheartened the men, and a successful
attack would raise their spirits. Bee estimated enemy strength at between four
and six thousand. He exuded confidence, for he knew the area and predicted
an easy victory. Magruder initially agreed but later postponed the attack because of supply shortages for the entire attacking force. He was able to provide
enough horses to remount two of the other cavalry regiments in preparation
for operations against the Federals around Indianola. In anticipation of further action, he placed all cavalry and two batteries of light artillery under
Buchel's command. Because Magruder delayed the planned attack and Banks
began withdrawing his troops toward New Orleans, the regiment had little
enemy contact until the middle of March.[23]

A heavy skirmish took place on March 13 near the city of San Patricio, in
San Patricio County, involving Capt. James Ware's company. The company

bivouacked at Camp San Fernando near Corpus Christi and patrolled from there. Ware also maintained a series of pickets and lookouts on Live Oak Point near Corpus Christi. In addition to leading a cavalry company, Ware administered the local cotton trade and secreted a large number of cotton bales for shipment south to exchange for military supplies available across the Rio Grande. The burden of managing the cotton, however, did not dissuade Ware from leading his troops in the field. On March 13, he led a detachment of his men as a component of a larger force commanded by Maj. Matthew Nolan. The combined units discovered a force of enemy cavalry camped in thick mesquite brush. After a sharply contested battle, about fifteen minutes in length, the Confederate cavalry completely routed the enemy. Nolan estimated the enemy force at 125 men, "well armed with Burnsides carbines, revolvers, and sabers." Nolan commanded only sixty-two men, most of whom were indifferently armed. "The enemy charged with about eighty men" and "fought most gallantly," being repulsed only "after a desperate fight and after a loss of much blood and property." According to Nolan, Ware and his men "acted with conspicuous gallantry" and "behaved coolly and bravely." An indeterminate number of Ware's men received wounds in the skirmish and were forced to remain in a camp in the brush until well enough to be transferred to a hospital in Corpus Christi.[24]

Magruder frustrated Banks in his attempt to move up the Texas coast to Houston and Galveston. Banks also failed in his stated goal of moving up the Colorado River to capture San Antonio and Austin. He managed briefly to interrupt the cotton trade along the Rio Grande, but the resourceful Texans just moved up the Rio Grande and continued the important trade. In February and March, 1864, Banks, under impetus from Washington, evolved a new plan to invade Texas through Louisiana and began to move his corps to New Orleans. He planned to move overland across Louisiana; head up the Red River to Shreveport, Louisiana; and thence march into the agricultural regions of East Texas.[25]

CHAPTER 10

"Our Time Is at Hand"

Between Alexandria and Mansfield, Louisiana, a distance of ninety miles, the terrain changes dramatically. Broad, flat, alluvial plains near the Mississippi River give way to rolling, pine-covered hills cut by steep ravines and bayous.

During the Civil War, a road ran from below Alexandria to Bayou Boeuf, which flowed into the Red River. This road passed through pine forests to Burr's Ferry on the Sabine and then, twenty miles from the Boeuf, intersected another road from Opelousas to Fort Jesup. From there the trace led north to Pleasant Hill, Mansfield, and Shreveport. Smaller roads crisscrossed the area and led to ferries on the Red River. Thick, red clay and sand composed the poor soil of the region. Roads became muddy, sunken forest paths bordered closely by dense pine thickets. Making travel along this wretched stretch of road even more difficult were the intermittent bayous and swamps that meandered among small hills and steep ravines. The only drinking water available stood in these infrequent bayous or in the even less frequent cisterns and wells in the region's scanty settlements. Before attempting any military operations in this sparsely settled country, Maj. Gen. Richard Taylor established several depots, or caches, of forage and supplies to sustain both soldiers and horses. Because of shortages and lack of support from the local populace, he confiscated a portion of his supplies and horses from civilians living up and down the Red River. The menacing character of this terrain caused one Union cavalryman to call it "a howling wilderness."[1]

Harboring lingering doubts about operations in this inhospitable country, Maj. Gen. Nathaniel Banks nevertheless acquiesced to a plan promoted by Maj. Gen. Henry W. Halleck and some influential New England politicians. Banks realized the positive effect that a successful military campaign would have on

fig. 16. Richard Taylor commanded Confederate forces opposing Nathaniel Banks's march up the Red River in Louisiana. Courtesy Jack McCormack Irish Collection, U.S. Army Military History Institute, Carlisle Barracks, Pennsylvania

his future political career, and this somewhat diminished his misgivings. As Banks planned his invasion of Texas through this menacing region of Louisiana, he realized the necessity of naval support. Through the intercession of Maj. Gen. William T. Sherman, Banks secured a commitment from Rear Adm. David D. Porter, commander of U.S. naval forces along the Mississippi River. Porter agreed to assemble a large naval squadron to move up the Red River and support Banks's operations. On March 12, 1864, Porter's flotilla of thirteen ironclads, four tinclads, five other armed vessels, and nearly forty transports began conveying ten thousand troops of the 16th and 17th Army Corps, commanded by Brig. Gen. Andrew J. Smith, up the mouth of the Red River. On March 15, the first of Porter's gunboats reached Alexandria, and Taylor ordered all Confederate units to evacuate the city.[2]

With the addition of Smith's troops to his own Army of the Gulf, Banks's army numbered approximately thirty thousand effectives, who enjoyed an abundance of food and leisure. Union troops also demonstrated their intention to destroy the economic foundation of the region. On April 1, Pvt. John Tyler Webb, 30th Maine Infantry, wrote in his diary: "Went into camp at 5 P.M. I fell out and got some bread baked. Had a boiled pig and stake [*sic*] for supper. Had cotton to sleep on. 200 lbs. costly bed. Saw cotton & a machine shop burning."[3]

By the end of March, Banks had forced Taylor (President Zachary Taylor's son) back two hundred miles along the road. Banks thereby came to control most of the roads below Pleasant Hill. Taylor's troops numbered only about 6,500. The previous December, he had sent Maj. Gen. Thomas "Tom" Green's cavalry division to aid in defending against the Federal incursions along the Texas coast. Now, the long retreat and the lack of troops from the Atchafalaya River galled Taylor. On March 31, he wrote to Lt. Gen. Edmund Kirby Smith, who was commanding the Trans-Mississippi Department: "It would have been better to lose the state after a defeat than to surrender it without a fight. The fairest and richest portion of the Confederacy is now a waste."[4]

After consolidating his army at Alexandria, Banks proceeded with a disorganized and ill-conceived march upriver. At Grand Ecore, refusing to conduct a reconnaissance for a more favorable route, Banks elected to leave the river and Porter's supporting 210 naval guns, to march along the stage road to Pleasant Hill. Although a preferable avenue of approach to Shreveport existed along the river road, Banks did not consult local guides fully and failed to locate this more expedient route. On April 3, he established a garrison at Grand Ecore and three days later started his imposing army up the narrow, inland corridor toward Shreveport. Webb reported that the men were foraging on the country and still eating well: "Had chicken stew for dinner. Full as a Tick." The Federal column marching overland numbered over twenty-five thousand combat and support troops encumbered with over a thousand supply wagons and ambulances. Ninety guns reinforced the Union column, and these gun carriages, with their supporting caissons, made a quagmire of Banks's only supply route, considerably reducing any hope of a steady advance.[5]

To complicate matters further, the column's march order was poorly conceived. Although Brig. Gen. Albert L. Lee's cavalry led the advance, his supply train obstructed the road between his mounted troops and their supporting infantry. Lee complained that, if he struck a strong Rebel force, the infantry could not be brought up rapidly to reinforce him. Banks assured him that Taylor would not fight before the Union troops approached Shreveport, and the column remained interspersed with supply trains and combat troops. Banks's haphazard organization proved a recipe for disaster.[6]

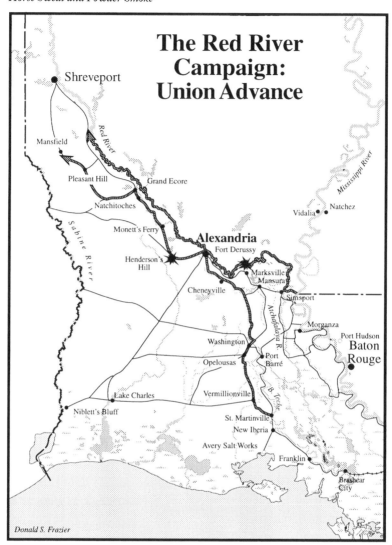

map 5. The Red River Campaign: Union Advance. Map prepared by
Don Frazier

When the Federals began to advance up the Red River in mid-March, Kirby
Smith ordered all available Confederate troops to move immediately to Taylor's
aid. From Arkansas, Brig. Gens. Mosby Parsons and Thomas J. Churchill
marched their small divisions toward Shreveport to add their strength to that
of the infantry under Brig. Gens. Alfred Mouton and John G. Walker. On
March 5, Kirby Smith ordered Maj. Gen. John B. Magruder to send Green's

cavalry division and all other feasible troops from Texas. Responding to this order, Brig. Gen. Hamilton P. Bee gathered six regiments of cavalry near the mouth of the Colorado River. In mid March, he rode from Columbus, Texas, toward Louisiana with his new brigade, composed of the regiments of Augustus Buchel, Xavier B. DeBray, Nicholas C. Gould, James B. Liken, Alexander W. Terrell, and Peter C. Woods. The Texas troops rode through the unusually cold spring weather and crossed the Sabine River at Logansport, then continued to Mansfield, twenty miles to the rear of Taylor's front line. On April 1, 1864, the first contingents of Texas reinforcements began to arrive in Louisiana. Because of delays en route, the cavalry regiments appeared in scattered groups. As one regiment rode past Taylor, sitting astride his horse in Mansfield, the Texans heard him call out, "Boys I'm glad to see you." April 5 dawned with a hard frost but developed into a fair, cool day, as Buchel's regiment rode into Mansfield. Early the next morning, Bee, his headquarters staff, and two other regiments reached Taylor's headquarters. Bee utilized the remainder of the day to reorganize the newly arrived cavalry regiments. When Bee reported to Green late that evening, Green designated Bee's unit as the 1st Division of Green's cavalry corps.[7]

As the first of Lee's three Union cavalry brigades advanced through Pleasant Hill, they pushed out about two hundred Confederate cavalrymen before them. Buchel's regiment, along with Bee's other cavalry, fought a strong delaying action on the road to Mansfield. At Wilson's Farm, three miles from Pleasant Hill, the Union advance guard encountered the Confederates "in considerable force," deployed in the woods with their left flank protected by a deep ravine. Green's "wild horsemen" resisted so strongly that the Federal commander dismounted and committed his entire cavalry brigade and a supporting battery of artillery to the line. Firing became intense on both sides, and the Confederates' obstinacy forced the Union commander to commit elements of another brigade to the expanding conflict. With loud Rebel yells and "great impetuosity," quick-shooting Texas horsemen charged into the Union front and right flank, dislodging the leading Federal brigade and driving it back into Lee's advancing reinforcements. Struggling up the muddy road, the combined strength of the two brigades eventually managed to stop what a Yankee trooper called the "fiery attack" of the onrushing Texas cavalry. After this repulse, the Confederate forces broke off contact, and the Yankee cavalry followed them along the road until near nightfall. During the withdrawal, Green commented to Buchel, "We haven't had much show yet, but we will give them hell tomorrow." At Wilson's Farm, Federal cavalrymen claimed twenty-seven Rebels captured, at the cost of eleven Federals killed, forty-two wounded, and nine missing.[8]

fig. 17. Edmund Kirby-Smith commanded the Confederate Trans-Mississippi Department. Courtesy Massachusetts Commandery, Military Order of the Loyal Legion and U.S. Army Military History Institute, Carlisle Barracks, Pennsylvania

Before dark fell on the cloudy and windy day, Green's cavalry, in strong positions ten miles from Pleasant Hill, again halted the Federal advance, and both sides spent a wet, miserable night in the rain near Carroll's Mill. Green deployed his cavalry regiments and the four-gun Val Verde Battery in a well-sited position behind a bayou at Carroll's Mill. In successive charges, Lee's units had failed to dislodge the determined Confederates. After again being abruptly halted, Banks's cavalry divisions bivouacked for the night along the narrow, rain-soaked road.[9]

During the day's fighting, the Federal force captured several Confederates and claimed many more killed and wounded. Confederate losses amounted to about 100, and Union losses totaled 225 killed, wounded, and captured. One of the prisoners, Lt. George Stone of Lee's cavalry, crossed into Confederate lines "so drunk that he could hardly ride." The tipsy lieutenant still flourished a canteen full of whiskey when captured. (No one reported what happened to the whiskey.) Thick pine woods forbade extensive use of mounted men, and most of the Union soldiers fought dismounted. The Texans spent the night sleeping along the small creek in line of battle. As on the Texas plains, they slept alongside their weapons and with their reins wrapped around their hands, ready to leap into the saddle and ride into action.[10]

The next morning, Green ordered Bee to delay Banks's advance guard as long as possible and rode away to assist Taylor in organizing his chosen battle line south of Mansfield. Bee immediately executed a tactical plan designed to hold up the Union cavalry and give Taylor time to prepare his defenses. Bee formed his regiments into three lines about five hundred yards apart. As Lee's advance guard pushed close to the first line, Bee instructed his men to fire several volleys into the advancing enemy and then hurriedly to mount and ride to the rear of the last regiment blocking the road. These tactics forced the Union troops to dismount and deploy into an attack formation each time they encountered one of the Texas blocking positions. After the Confederate cavalry abandoned a position, Lee's cavalry had to recover their lead horses before they could advance, slowing the Union army's progress. The dense woods and hills greatly favored Bee's tactics while frustrating the Federals. At one point during the retrograde operation, Buchel's regiment ambushed the Union advance guard, inflicting heavy casualties. In this manner, Bee managed to impede Banks's progress for over seven hours, while Taylor readied his battle line at Mansfield.[11]

Although achieving tactical success, the Texas horsemen experienced some setbacks while opposing the Union cavalry. Before the day's fighting commenced, a few of the Texans must have slept late and found their breakfast rudely interrupted. As they advanced, the 3rd Massachusetts Cavalry discovered corncake and bacon recently cooked and spread out on logs.[12]

Breakfast, of course, was not the only casualty. Amid the whine of Federal minié balls, Capt. James S. Bigham grabbed the reins of his horse, leaped into the saddle, and galloped back toward a secondary position. As he rode away, a bullet struck him from behind in the upper part of a leg. He reached around and, with only his fingers, extracted the bullet from the fleshy part of his leg. Exasperated at being hit from the rear, he held out the bloody hunk of lead to Wight, who rode beside him, saying, "I woudent care a damn for that if it was in front." Wight remembered, "It developed in to a bad wound." After a morning of exchanging gunfire with the blue-coated Yankees, the 1st Texas Cavalry, along with Bee's other units, rode back through the Confederate main line shortly after noon.[13]

Based on his cavalry's intelligence reports, Taylor knew that Banks's advancing column was strung out for twenty miles along the Pleasant Hill Road. In order to exploit the lack of cohesion in the Federal column, Taylor analyzed the terrain and prepared his army to fight three miles south of Mansfield. He realized that, if Banks passed through the town, the Federal commander could proceed to Shreveport on any or all of three different roads. Kirby Smith lacked sufficient forces to stop Banks if the Union column split up. Taylor chose a point where the Pleasant Hill Road ran northwest to southeast through the center of a clearing 800 yards wide and 1,200 yards long. A fence bordered the north side of the clearing and separated it from the pines. Another fence extended along the west side of the clearing. To oppose Banks's approaching army of over 25,000 effectives, Taylor deployed 5,300 infantry, 3,000 cavalry, and 500 artillerymen. Within twenty-four hours, he expected Churchill to arrive with 4,400 additional troops.[14]

Churchill could not be counted on to arrive for the initial battle, so Taylor disposed his available units across Banks's line of advance. Walker's Texas Infantry Division occupied positions immediately to the right of the Pleasant Hill Road, which ran across the clearing from northwest to southeast. To cover Walker's flank, Bee ordered Terrell's and Buchel's regiments to the extreme right of his line. DeBray and a battery of artillery remained in reserve on the road a short distance behind the main line. Mouton deployed his division to the left and across the road from Walker. To the far left of the Confederate line, Brig. Gen. James P. Major's division of dismounted Texas cavalry took up positions in the pine woods on Mouton's left. (Major's men previously had been dismounted to provide required infantry; but, as proud Texans, they refused to surrender the cavalry designation.) Walker and Mouton each had two artillery batteries supporting their divisions. Taylor held other batteries in reserve, because the heavily wooded terrain restricted effective employment of all his cannon.[15]

Taylor and his men remained confident and resolute as the first elements of approaching Federals disputed the Confederate hold on the Mansfield Road. Riding along his front lines inspecting his dispositions, Taylor paused and declared to Brig. Gen. Camille A. J. M. de Polignac of Mouton's division, "Little Frenchman I'm going to fight Banks if he has a million men." An entry in one of his men's diary echoes Taylor's bravado: "We are ready and eager to meet the damned rascals." About one hundred mounted Federals, shouting "Sooe Sooe" as if driving hogs, pushed the Confederate cavalry skirmishers into the waiting lines, but the overzealous Yankees received heavy losses in a shower of bullets from Mouton's Louisianans. Viewing the scene, Felix Pierre Poche described the Union cavalry as fleeing "in great disorder," leaving ten wounded and several dead horses behind. Meeting a stubborn defense, the leading units of Banks's 13th Army Corps, under Brig. Gen. Thomas E. G. Ransom, deployed in the woods opposite Taylor's line and waited for reinforcements to come up. Light skirmishing and sniping between sharpshooters continued between the lines for about two hours. This skirmishing indicated a shift of Union troops from the left to the right, unveiling Banks's intention to turn Taylor's left flank. When Banks arrived at the point of contact, he had ordered Lee to hold in place and sent orders back for Maj. Gen. William B. Franklin "to hurry forward the column" and close up with his supporting infantry.[16]

To counter these Federal movements, Taylor ordered significant modifications to his defensive configuration. He redeployed Brig. Gen. Horace Randal's brigade of Walker's division across the road to strengthen Mouton. He then shifted the entire Confederate line to reinforce his left. To bolster Major's position, he sent Terrell's cavalry over to the Confederate far left and directed DeBray's regiment to join Buchel on the right. During these redeployments, Buchel maneuvered his cavalrymen to the extreme right of the Confederate line. Skirmishers deployed in the field on both sides of the road masked the Confederate movements. Pvt. Levi Lamoni Wight, Company E, recalled that, as Buchel rode among his men, he told them in so many words, "Our time is at hand. Boys you will soon see blood until you are satisfied."[17]

At 4 P.M., Taylor became impatient with the intermittent skirmishing and, surmising the enemy maneuvers to be incomplete, ordered Mouton to launch an attack from the left. Mouton's division charged through a murderous fire, and he, along with many other officers, fell before it. Poche wrote that the fusillade "beat our soldiers down even as a storm tears down the trees of a forest." Despite heavy losses of men and officers, the attack never faltered or became disorganized. Polignac took command of Mouton's division, and the screaming Confederates relentlessly pressed on. On the Confederate left, Major's dismounted Texas cavalry kept pace with Polignac's advance, forcing the enemy back and turning its right flank. Randal supported the attack by advancing his regiments by echelon from the left. Green commanded all actions on the left of the road, while Taylor maintained overall authority. When the attack was well developed on the left, Taylor ordered Walker forward and directed Bee to sweep around to the enemy's rear with Buchel's and DeBray's cavalry. Brig. Gen. William R. Scurry of Walker's division deviated to the right and broke through the blue-coated line to the high road at the rear of Banks's front line of defense.[18]

Buchel's and DeBray's advancing cavalry, although impeded by thick woods, overran all enemy opposition. As they began to retreat, the Federals attempted to form secondary lines of defense on the piney ridges, but the screaming Texans swept away every line as soon as it formed and captured almost every gun before it could be brought to bear. Only a few Federal batteries managed to

fig. 18. William B. Franklin
served as second-in-
command under Banks in
several 1863-64 campaigns
in Texas and Louisiana.
Courtesy Massachusetts
Commandery, Military
Order of the Loyal Legion
and U.S. Army Military
History Institute, Carlisle
Barracks, Pennsylvania

unlimber their guns and fire on the advancing Rebels before they were captured. For five miles, the exuberant Confederates drove the Yankees rapidly
and steadily back. The lead divisions of the U.S. 13th Army Corps broke and
ran, beginning a rout. As both Federal flanks gave way, Franklin ordered the
3rd Division of the 13th Corps to hasten up and bolster his collapsing line.[19]

Bee's two cavalry regiments pressed through the pine woods and ravines,
driving the 3rd Massachusetts Cavalry and 165th New York Infantry before
them. A Massachusetts cavalryman lamented that their men "dropped like
autumnal leaves before an October gale." The 3rd Massachusetts Cavalry alone
lost 67 men and 121 horses in less than thirty minutes. The Texans crossed Seven
Mile Creek toward what was thought to be a routed enemy. Riding at full speed
toward the blue-coated enemy, the cavalry expected to exploit the successes of
the infantry. Instead, they ran headlong into Brig. Gen. Robert A. Cameron's

3rd Division, U.S. 13th Army Corps, which had barely established a new defensive position.[20]

Cameron's fresh infantry moved into well-posted positions on a hill overlooking the battle, but even a vigorous burst of defensive fire from these troops failed to stop the onrushing Rebels. As "musket balls whizzed through the air," portions of A. L. Lee's cavalry halted their retreat and swung their horses around to form a line behind and reinforcing the beleaguered infantry. After an initial repulse, the Texas cavalry, in a charge that mingled with Walker's infantry, chased the Federals from their newly formed line. All along the line of battle, Confederate onslaughts shattered Union confidence. Detailed as a courier on Green's staff, Pvt. H. C. Medford of Col. Walter P. Lane's 1st Texas Partisan Rangers penned his impressions of the fierce fighting: "The strife of this battle is terrible. Many of our men are falling. The whole heavens are replete with destructive missiles. There is not a safe place anywhere on this battlefield." When the 13th Corps line broke, Medford recalled thinking, "It is Bull Run time."

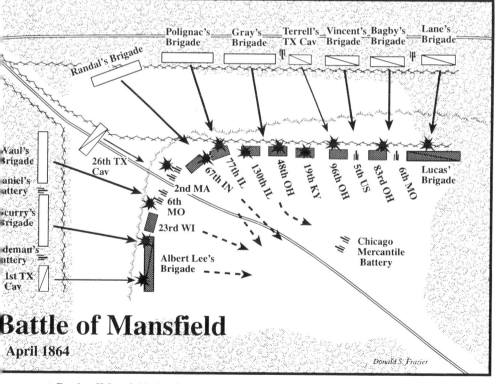

map 6. Battle of Mansfield, April 8, 1864. Map prepared by Don Frazier

Courageously but futilely, Banks rode along his line, attempting to rally his men as the retreat became a complete rout. "Form a line here," he cried as his line crumbled. "I know that you will not desert me." But his soldiers ignored his pleas and bolted before the howling Rebels. A Federal officer attempting to bring up reinforcements later complained about knees badly bruised by the terrified mob of Union troops sprinting to the rear. At one point he observed a line of fugitives "tailed out behind a single tree in an effort to escape the singing Minie balls."[21]

As Taylor's men pressed their advantage, most Union soldiers joined the rush to the rear, crying, "The day is lost." Complete chaos engulfed the head of the Federal column. Panicked teamsters attempted to turn their wagons around on the narrow road. The frightened men lashed at their teams and turned their wagons into one another, locking wheels and clogging the road. When their wagons became ensnared, the terrorized teamsters cut their traces, mounted their mules, and raced away toward Pleasant Hill. This simply added a jumble of men and horses to the wagons and discarded equipment that choked the road.[22]

As a result of the confusion, Taylor's army captured an enormous amount of abandoned war materiel. Twenty pieces of artillery, an estimated one thousand horses, and the entire supply train of the Union cavalry corps, which totaled over two hundred wagons, fell into Rebel hands. Dr. Frank Rainey, a member of Green's staff, reported that several of the wagons were labeled "Austin, San Antonio, Houston, Galveston, and etc." Rainey recounted that the battle "knocked Banks' plans into a cocked hat." Kegs of whiskey found in the wagons made the Confederate victory even more savory.[23]

Despite heavy losses in men and horses, the advancing Confederates swept all before them until approaching darkness and another Union division blunted their charge. As daylight faded and the woods grew dark, Brig. Gen. William H. Emory's 1st Division, 19th U.S. Army Corps, eventually pushed forward through the fleeing mob and massed on a hill overlooking a vital creek that meandered through a peach orchard called Pleasant Grove. Above the fray, Emory shouted, "Men you must hold this position at all hazards. Before the enemy gets past here they must ride over me and my little grey mare."[24]

Advancing Rebels rushed headlong into a massed point-blank fire from the leveled rifles of Emory's men and a "storm of lead and hail swept on the Confederate Army . . . leaving the ground covered with the bleeding forms of the killed and wounded." A Confederate officer later recalled, "The very air seemed dark and hot with balls and on every side was heard their dull crashing sound as they struck that swaying mass, tearing through flesh, bone, and sinew." This overwhelming fusillade of musketry stopped the Confederate advance along the little watercourse. For both sides, control of the water was tactically imperative, and Taylor ordered the enemy driven from it. Weary Confederate officers rallied their tired men for another rush forward. There was no artillery available for either side, and the soldiers fought with only the muskets and pistols of the cavalrymen. When darkness fell, the Rebels camped on the stream while Emory's five thousand men shivered in the cold night air and looked thirstily toward the water from some four hundred yards away.[25]

Bee called this action the Battle of the Peach Orchard and insisted that the gory struggle was an engagement completely separate from Mansfield. Wight recalled that, during the heat of the battle, "the bullets was flyining [*sic*] thick and fast." Ignoring the rifle fire crackling around him, Buchel remained mounted throughout the fighting, while his adjutant led his mount behind his commander, imploring, "Colonel for God's sake get off your horse." Disdaining the danger, Buchel retorted curtly, "When I want your advice I will ask you for it." Leading Company D through the orchard, Capt. James C. Borden fell severely wounded, and Pvt. George S. Gayle reported Borden "not fit for future service." J. M. Thompson had his horse shot from under him and recalled that three enemy bullets struck his rifle, "once when aiming at [a] Federal officer." Thompson reported that all his company officers were either killed or wounded and that a sergeant led the company when darkness forced a halt to the fighting. Wight remembered the Peach Orchard as the bloodiest phase of the Battle of Mansfield.[26]

During the night, Banks's confidence waned, and he ordered a withdrawal. On Saturday morning, April 9, Buchel's and DeBray's regiments pursued the Union army's rear guard back down the road to Pleasant Hill. A few hours of the hardest fighting ever to occur in the Civil War west of the Mississippi River had sent Banks fleeing down the road before a considerably inferior force. For fifteen miles, dramatic evidence of the Union rout littered the road. Scattered equipment, discarded weapons, burning wagons, and abandoned ambulances choked the track toward Pleasant Hill. Union artillerymen had deserted their guns, while infantry and cavalry bolting from the battlefield threw away their arms and accoutrements as evidence of panic and disorder. Medford wrote that Union equipment littered the battlefield and "dead and dying lay on every side of [the] road." He remembered that dead horses and men covered "9 square miles" and that "Negroes and stragglers [were] robbing the dead." Pvt. William Kuykendall, riding to rejoin Company D after an extended illness, rode through Mansfield after the battle and described further the "grewsome [*sic*] evidence of the struggle . . . on all sides—dead men, dead horses, abandoned camp equipage, muskets, etc. were observed all along the roads."[27]

The spirited Texans chased the Yankees for fifteen miles before meeting any resistance, taking over a hundred Union stragglers and abandoned wounded as prisoners along the way. Wight wrote that "duering the day we drove the cowerdley devels [*sic*] to Plesent Hill." Not until after 9 A.M. did the lead elements of the cavalry meet strong opposition from fixed positions in front of Pleasant Hill. Bee halted his horsemen to reconnoiter the Federal lines. To determine the strength and extent of the Union positions, he sent Buchel to the left and Richard Hardemann's horsemen to the right of the stage road. Buchel reported that the Union right rested on a steep, wooded ravine and extended only a short distance into the timber. Hardemann's scouts, however, indicated that the Federal line stretched for more than a mile into the pinery on the Confederate right. Such indisputable evidence of Federal strength surprised Bee after the previous day's events. He decided that his cavalry had no business assaulting such a strong, entrenched position. After Green arrived on the scene and took command, he toured the lines, agreeing that the cavalry should not attack alone. He ordered his horsemen to continue to probe the Federal defenses while they waited for Taylor to bring up his infantry and artillery.[28]

Banks's line extended across a plateau from College Hill on the left to a wooded hill on the right of the road to Mansfield. The Federals' most advanced infantry occupied a steep-sided, pine-wooded gully, which they had reinforced with a barricade of fallen timber. The main line of resistance and the artillery supported forward outposts that were placed in the gullies north of the plateau. An open field several hundred yards wide separated the outposts from the primary Union defenses. Banks's positions held about eighteen thousand men, including troops who were fresh and had not been engaged previously.[29]

Taylor's infantry did not arrive on the scene until well after noon. After the long, dry forced march from Mansfield and Keachiee, the men required immediate rest and water before they could be expected to attack an entrenched enemy. Taylor allowed his exhausted foot soldiers to recuperate for two hours, while he considered his tactical plan. Throughout the early afternoon, as the infantry rested, Bee's cavalry incessantly annoyed the Yankees, feinting right and left of the line seeking to determine exact locations of Union troop dispositions.[30]

At 3 P.M., Taylor completed his plan of attack and deployed his command to storm the Union line. He sent Churchill's men to the woods on the right, with orders to maneuver far enough to the right to attack and roll up the Union left flank. Three regiments of cavalry screened Churchill's right with orders to drive to the Natchitoches Road and cut off any Union retreat in that direction.

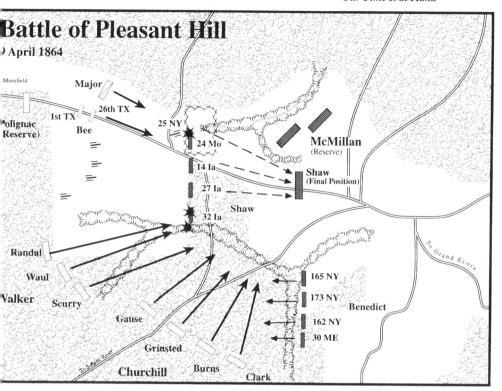

Battle of Pleasant Hill
April 1864

map 7. Battle of Pleasant Hill, April 9, 1864. Map prepared by Don Frazier

Walker formed his "Greyhounds" to Churchill's left and extended his line to make contact with Major's dismounted cavalry on the Confederate left. Green commanded the attacking troops to the left of the road and ordered Bee to hold Buchel's and DeBray's cavalry on the road in the center. When the Federal line weakened, Green planned to wield his cavalrymen as shock troops by smashing a mounted charge through Pleasant Hill and exploiting any breakthrough made by the Confederate infantry. Polignac's small, battered division constituted Taylor's only reserve.[31]

To divert attention from Churchill's attack, Taylor, at approximately 4:30 P.M., ordered Green to open with his artillery on Federal batteries posted on high ground along the Pleasant Hill road. Without supporting infantry, Confederate artillery raced forward to within two hundred yards of the Federals, unlimbered their guns, and commenced a rapid fire on the opposing batteries. Accurate, point-blank fire by Green's artillery created such havoc in a Union battery in the center of the line that it limbered up and wheeled to withdraw.

A Federal brigade commander reported that this battery left one gun and caisson on the road and "disgracefully left the field."[32]

About 5 P.M., a fusillade of musketry and a chorus of furious yells echoed through the pines, indicating Churchill's attack on what Confederate officers judged to be a demoralized enemy. When Green heard the tumult of battle to his right, he ordered his sixteen guns of the cavalry corps, most of which had been captured the day before, to commence a rapid fire upon the bluecoats' positions. Answering fire from over forty Federal guns aptly demonstrated that the Confederates confronted a significantly different force than the one they had faced the day prior. Wight wrote, "Brave men [were] melting before the blazening [*sic*] cannon . . . and dead men were in piles."[33]

When Walker heard the raucous noise of Churchill's assault, he ordered his division forward. His advance and the wheeling Federal batteries to his front led Green to assume, mistakenly, that the time had come to launch his mounted attack. To Buchel's dismay, he ordered Bee's cavalry forward. Green concluded that the Union line had wavered under Confederate pressure, and he hoped to exploit the enemy's confusion. Earlier reconnaissance and skirmishing had revealed to Buchel that the 24th Missouri Infantry occupied hidden positions that extended perpendicular to the main Federal line of defense and that their field of fire covered the open ground over which his cavalry must charge. Cpl. William H. Hudson, Company G, remembered that Buchel, "of known military knowledge and bravery," immediately comprehended that any mounted assault against the entrenched Federal positions would needlessly expose his troops to an enfilading crossfire and futile casualties. Consequently Buchel dispatched a courier to Green to stop or postpone the attack. Wight, in his homespun language, recorded Buchel's message as, "Tell the Genl that I can efect nothng but a sacrafise of men in [a] charg rite now from my possion." Green refused Buchel's request and, in his reply to the courier, insinuated that Buchel displayed cowardice. Recognizing the hopelessness of the charge, Buchel told his men that he could not order them into such an ambuscade but would follow orders and charge alone. His loyal Texas regiment raised a cheer, threw their hats into the air, and loudly vowed to follow their colonel in any attack.[34]

Late that afternoon, the slanted rays of the ebbing sunlight filtered through the thick pines and glinted off the drawn sabers of Buchel's and DeBray's cavalry as the Texans massed for their charge. The Missouri infantry, lying in concealed positions, watched the Confederate cavalry across the clearing to their front form into columns of fours, readying to assail the Union line. With a loud Texas yell, both regiments burst into the open field and rode toward the

fig. 19. Thomas Green commanded the Texas Cavalry Corps until his death at Blair's Landing on April 12, 1864. Courtesy Archives Division, Texas State Library, Austin

enemy at a gallop. One Federal defender wrote, "Their cavalry came upon us like a hurricane. Their excited horses with open mouths and distended nostrils came like a herd of wild buffaloes stampeded by a prairie fire." Another Federal private described the Texans' charge:

> Over 300 cavalry came dashing along at full speed with their sabers drawn and yelling at the top of their voices. Captain Jones . . . told us to lay still until he gave us orders to fire. When they were within one hundred yards Jones hollered, "to your feet and boys let them have it!" He had hardly got the words out of his mouth when all of us were on our feet and such a roll of musketry I never want to hear again. I could see the poor fellows fall from their horses at every shot we fired at them. They were truly brave fellows or they would have never ventured up so close.[35]

Pandemonium spawned by a crossfire of musketry, cannons' roar, clouds of powder smoke, plunging horses, and men literally blasted from their saddles caused the mounted attack to disintegrate. A Yankee officer reported, "Riders

fig. 20. Xavier B. DeBray and his regiment accompanied the 1st Texas Cavalry on almost every campaign in 1863-65. Courtesy Archives Division, Texas State Library, Austin

reeled and fell senseless [and] horses were struck as dead as if a bolt of heaven had riven the very air . . . the scene was an appalling one." Some of the men broke and ran for refuge from the converging fire in a ravine, as nonplussed officers attempted to withdraw their surviving troops from the trap.[36]

Swept by devastating fire from front and flank, DeBray's regiment returned to the Confederate lines with a loss of one-third of its number. Medford wrote, "The dead and wounded lie thick, [on] all parts of the field." Both Bee and DeBray received injuries in the fruitless attack. DeBray's horse, shot dead near the enemy's lines, pinned the colonel to the ground by trapping his boot in a stirrup under the fallen animal. Slipping his boot off his injured foot, DeBray, using his saber for a crutch, limped back toward safety while rifle balls cracked around him. When asked by Taylor if he were wounded, DeBray replied, "No general. I am slightly hurt, but as you may see I was sent on a bootless errand." "Never mind the boot," replied Taylor. "You have won your spurs." During the engagement, Bee had two mounts shot from under him and acquired some bruises from resulting falls.[37]

Buchel halted his troopers before they entered the killing zone and withdrew them to the protecting woods. He dismounted his regiment, moved them to the left, and organized an attack that dislodged the Missouri infantry and drove them back into the main Federal lines. Buchel remained on horseback during the attack, which made him an easy target. At the edge of the enemy lines, his horse shot from under him, Buchel fell with seven serious wounds. A short time later, men of the 14th Iowa Infantry found him, took his name and rank, and left him where he lay.[38]

The 1st Texas Cavalry completely routed the Missouri infantry from their positions, but a Union counterattack forced the Texans back. During this fray, according to the 16th Indiana Cavalry Regiment, fighting dismounted as infantry, it captured the flag of the 1st Texas Cavalry and several of its lead mounts. Lt. Col. William O. Yager, realizing how precarious the battle was at this juncture, seized the initiative and took command of the regiment. He led a counterattack that again broke the Union lines. Wight recalled that an artillery battery firing "grape and cannister" supported the attack: "We broke their ranks and in five minets [*sic*] the enemy was flying." As they advanced, his men found Buchel, mortally wounded, lying in the abandoned Union bulwarks. Hudson and three others "laid him gently on a captured Yankee blanket" and moved him to an ambulance. As they carried their bleeding colonel from the scene of conflict, Buchel murmured, "Let me pass to the front." Although grievously wounded, Buchel still sought to be at the forefront of his men during battle. When told that the Yankees had been driven back, he seemed to relax and whispered, "That is good."[39]

Both Bee and Taylor later claimed to have been at Buchel's side when he died at Bee's headquarters two days later. Bee remarked that the fallen colonel's death was "a irreputable loss to our cause and his adopted country." Taylor added his respect for Buchel, saying, "The fatherland sent no bolder horseman to Rossbach or Gravelotte."[40]

On the Confederate right, Churchill advanced three-quarters of a mile and discovered he had not moved far enough to sweep around the Union left flank. He mistook the Sabine Crossing Road for the Jesup Road. Realizing his mistake, he ordered his command to move farther to the right but still failed to shift far enough to hit the enemy line on its extreme left. About 5 P.M., the Confederates drove in the Federal 16th Corps pickets and, with a Rebel yell and loud rattle of musketry, chased them back into the main Federal positions. The corps line stretched along a ditch that Churchill's men, using clubbed muskets and bayonets, cleared of bluecoated soldiers. As Churchill's men broke through Banks's second line of defense and pushed into Pleasant Hill, a coun-

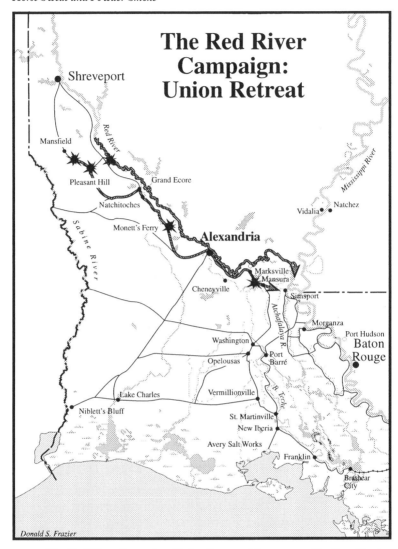

map 8. The Red River Campaign: Union Retreat. Map prepared by Don Frazier

terattack by Brig. Gen. A. J. Smith's 16th Corps struck the exposed Confederate right flank, stalling Churchill's advance.[41]

To Churchill's left, Walker met strong resistance in the woods fronting the plateau but pushed the enemy back from the gully. The fresh Union 16th Corps, however, saved Banks's left and center. As Churchill's infantry recoiled from the vigorous counterattack on their flank, they collided with Walker's advance, further muddling the situation. Smith threw his men in at this critical juncture, and their determined resistance made the fighting "close and bloody." Amid choking clouds of powder smoke, the grimy, wild-eyed men met face to face, firing at point-blank range and using their bayonets to deadly effect. Although meeting intense resistance, Walker's center and left brigades fought to the outskirts of Pleasant Hill and tenaciously held that line. Incapacitated by a groin wound, Walker was carried from the field. Walker's foot soldiers on the right flank, momentarily leaderless and subjected to a desperate defense, with what a Union major described as "an incessant and destructive fire," fell back from the Federal barricades.[42]

Smith's counterblow had shattered the continuity in the thick woods on Taylor's right. The fighting became very confused, as lost and mingling units disrupted coordinated attacks. Confederate officers rallied their men time and again but could not force the Federals out of their positions. Confederate officers prevented a complete disaster but could not inflame their men sufficiently for another advance. Amid the swirling smoke in the murky forest, some confused Rebel infantrymen fired on each other, just as they had on the previous night. Taylor, disillusioned, ordered his infantry back to reform at the edge of the open field.[43]

fig. 21. "Repulse of the Rebels at Pleasant Hill, Louisiana." From *Harper's Weekly*, May 7, 1864.

On the left, the Confederates met with more success. As the day waned, Major's dismounted cavalry worked their way around through the wooded ravines to the right flank of the Federal line. While Major's men pressed their assault, Bee combined the remnants of his now dismounted cavalry and joined an attack with Polignac's infantry, which had been ordered into the fray. Describing the Confederate attack, a Union colonel wrote, "We met them with a determined fire," loosing several volleys into the advancing Rebel ranks, and for two hours "the rattle of musketry was incessant and deafening." The close-quarter battle continued, both sides hotly engaged and firing continuously until darkness fell. Although inflicting over five hundred casualties on their enemy, a significant number of Bee's cavalrymen went down in a futile effort which Taylor later described as a "gallant" and "premature" charge that "cost valuable lives."[44]

With their flank turned and Polignac's decimated division added to Bee's yelling Texans driving into their front, the Union line began to crumble. In the gathering darkness, the Texas cavalrymen occupied several abandoned Federal artillery positions and continued to advance toward Pleasant Hill.[45]

In the twilight and the confusion of battle, some Confederate units fired on one another, further intensifying the bedlam in the thick pines. Pushing through the dark woods and billowing clouds of powder smoke, the scattered Confederate units mistook their own troops for retreating Yankees and fired at the fleeting figures moving through the darkening forest. Buchel's men directed a fusillade into Major's advancing dismounted cavalry. Thinking Buchel's men were Yankees, Major's perplexed troops returned their fire. Adding to the turmoil in the jumbled Texas outfits, Walter P. Lane's Partisan Rangers, moving in from the far left, also fired into Major's attacking force. To prevent needless casualties, Confederate officers halted their advance and drew back their men. As night engulfed the battlefield, both sides disengaged, many Confederates drawing back toward Mansfield.[46]

At 9 P.M., Taylor ordered Bee to "return to the battlefield, picket up to the enemy's lines, and give him [Taylor] the earliest report of their movement in the morning." Bee moved four companies of Buchel's regiment forward and deployed them in the gloom to act as pickets. At 10 P.M., the 1st Texas Cavalry reestablished the line held at dark and slowly crept toward the enemy. In a few moments, a crackle of musketry and muzzle flashes lit up the darkness like chain lightning. Blundering into enemy pickets, the surprised cavalry discovered that the Yankees had not yet retreated a step. After a few sporadic volleys, the firing soon ceased, and the remainder of the night passed without alarm. The woods echoed with the ring of axes, a few shouts, jingling harnesses, and the rumble of moving wagons until midnight, when all became quiet. Wight, on forward picket, discovered a "Yanke" so soundly asleep that the Texan took his "gunbelt[,] cartridges[,] and overcoat." Wight wrote to his wife, "I do not think the felow had any business sleeping at sutch a time when his friends needed his healp."[47]

At daylight, the Texans cautiously advanced and shortly found themselves in abandoned Union positions. Before sunrise, Bee occupied the house in Pleasant Hill that Banks had used as headquarters the previous night. Several of Banks's senior officers assumed that they had suffered another defeat at the hands of what they thought to be Taylor's superior forces and enjoined him to retreat to Blair's Landing or Grand Ecore. Other officers, such as A. J. Smith, disagreed and advocated a Union army attack the next day. When advised of Banks's decision to retreat, Smith proposed that Franklin arrest Banks and take command of the army. Franklin asked, "Smith, don't you know this is mutiny?" Then Smith acceded to the retreat.[48]

As the combatants disengaged during the evening of April 9, both sides began to reorganize and assess the mayhem of the preceding two days. Dead men and horses littered the entire area from Mansfield to Pleasant Hill. Medford articulated the sentiments of the combatants when he wrote, "This fierce encounter has been dreadful on both sides." While the Federal army hastily evacuated Pleasant Hill, most Confederates trudged six miles rearward to where water and supplies waited. Taylor ordered the majority of his cavalry back to Mansfield to forage and rest, as they had been fighting for four consecutive days. Men and horses had been without food for over forty hours. Bee brought up his supply and forage wagons from the millstream. Soldiers from the 1st Texas Cavalry on the picket line nonetheless received little sustenance as they stood shivering in the dark. Cpl. J. M. Thompson complained that he had "no food for four days and [the] first was raw bacon and no bread." The only water available was in the wells and cisterns of Pleasant Hill, and Banks's troops had drained them almost dry.[49]

Taylor ordered Bee to organize his mounted regiments and pursue the retreating enemy at first light. In their hurried evacuation, the Yankees abandoned unburied on the battlefield over four hundred wounded and their dead. With cold darkness enveloping the battlefield, Buchel's Texans listened all night to the pitiful groans and delirious shrieks of the wounded: "Oh, I'm freezing," "For God's sake bring us some water," and "Send someone to get me." Such cries rent the chill night air and sent shivers down the Texans' spines.[50]

The Federals, however, did not suffer alone. Confederate veterans later reported heavy casualties. One Texas soldier wrote, "Our men lay in heaps. Grape and canister piled up the dead in the open fields and our wounded were coming out, shot in every conceivable form." Another Texas trooper reported that the Confederates lost as many as 2,500 men killed outright. Lt. Col. Louis A. Bringier, a Louisiana officer, wrote his wife about the "terrible contest that took place." He stated, "We men decided to win or die." A Texas veteran of the battle said that at Pleasant Hill they counted over 1,200 Union dead and 400 wounded left on the battlefield. Poche described many of the dead, "the greater number of whom were mutilated." Some were "without heads" and "completely mangled," with arms and legs missing. One Confederate lay "with his ribs crushed, leaving his entrails exposed to view and one could see the flies crawling all over them." In two days of fighting, Banks had lost over 3,700 killed, wounded, and missing; while Taylor reported total casualties of 2,626. His most serious losses at Pleasant Hill were in Buchel's and DeBray's cavalry and W. R. Scurry's brigade of Walker's division.[51]

Kuykendall, still trailing his unit, retold his experiences and observations as he surveyed the battlefield: "Passing a field hospital beside the road not far from Pleasant Hill were observed piled up along the wall of a gallery of a small house a great number of amputated limbs of the unfortunate wounded." He described the entire scene as "a regular charnel house of death, where friend and foe had lain down [their] lives in support of a mere question of principle. The very atmosphere protested as the foul stench from decaying man and beast filled the nostrils . . . friends had died in full enjoyment of 'vigorous' manhood [and] immolated themselves on the altar of their country."[52]

After viewing the carnage, Kuykendall believed war to be "unrelenting and barbarious in its every aspect." He recollected that, in the two days of fighting, "our regiment lost about sixty killed and wounded." Incomplete records reveal that the 1st Texas lost nine killed, fifty-one wounded, and four missing during the fighting on April 8 and 9. Wight wrote that both Capt. James Swan Bigham and a Lieutenant Kercondin [Kuykendall] "was wounded the second day of the fight." He did not know the "precise nomber" of casualties, but "of our regiment" he believed there were twenty men "kiled ded on the field" and eighty men wounded.[53]

Promoted to colonel, Yager replaced Buchel as commander of the 1st Texas Cavalry and led the unit through the balance of the war. At first light on April 10, Bee placed him in command of a cavalry unit comprising Buchel's regiment and the remnants of DeBray's unit and sent them in pursuit of what Medford labeled "panic stricken and cowardly Yankees." Yager's weary Texans rode through the frosty morning, following the retreating Union troops for over twenty miles to the double bridges before Grand Ecore. The fleeing Yan-

fig. 22. "Rebel attack on gunboats in the Red River." From *Harper's Weekly,*
May 14, 1864.

kees burned the bridges, terminating Yager's advance. During the morning,
the cavalry passed many broken and burning wagons, discarded equipment,
and destroyed materiel. The mounted Texans captured another one hundred
Federal stragglers and returned to meet Bee with the captured men and equipment. "You must know that we was a worn out set of men by the time the fight
was over," Wight wrote in a letter to his wife. Wight recounted that, during
the march from Texas, Buchel's men "only got 4 hours [sleep] out of 24" and
only a short rest "before we went into the fight."[54]

Although the fighting had been bloody and the living conditions harsh, the
Texas horsemen kept their sense of humor. When guards marched several
companies of New York Zouaves, captured by the 1st Texas Cavalry, into the

Texas encampment, the Confederate troops feigned astonishment at the Yankee troops' baggy, red, bloomerlike pantaloons and "dainty little red hats with tassels." The Texans gasped incredulously as they threw down their weapons, vowing that they would quit and go home before they would fight any more women. Many Zouaves missed the joke and protested loudly that they were men, not women![55]

CHAPTER 11

"The Limits of Endurance Have Been Reached"

Maj. Gen. Nathaniel P. Banks marched his disheartened Union troops into Grand Ecore and attempted to defend himself from attacks, both Union and Confederate. Adm. David D. Porter reported that the "Army here had met with a great defeat, no matter what the generals try to make of it." He called the "whole affair . . . terribly mismanaged." Lt. Gen. Ulysses S. Grant declared the battle at Pleasant Hill a disaster. While Banks attempted to put the best possible light on the situation, Brig. Gen. Hamilton P. Bee and his Texas cavalry occupied Natchitoches, four miles from Grand Ecore. Banks believed that Maj. Gen. Richard Taylor had twenty-five thousand men opposing him and spent several days ringing Grand Ecore with an abatis strengthened by a network of entrenchments and rifle pits. Not a day passed without some skirmishing between the Texas horsemen and the Union soldiers occupying Grand Ecore. On April 11, Pvt. John Tyler Webb, 30th Maine Infantry, penned a note in his diary describing one clash with the Confederates: "Saw 400 Rebs firing [at] the owner to my Hat. I could not see giving it up to them. Killed, wounded, & missing 142." Bee reported seven days of continuous fighting around Grand Ecore. Pvt. Levi Lamoni Wight, Company E, recalled that, from Mansfield to the end of the campaign, his company joined in seventy-eight days of continual combat with the Yankees.[1]

Veterans of the Red River Campaign recounted several engagements along the Red River between Porter's flotilla and Taylor's depleted Rebel army. In describing his operations in the vicinity of Grand Ecore, Bee added proudly that his cavalrymen had curtailed Union operations, as the Texans continued to drive the enemy cavalry back on their artillery and infantry support. On

April 15, Lt. Gen. Edmund Kirby Smith ordered all but Polignac's infantry to march toward Arkansas. This left Taylor with only his cavalry and one over-tired infantry division of less than two thousand effectives. Amazingly, a Confederate force of hardly five thousand continued to intimidate over twenty-five thousand Federal soldiers.[2]

Pvt. William Kuykendall's diary expounded upon the vicissitudes of life as experienced by the 1st Texas cavalrymen around Grand Ecore. Trains of packhorses and mules hauled food and supplies to the Texans' forward positions. Occasionally, because muleskinners lost their bearings on dark, unfamiliar roads, troops went without resupply for two or three days. Initially detailed to guard supplies and escort trains of pack mules, Kuykendall, bent on fighting the Yankees, exchanged duties with "a constitutional coward in the company who seemed utterly incapable of facing an enemy."[3]

The change in duty afforded the eager private some immediate excitement while on picket duty under Sgt. Jack Dickey with Pvt. Hugh Bourke and Pvt. Wallace, the latter "a half witted fellow." Dickey and Kuykendall moved forward for an open view of the road into Grand Ecore and spotted an enemy infantry squad advancing toward them. Kuykendall raised his rifle to fire, but Dickey yelled to run for the horses, as the enemy "was in full charge." The other privates mounted their horses and fled, allowing Dickey's horse to break its headstall and escape with the sergeant's saddle—a calamity at this stage of the war. Dickey dodged through the trees on foot and eluded the pursuing Federals. Kuykendall jerked his reins loose from a branch and vaulted into the saddle, reining the excited animal toward the rear. "The Yanks were within forty paces ordering me to surrender." Slapping spurs to his mount, Kuykendall rode among whizzing bullets for two hundred yards, then swung his horse around to face his pursuers, but "my horse refused to stand and I did not fire." Kuykendall's company hurriedly came to the rescue and "chased [the] Yanks back down the road." After resuming their original picket post, Dickey and Kuykendall guaranteed the others that "if they left us again we would fire on them."[4]

Dickey and Kuykendall again left the others to guard their horses, and this led to more excitement. The jittery horse guards reported another enemy squad moving up from their right. Dickey and Kuykendall hurriedly returned and leapt to their saddles, and the detail galloped to verify how large an enemy force the nervous men had glimpsed slinking through the woods. Kuykendall griped that no enemy was in view; the "only animate object visible was an old brindled cow contentedly browsing in the distance."[5]

Banks concluded that he must comply with Grant's orders to return A. J.

Smith's corps to Maj. Gen. William T. Sherman and discontinue his campaign in preparation for an advance on Mobile, Alabama. Besides, he had had enough of the continual harassment by the Confederate cavalry. Consequently, on April 21, he ordered another retreat southeast toward Alexandria. Confederate Gen. John A. Wharton, who commanded the Confederate Cavalry Corps after Green's death at Blair's Landing on April 12, ordered Bee to move his cavalry division to Monett's Ferry on the Cane River and prevent Banks from crossing. On April 21, Bee assembled his men and left the vicinity of Grand Ecore, relocating forty miles toward the ferry, where he arrayed his meager force to challenge Banks's retreating cavalcade.[6]

Along with Bee's other regiments, the 1st Texas Cavalry established defensive positions astride the road to Monett's Ferry, blocking Banks's retreat. Through some unexplained Confederate complacency, the Union advance guard surprised the regiment at breakfast. A cousin of Kuykendall, Lt. Jim Tom of another regiment, had come to visit, bringing a portion of his "flower" ration, considered "too great a luxury for a private soldier," and the two cousins planned to "fare sumptuously on flap-jacks and molasses." Kuykendall lamented that "the Yanks swindled us [out of] that splendid repast." At dawn a bugle sounded, and the entire command saddled up, as one of Bee's aides "[was] rushing hither and thither through camp," declaring "in frenzied exclamations that the enemy was upon us." The regiment formed into line of battle as a company commanded by "Cpt. McNelly [was] gallantly combating the advance of the enemy now almost within rifle range." Attacking the lead elements of Banks's column, the Texans temporarily halted the Union advance, and the "only loss sustained was breakfast, dinner and supper." Col. William O. Yager detailed Companies D and I under Capt. Solomon C. Geron to act as rearguard skirmishers, as the Texans fell back before a superior force.[7]

At sunset, the 1st Texas Cavalry settled into defensive positions just north of Monett's Ferry but lingered there only a few hours. At 1 A.M., the regiment received word to cross south of the Cane River and await further orders. According to Kuykendall, the men reacted with alacrity, since they had been almost constantly in the saddle and "without nourishment" for nearly two days. Their anticipation of any rest and food was quickly dashed, however, as Bee ordered eight companies of the regiment into a position eight miles south of the ferry. Rumors of a Federal force marching north from Alexandria to Banks's relief necessitated that Bee prepare to defend both his front and rear. Geron's squadron remained with the roughly two thousand Texas cavalrymen who were preparing to prevent any Union crossing of the ferry.[8]

On the morning of April 23, Bee discovered Banks advancing on his small command with the preponderance of the Union army. At 8 A.M., Banks massed his forces in the edge of a swamp about twelve hundred yards from the ferry. He sent both cavalry and infantry skirmishers forward to test the Confederate defenses, which Kuykendall described as "stretched so thin as to be little more than a skirmish line." He remembered that Confederate cavalrymen were digging emplacements south of the river "with such implements as they could command." Most of Geron's squadron occupied positions in the main line of defense, while a ten-man squad guarded two field pieces sent to reinforce the right of Bee's line. Kuykendall and the rest of the detail thought they were screened from observation by a stand of pine trees, but "evidently such was not the case." Enemy gunners fired on the Confederate detachment before the Texans had time to swing the guns into firing position. The first Yankee shell landed "within 20 feet of one gun but failed to explode and [inflicted] no damage." Kuykendall related that this shot initiated a long artillery duel. About mid-afternoon, Bee directed Geron and his men to rejoin their regiment south of Monett's Ferry; the 1st Texas Cavalry did not participate further in the battle at the river crossing.[9]

At 10 A.M., a large Federal force crossed Cane River two miles above the ferry and moved down on Bee's left. Another column attempted a crossing four miles below Bee's main defensive positions. Approximately fifteen thousand men were facing Bee's center. Bee did not have the troops to counter what he perceived to be a double envelopment of his position. Bee's cavalry, without infantry support, held the left and center against the assault of ten thousand Federals for over two hours, but advancing Union infantry slowly drove the Confederates back until the main positions on a hill overlooking the ferry could be defended no longer. Bee shifted troops from his line and reinforced his extreme left. The Federals renewed the attack and met a massed fire of twelve hundred muskets and an artillery battery firing double-shotted canister at close range. The heavy fire temporarily halted the Union advance.[10]

Part of DeBray's cavalry stubbornly resisted the crossing of Federal cavalry at the ford below the ferry, but the thin Confederate line gave way, and Banks finally turned Bee's flanks. Bee consulted with brigadier generals Arthur P. Bagby and James P. Major and decided to withdraw. As the retreat began, the Federals opened fire on his center with forty pieces of newly emplaced artillery. Through the shrapnel and smoke of an intense barrage, the Confederate cavalry retired at a walk and steadily returned fire against the advancing enemy. Bee lost about fifty men killed and an artillery wagon, along with several horses. Banks admitted to losing six hundred men killed and wounded, listing himself among the wounded.[11]

Bee's two thousand men held the ferry for about seven hours, but he withdrew to save his small command. He fell back to Beasley's Plantation because his men lacked sufficient provisions. Some men were starving; the woods, set ablaze by the battle, provided no grass or forage for the Texans' horses. Bee had ordered his supply train removed to prevent its capture, and he was compelled to retreat twenty-seven miles to rejoin his wagons at Beasley's. He expected to continue resisting Banks's advance but changed his plans because the retreat was longer than anticipated and rations and ammunition were in critically short supply. To lead them along unfamiliar trails to rejoin Bee's horsemen at Beasley's, the 1st Texas Cavalry employed local citizens as guides. Kuykendall endured the same experiences as many other Texans between April 23 and 26. He spent nearly two days and nights "continually under the saddle with-out rest [or] provender. My horse became so greatly jaded that I was forced to stop [and] rest him." The weary cavalryman tied his mount to a sapling and, using his saddle blanket, was "soon in the arms of morphius [*sic*]." With little rest and fewer provisions, the dauntless Texas cavalrymen continued to harass Banks and slow his advance along Bayou Boeuf. Due to the cavalry's mobility and their stubborn attacks, Banks believed that he confronted a larger force than in fact was badgering the retreating Federals.[12]

To hinder the Confederate pursuit and punish others for their misery, Banks's rearguard under Brig. Gen. A. J. Smith burned everything in the retreating Federals' wake, including slave quarters and chicken houses. They set every house ablaze, allowing women and children only moments to flee, with nothing but the clothes on their backs. Union cavalry and infantry drove off or killed all the livestock they discovered, and what valuables they could not carry away, they burned. They threw animal carcasses into wells and shot cisterns full of holes, forcing the populace and the pursuing Rebels to drink from the fouled streams. Webb related how he feasted on "Fried Fresh Pig and [slept on] a nice cotton bed 100 lbs. for 4 of us." Another eastern soldier wrote, "The wanton and useless destruction of valuable property has well earned his [Smith's] command a lasting disgrace." On April 24, Taylor reported that the "destruction of this country by the enemy exceeds anything in history. For many miles every dwelling-house, every negro cabin, every cotton-gin, every corn-crib, and even chicken-houses have been burned to the ground; every fence torn down and the fields torn up by the hooves of horses and wheels of wagons. Many hundreds of persons are utterly without shelter."[13]

Kuykendall summarized what he called the "ruthless barbarity [and] vandalism of [the] enemy in the smoldering ruin that marked the cite [*sic*] of once happy homes." Before the battle at Monett's Ferry, units of the 1st Texas Cav-

fig. 23. Andrew J. Smith
gained a reputation for
wanton destruction of
private property during the
Red River Campaign.
Courtesy Massachusetts
Commandery, Military
Order of the Loyal Legion
and U.S. Army Military
History Institute, Carlisle
Barracks, Pennsylvania

alry had occupied a post near the "palatial residence and property" of a wealthy planter who had fled before the advancing enemy. The planter's wife remained in the house, fervently hoping that the Yankees would not harm her and would spare her opulent residence, even though, during Banks's advance, she "had been offered every indignity." Kuykendall's squadron left before the main battle but, upon returning, learned that the "forebodings of this defenseless lady were fully realized." To the Texan's complete dismay, "the magnificent building together with the out-houses was a mass of smoldering ruins." Neighbors told Kuykendall that the Yankees ejected the lady without so much as a change of clothes. This pitiless Yankee behavior prompted him to comment, "Such incidents characterized the ruthless war waged by a reputed civilization against the people of the South."[14]

Late in the day on April 26, in what Webb described as a "hard March," the last of Banks's column finally staggered into Alexandria, where the Union army was forced to remain for over two weeks. The next morning, Banks's men realized that they were surrounded by Confederate troops, who attacked them daily and, according to DeBray, "annoyed them by every possible means." The

1st Texas Cavalry, now brigaded under Brig. Gen. Arthur P. Bagby, daily ranged the countryside near Alexandria, assailing the surrounded Federals at every opportunity. Bagby's brigade, along with Wharton's other vociferous Confederate cavalry, controlled the bayous and roads leading to Alexandria and for several days cut Banks off from all communication with the Mississippi River.[15]

On the same day, as Banks exhorted his commanders to consolidate their perimeter around Alexandria, the 1st Texas Cavalry participated in a dawn-to-dusk battle to push Union outposts back into the city. At McNutt's Hill, three regiments of Bee's cavalry, including the 1st Texas, attacked Federal outposts along Bayou Rapides, twelve miles from Alexandria. Subtly chastising Kirby Smith for his lack of support, Taylor, describing the combat, reported, "Without food for man or horse, our men seem animated by a determination to quench the incendiary fires lighted by the vandals in their blood. If pluck and energy can supply the place of numbers we will yet reap the harvest of which the seeds were sown at Mansfield and Pleasant Hill."[16]

Unluckily, Col. Edmund J. Davis's "renegade regiment" of Texas Unionists opposed the resolute 1st Texas' advance down the bayou. Kuykendall recounted that Davis's unit, "composed of worthless vagabonds who were a . . . disgrace to the land that gave them birth," offered little resistance to the Confederate assault. "[We] drove him from his position" with little effort and continued to do so "several times during the day" with "but slight casualties." (Again, Kuykendall's sentiments about Federal Texans were hardly impartial.) Losing one killed and two wounded, Yager's troops pushed the enemy back about nine miles and then, since they had outdistanced the regiment supporting their left flank, halted their advance about three miles from Alexandria.[17]

Dismounting, Yager's Texans advanced warily along the bayou toward Davis's troops, who mistakenly surmised that the Confederates had discontinued their attack and retired from the line. Kuykendall remarked, "They were engaged in preparing their repast." Observing the Texans stealing through the foliage, Yankee pickets fired and wounded Pvt. Pendleton Love, Company C. Yager yelled, "Boys let us charge!" Kuykendall described the spontaneous onslaught as a "most perfect disorder" "not unlike the advance of a herd of stamped [*sic*] Texas beeves." The "Yanks" fled in a disorder as great as the Texans' charge, "leaving their 'hardtack' and coffee as trophies to the victors." Confederate spoils also included an "officer's horse and accoutrements."[18]

Most of the hungry Texans halted in the Union camp, while a few of the cavalrymen chased the retreating Unionists farther toward Alexandria. Those remaining in camp sprinted for "the abandoned grub and seized upon and devoured the last vestige of it." The troops who followed the Yankees took positions behind a fence in case of a counterattack. Col. Richard Hardemann, called "Old Gotch" because of the way an old injury forced him to cant his head, rode up and admonished the Texans to wait until the Federal troops "got into close range." Then, he said, "Boys give them Hell!" When the enemy did not appear, Kuykendall and his companions returned to the Union camp: "Alas, too late to even secure the crums [*sic*] as it had all disappeared as if by magic."[19]

On May 5, Bagby's brigade joined in a fight that began at dawn and was, as Taylor described it, "brisk and well sustained for several hours." This engagement occurred on the Bayou Robert Road about eleven miles from Alexandria. Banks's infantry "gave way and retreated toward Alexandria," with yelling Texas cavalry in pursuit. Banks's army remained cut off from downriver reinforcements and consequently began to suffer from a lack of supplies, especially fodder for the horses and mules. The U.S. cavalry could not fulfill its duties because of the poor condition of its mounts; those captured by Rebel forays were described as little more than skeletons. Taylor ordered his cavalry to remove all grain and forage from any plantation within reach of the Federals. He told Kirby Smith, "We will play the game the Russians played in the retreat from Moscow." As Taylor put it, "My little force of scarce 6000" horsemen and infantry kept Banks's army, which had been reinforced to 31,000, including over 5,000 cavalry, bottled up inside a double row of zigzag trenches surrounding Alexandria.[20]

Posted at Wells' Sugar Mill, three miles south of Alexandria, the 1st Texas Cavalry sat astride Banks's main overland supply route and incessantly clashed with Union forces. Five companies of the regiment remained on picket duty, while the other five rested in camp a few miles back in the swamp. Every twenty-four hours, the troops rotated to allow the men and horses short respites that were "greatly enjoyed and much needed" after their recent hard service. Kuykendall reported "almost daily skirmishes with Yankee outposts," but the sugar mill was the main "bone of contention." The sugar and molasses stored in the sugar house afforded "too great a temptation to our half starved troops to be overcome." Several cavalrymen conceived a plan to "storm the sugar house," which "we did driving the Yankees from the premises" and taking "possession in the name of the Confederacy." Filling their haversacks with all they could carry, the Texans returned to their picket duty. When the hungry Texans exhausted their supply of sugar, they again assaulted the mill, drove out the Union defenders, and once more filled their haversacks with sugar and molasses before repairing to their posts.[21]

The sugar mill and associated buildings stood on the banks of a small bayou, and the Federal infantry took advantage of the protection afforded them by the building's walls. Open fields offered excellent fields of fire, but the Union troops "usually beat a hasty retreat" whenever attacked. Finally Federal officers tired of losing control of the mill and brought up reinforcements of cavalry and artillery, changing the balance of power along the bayou.[22]

Troopers of Company D soon encountered the Union reinforcements along the bayou. Charged with forcing the Yankee pickets north of the waterway, five Texans unwittingly rode into twenty blue-coated cavalrymen. Only seventy-five yards and the small bayou separated the two forces. Kuykendall related that a few small trees offered the Texans' only protection, "of which we were not slow to avail ourselves." The Federal horsemen took cover in a large thicket as a brisk exchange of rifle fire commenced. The outnumbered Texans fired at the smoke from the enemy's rifles; because the Union cavalrymen hid in the thick brush, the Confederates could not distinguish individual targets. Kuykendall described a heavy volume of fire issuing from the Yankee positions; "their missiles" frequently struck the diminutive trees providing the only cover for the Rebels. The Texas private continued with his account of the fray: "I observed a bluecoat crawling on his all-fours up the bayou with the evident intention of uncovering our position and picking us off one at a time." Immediately realizing the dire consequences of even one soldier's firing from an enfilading position, Kuykendall, "with all possible deliberation[,] fired upon him." As the smoke from the Confederate's rifle cleared, "my man disappeared from view as if he had been spirited away." Kuykendall prided himself on his marksmanship and had every confidence in his musket, to which a gunsmith had added a "hair trigger" and "silver bead" front sight to improve its accuracy. According to the beleaguered Texan, this was the only shot "I ever fired upon the result of which I felt my life depended." He never determined whether he hit the crawling man, but the firing stopped on both sides and the opposing forces slowly disengaged. This short, furious skirmish ended the conflict over Wells' Sugar Mill.[23]

While camped south of Alexandria, the 1st Texas Cavalry waged a campaign against antagonists more insidious than Federal soldiers. Kuykendall's diary explains how "loathesome insects known as 'gray-backs' infested our command." Due to lack of supplies, "our wardrobe consisted of but a singlesuit," and eliminating the obnoxious bugs "was indeed a difficult matter." Lt. Landon C. Preston secured a thirty-gallon sugar kettle, which several men filled with water. Then they started a fire, "in [the] mode of a washwoman." The Texans were "determined to rid ourselves of them [lice] by heroic means" and stripped off all their clothing and placed it, along with their blankets and hats, into the boiling water.

No sooner had they hung out their wash to dry than, "to our chagrin[,] a bugle call was heard." Quickly donning their sopping clothing, the men joined their company's formation. Remembering his humiliation, Kuykendall wrote, "I am sure that those of Jeff Davis' veterans never made a more ludicrous appearance than did we." The bugle calling the regiment to "boots and saddles" signified Banks's continued retreat down the Red River.[24]

When Porter's flotilla steamed back into Alexandria, the Federal admiral discovered the water so shallow that his deep-draft ironclad gunboats could not continue downriver. A rise in the depth of the water over the falls was necessary before his vessels could negotiate the ledge of exposed rocks blocking the river. Porter's predicament placed Banks in a quandary. Should he abandon Alexandria, destroying the stranded gunboats to prevent their capture, or remain with Porter indefinitely? Burning the stranded ironclads would be another major catastrophe—Porter already had been forced to blow up the grounded *Eastport.* To save both his and Porter's military reputations, Banks had to remain with the navy until some solution could be found that would save the gunboats.[25]

Between May 8 and May 13, Lt. Col. Joseph Bailey, chief engineer of Maj. Gen. William B. Franklin, improvised a series of dams that finally allowed Porter's flotilla to negotiate the shallow waters over the falls. Freeing Porter to steam downriver enabled Banks to continue his retreat, devastating the countryside as his army trudged toward Simsport. Although the Federal commander had offered rewards for such evidence "as will convict the accused of incendiarism before a general court-martial," Smith's departing infantry, using a mixture of turpentine and camphene, ignited a conflagration that consumed more than twenty-two blocks of the city of Alexandria. Clouds of black smoke from burning buildings billowed over the countryside in the wake of the retreating U.S. troops. One Union infantryman's narrative of the renewed retreat described how, on one occasion, he had counted nineteen sugar plantations burning. Later he "saw the ruins of many more."[26]

Union troops retreating before the dogged Texas cavalrymen found daily life full of misery. In addition to persistent cavalry raids, many Yankees complained of the terrible swamps, quicksand, bayous, alligators, water moccasins, and mosquitoes. Federal soldiers wrote home after the battles up and down the Red River about the horrors of their retreat. Wreckage of all types choked the river and roads. Decomposing bodies of men and animals floated downstream or lay on the river banks with buzzards picking at them. River water was foul, but many times it was the only drinking water available to the dispirited Yankees. The countryside proved a terror for the retreating Federals; but for lack of ra-

fig. 24. "Porter's gun-boats passing the dam in the Red River, near Alexandria." From *Harper's Weekly*, June 18, 1864

tions, it was ideal for the deadly Confederate sharpshooters. One Texas cavalryman complained, "For thirty days we had practically nothing to eat."[27]

The 1st Texas Cavalry constantly beleaguered the retreating Federals and joined in the final engagements during the closing days of Banks's abortive expedition. On May 15, on the Avoyelles Prairie near Marksville, they joined with other cavalry units under Bagby to turn back the Union advance several times. Only major Federal reinforcements shoved the obstinate Texans aside, allowing Banks's column to continue. Challenging the Federal advance guard at this action, the 1st Texas Cavalry lost Pvt. James O'Dougherty, Company A, mortally wounded, and at least four other men captured. The next day at Mansura, Taylor drew his entire force on line to oppose the Federal procession downriver. Yager's horsemen screened the Confederate right and turned back several lines of Union skirmishers. The four-hour battle was on an open prairie, which Taylor described as "smooth as a billiard table." Since the conflict was mainly an artillery duel, the 1st Texas Cavalry suffered no casualties. Webb characterized the opposing lines of battle as a "Grand display of Troops."[28]

On Tuesday, May 17, Yager, with the 1st Texas and 2d Louisiana cavalry regiments, made a slashing mounted attack on the Union rearguard. The yell-

fig. 25. Banks's troops had to contend not only with Confederate soldiers, but also with alligators, water moccasins, and mosquitoes. Courtesy Gene Swinson, Baird, Texas

ing Confederates cut into the Federal wagon train near Yellow Bayou. The Negro soldiers of the Corps d'Afrique, which comprised the guard for the supply wagons, fled before the barking pistols and flashing sabers, as the yelling Confederate cavalrymen drove through the surprised Federals. Yager's troopers claimed to have killed several white officers as the Negro guards fled. The Union 16th Corps controlled the road, however, preventing Yager from driving the captured wagons back into Confederate lines. The triumphant Rebels destroyed a large quantity of valuable military supplies and equipment abandoned by the scattered guards. To prevent the Federals from making further use of the rolling stock, the Confederates burned the wagons and their contents before galloping away into the pines.[29]

The next day at Yellow Bayou, the 1st Texas Cavalry fought its last major engagement of the campaign. Taylor brazenly massed his five thousand men for a frontal attack on a Union infantry division and cavalry brigade that covered Banks's retirement across the Atchafalaya River. Wight remembered that the 1st Texas Cavalry galloped in a headlong dash to arrive in position for the assault. "In such a ride as this if a man fell from his horse he would allmost sertenly be tramped to death" [*sic*].

The regiment, posted on the far right of the Confederate line, attacked about 9 A.M. and, with infantry support, sent the Federal skirmish line fleeing through the timber. According to Wight, one of his squad mistakenly shot a dismounted Confederate, thinking he was a Federal picket. A second line, composed of Federal cavalry, also broke before deadly fire from the onrushing Texans. Subjected to heavy artillery and rifle fire, the Union left began to retreat; only reinforcements of both infantry and artillery, hastily moved into position, checked

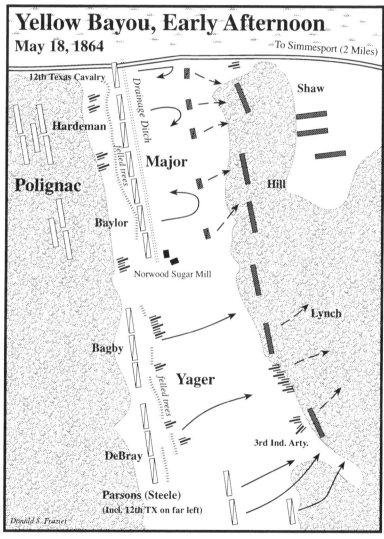

map 9. Yellow Bayou, Early Afternoon, May 18, 1864. Map prepared by Don Frazier

the Confederate advance. When the Union cavalry attempted a counterattack, the Texans compelled them to fall back behind a line of protecting infantry. Twice, Federal units forced Taylor's attackers back; twice, renewed Confederate assaults drove the Union brigades back into their original positions. Near evening, muzzle blasts from the cannon set the forest ablaze; under heavy pressure from Federal artillery firing double-shotted canister, Taylor finally retired from the battlefield. Describing the scene, a Union colonel wrote, "All poured such a murderous fire into the ranks of the enemy that he was compelled to fall back in great disorder." In this violent, see-saw engagement, a few Confederate units suffered heavy casualties. The 5th Texas Cavalry, for instance, had only 7 soldiers able to fight at the end of the day. Total Confederate casualties numbered an estimated 608, while Union units lost 28 killed, 226 wounded, and 3 missing. The 1st Texas Cavalry, fighting on the periphery of the major attack, suffered only 7 wounded and a few crippled horses.[30]

The following morning, Banks completed his retreat across the Atchafalaya River, ending his Red River Expedition. Taylor believed that Kirby Smith had snatched a magnificent victory away from him by ordering all but Polignac's infantry to Arkansas to oppose the Union advance there. He wrote, "I feel bitterly about this because my army has been robbed of the just measure of its glory and the country of the most brilliant and complete success of the war." His army, however, had reached the end of its ability to fight any major engagements. On May 19, he reported that he and his men were suffering from sickness and exhaustion: "The limits of human and equine endurance have been reached."[31]

After the battle at Yellow Bayou, the 1st Texas Cavalry, along with several other mounted units, relocated to the vicinity of Fort DeRussy, where they were reorganized before further operations. In early September, 1864, the regiment became part of a brigade of Texas cavalry commanded by Alexander W. Terrell. Yager's 1st Texas Cavalry, Terrell's own 34th Texas Cavalry, and James P. Liken's 35th Texas Cavalry constituted the new unit. The brigade came under the command of Acting Brigadier General Bagby's division, which was deployed on the Atchafalaya River along a twenty-mile front between Simsport and Morgan's Ferry.[32]

As part of Terrell's brigade, the 1st Texas Cavalry participated in its last known combat of the Civil War. On September 17, about six miles west of Morganza, Louisiana, four thousand Federals, supported by at least one battery of artillery, attacked Terrell's brigade in an attempt to cross the Atchafalaya River in force. Accurate carbine and musket fire from the Texas sharpshooters prevented the Federals from crossing the river, and they withdrew temporarily.[33]

Anticipating another Union crossing attempt, Terrell moved his men to Morgan's Ferry. His twelve hundred cavalrymen confronted over four thousand Union troops, reinforced by at least twelve pieces of artillery. This wide, deep segment of the Atchafalaya, however, strengthened the Confederate defenses, as it could not be crossed by cannon or wagon except by ferry or bridge. About 2:30 A.M. on September 20, Terrell's secret outpost warned him of the advancing Federal cavalry. As daylight filtered through the pines, the Union troops, supported by four guns, attempted to bridge the river at Mussel Shoals Bayou south of the Rebel positions. Union soldiers also cut a road to the bayou out of range of Terrell's artillery. The Federals managed to float two cannons on improvised rafts across the river north of the Confederate fortifications and rolled the guns into position, enfilading Terrell's redoubt.[34]

Outnumbered, outflanked, and short of ammunition, Terrell ordered a retreat. The artillery limbered up and moved out first. After their crews moved the guns and caissons well away from danger, most of the remaining Texans mounted and followed. Three companies of horsemen remained behind to act as skirmishers and to delay the Union crossing as long as possible. By three o'clock, despite the outnumbered Texans' best efforts, the Federals occupied the vacated Confederate positions. Yager's regiment fell back northward to Simsport and from there to Evergreen. As his regiment retreated, Yager left pickets along the road to warn him of any advancing Union cavalry. Surviving records furnish no confirmation that the regiment participated in any other major actions during 1864. In December, along with the rest of the brigade, Yager's regiment established winter quarters at Alexandria.[35]

In October, Wight wrote to his wife, "We are living very well at present." He reported that, although a cold north wind blew and "it is a raining," he still had his warm overcoat and lived in comfortable quarters. He and his messmates stripped planks from a fence to repair a damaged house, in which, he penned, "we have our bunks fixed up very nice." Rations issued consisted of beef, cornmeal, sugar, and molasses, which the men supplemented with dried beans, peas, persimmons, pawpaws, and some grapes. For a few weeks, the men were, as Wight put it, "not doing very bad." Conditions changed considerably in early 1865, however. Wight wrote home that he needed a cotton shirt, an overshirt, a pair of pants, drawers, and, along with a pair of shoes, four or five pair of socks. The destitute private's letter summarized his plight: "I need money bad."[36]

Moving into winter quarters apparently did not quell Yager's desire for campaigning against the Yankees. On February 16, 1865, Brig. Gen. W. R. Boggs, Kirby Smith's chief of staff, in a letter to Lt. Gen. Simon Bolivar Buckner, who was commanding the District of West Louisiana after Taylor's departure, responded to Yager's idea of relocating his regiment to the east bank of the Mississippi River. Kirby Smith realized the difficulty of transporting troops across the Federal-controlled river, believing any such moves "impractical," but he authorized such a move with some stipulations: "It can only be done by the individual consent and cooperation of the men comprising the command." Kirby Smith authorized Wharton to permit commanders to cross the river with their units if "a majority of the men are willing to cross the Mississippi and will give their individual efforts to make the attempt successful." Wharton received authorization to transfer men from one unit to another, allowing soldiers who wished to fight east of the river to join units that were attempting to shift their operations to a more active department.[37]

Whether Yager engineered a successful crossing of the river by his regiment remains in doubt; none of his cavalrymen's known correspondence records such a move. Nevertheless, on March 9, 1865, Union officers reported about fifteen hundred Texas cavalry near Port Gibson, "with the intention of crossing the Mississippi to go home." A Confederate command at Union Church, near Fayette, Mississippi, reportedly included one hundred troops commanded by Yager. Although these reports remain unsubstantiated, a modest contingent of the 1st Texas Cavalry may have campaigned on both banks of the Mississippi River.[38]

CHAPTER 12

"A Tribute to the Cavalry Branch of the Service"

In December, 1864, Lt. Gen. Edmund Kirby Smith, commander of the Trans-Mississippi Department, took several drastic measures to alleviate a severe shortage of horses. Initially he ordered most cavalry units in his command dismounted; he maintained control over an abundance of mounted units but infantry were scarce. On December 9, he ordered Maj. Gen. John B. Magruder to dismount all his cavalry. He then instructed Maj. Gen. John A. Wharton to dismount nine of his regiments, leaving only the best disciplined and equipped regiments as cavalry. The 1st Texas Cavalry retained its mounts. Disgruntled, the dismounted units sent their horses to artillery batteries. In the spring of 1865, despite an abundance of horses in Texas, the 1st Texas Cavalry experienced a shortage of reliable mounts, and many men obtained permission to return home to acquire fresh horses. Many of these men never returned to the regiment. The war ended before they procured horses and made their way back to Louisiana.[1]

After large Confederate armies surrendered in both Virginia and Tennessee, many Confederate soldiers lost heart and left their units to return home. Despite the fact that other Texas units were disintegrating around it, the 1st Texas Cavalry maintained its discipline, returning to Texas and dispersing only after receiving official orders. One Confederate commander wrote, "It is a tribute to the cavalry branch of the service that they showed up as well as they did under these very trying conditions when so many of our comrades in arms, especially those in other branches of the service had weakened and left, unmindful of their duty to remain subject to the end." The 1st Texas Cavalry disbanded on April 30 at Wildcat Bluff on the Trinity River between Dallas and

Corsicana, but many companies remained intact, as the men wished to remain together until they rode into their home counties. Most of the war-weary men simply wanted to go home to good food and their families.[2]

The Civil War irrevocably changed the tactics and ideas of cavalry employment. Cavalry units, especially the 1st Texas, combined lessons learned fighting Indians on the frontier with European military doctrine. European commanders generally employed cavalry only to support the infantry and to act as scouts, couriers, and guards for high-ranking officers. Fighting Indians required troops to make long, hard marches with little food or water. Texas horsemen also slept on the ground, sometimes with their reins wrapped around their hands, ready to rise and ride at a moment's notice. Combining frontier and European tactics made Texas Civil War cavalry an autonomous arm when accompanied by artillery and supply trains. Important cavalry missions included reconnaissance, screening, flanking attacks, and rapid exploitation of any breakthrough in enemy lines. The 1st Texas Cavalry operated far from the main bodies of troops and at times fought like dragoons, both mounted and dismounted as infantry.[3]

Maj. Gen. Richard Taylor and every other senior officer who commanded the Texas cavalry commented on their bravery and devotion to duty. All considered the Texans to be excellent horsemen, skilled marksmen, hardy, fearless, and self-reliant. Taylor remarked that the Texans were "always up there where you could smell the patching." Maj. Gen. John A. Wharton, in a general commendation, praised all his cavalry: "The history of no other campaign will present the spectacle of a cavalry force capturing and killing more of the enemy than their own numbers. This you have done and in so doing have immortalized yourselves and added new luster to Texas." The Texans never refused to charge when asked, and their cacophonous yells so intimidated some Federal units that they fled from the field of battle. After the battle at Mansfield, a Yankee prisoner reported, "It was them durn Texans hollerin' that scared them [Union infantry]" and caused Maj. Gen. Nathaniel P. Banks's line to break and run. Other veterans reported that the Texas yell had been heard for miles over the noise of cannon and musketry. Robert A. Newell, a Louisiana soldier who observed many Texas cavalry units, did not consider the mounted Texans quite so impressive. He wrote, "The[y] don't at all look like soldgers [*sic*]." He believed that, if the Confederacy had no better troops, "Louisiana was in a bad way." In his opinion, the Texans "looke more like baboons mounted on gotes [*sic*] than anything else." Unfortunately for Banks and his Union army, the Texans fought more like lions than baboons.[4]

Brig. Gen. Hamilton P. Bee also praised the 1st Texas Cavalry for its bravery and fighting spirit. Battle, sickness, and the other exigencies of extended combat reduced the strength of the regiment. Hardships and shortages, however, never caused the men to falter in carrying out their orders. Bee claimed for his men "the highest place for their gallantry, patience and endurance of fatigue, and never failing enthusiasm, and the fact that they held their positions for so many days, fighting the enemy's cavalry and driving them back on their artillery and infantry" without support. He declared that the Texans' performance of duty "stamps the soldiers worthy of the cause of which we fight."[5]

Arming the troopers with sabers, Col. Augustus Buchel trained the regiment as a predominantly cavalry fighting force; as a result, it garnered special recognition from Taylor. The Texans' preeminence in mounted tactics prompted Taylor to label the regiment "genuine cavalry." Excepting only Buchel's and DeBray's regiments, he referred to all other mounted units as "horse," not cavalry. He judged all other mounted units to be merely mounted infantry, not true cavalry. The 1st Texas Cavalry gained Taylor's respect for its ability to execute a variety of missions successfully. In general, independent Texans often ignored routine camp duties and roamed about at will. Only when a battle seemed imminent could they be kept together. Because of his admiration for the Texans' fighting spirit and ability, Taylor did not punish their transgressions. The 1st Texas Cavalry, known for its discipline and reliability, probably had a few men who succumbed to wanderlust, but available documents fail to indicate any tendency for the troops not to follow orders; they remained a cohesive fighting organization. Taylor may have favored Buchel's Texans, too, because their commander had served under, and been well respected by, Taylor's father.[6]

German immigrants in the regiment especially impressed Taylor. He wrote, "They had the idea they were fighting for their adopted country." Taylor explained that the immigrants conducted themselves "markedly different" in combat from those Germans whom he had confronted in the Federal army in Virginia. In Taylor's opinion, Texas German immigrants fought bravely and well, while those in eastern Federal armies broke and ran more often than not. Significantly, research indicates that more German immigrants served in Texas's Confederate units than most historians believe. Several Texas units, both cavalry and infantry, contained substantial numbers of German volunteers. German settlers, both native-born and immigrant, comprised almost the entire membership of some Texas units, such as Company E, 1st Texas Cavalry. Ironically, the unit that pursued German Unionists on the Nueces River became part of a regiment not only commanded by German immigrants but also containing numerous soldiers of German ancestry. Available records fail to show any animosity between Joseph Taylor's battalion and Germans in the regiment. Since many of the volunteers from German settlements enlisted in Frank van der Stucken's Company E and appeared to be advocates of states' rights, they may not have had much sympathy for German Unionists. Many German immigrants, because of experiences under oppressive governments in Europe in the 1840s, feared loss of freedom at the hands of another totalitarian state. In general, they supported the Union but believed that the U.S. government failed to protect their individual rights fully. During the secession crisis, one wrote, "We are convinced that the people of the United States do not enjoy the liberties guaranteed to them by the Constitution."[7]

Muster rolls of the 1st Texas Cavalry indicate that men from exceedingly diverse occupations and nationalities joined the regiment. Descriptive entries also reveal that, on numerous occasions, several members of the same family enlisted in the same companies. Names, physical descriptions, and places of residence and of birth indicate obvious father, son, and brother connections in several units. Farmers, stockmen, sailors, preachers, and teachers signed up to fight for Texas. While the list of occupations is too long to enumerate, almost every profession and trade appears in regimental rosters, from doctors and lawyers to druggists, jewelers, saddlers, students, and those with no occupation at all. By a great margin, farmer was the predominant occupation, followed by stock raiser and *ranchero*; "rancher" and "cowboy" were not terms used during this era. Interestingly, those born in the U.S. appeared on rolls as *rancheros* and those born in Mexico as herders. Whether such designations indicated the type of stock management practiced or ethnocentricity could not be determined.[8]

Enlistees of all ages came from almost every state in the Union and several foreign countries. Southern and border states, however, contributed the majority of regimental soldiers. Not only did soldiers of German descent enlist, but so did a large number of individuals from Ireland and Scotland. England, France, Mexico, Canada, and Spain were represented, too. Ages ranged from thirteen to fifty-eight, and height from six feet four inches down to four feet ten inches. A significant number of the men were six feet tall or taller, making the regiment's median height taller than that of the average man, who at the time measured five feet seven inches. Dispelling the popular conception of men's heights, unhappily for some native Texans, the tallest man in the regiment was born in Rhode Island.[9]

Compared with other Confederate units, veterans of the 1st Texas Cavalry displayed a remarkable sense of duty. They remained at their posts despite serious problems at home. Service records portray soldiers who, rather than deserting their comrades or forsaking their oaths, requested furloughs through proper military channels. In February, 1863, Pvt. D. B. F. Rhodes, Company H, citing serious family problems at home, requested a sixty-day leave. Unforeseen circumstances had forced his family out of their home, and they desperately needed permanent shelter. The same month, Pvt. L. C. Scott, Company K, asked for sixty days to "see to the comfort of his family," as they were ill and had no one to care for them. Frank M. Vivian, Company B, applied for a leave to return to Goliad, where his mother lay ill and had "no one to provide for her wants and even were she well could not provide the necessaries of life" because "provisions are very scarce." To be sure, said Vivian, "I know that every soldier should now be in the field," but he submitted his request under very troubling circumstances and never absented himself without leave. Several families suffered major outrages at the hands of their neighbors, but regimental troops appealed for permission for leave, rather than rushing home to protect their families. "Renegades infesting" Gillespie County burned all "houses pens and pastures" of Captain Frank van der Stucken's farm and placed his wife and five children "in danger." "Buschwackers [*sic*] of that region of the country" also ambushed his brother, firing several shots at him but, fortunately, missing. Pvt. Levi Wight and Charles Wahrmund experienced similar difficulties. "Deserters and other disloyal men," drove off their neighbors and left Wight's wife and three children and Wahrmund's wife and six children in "imminent danger" of attacks by renegades and Indians. Wight's family moved from Llano to Burnet to escape persecution. Both men simply asked permission to return home for a short time to insure the safety of their families and to "provide shelter and subsistance [*sic*] for them" until the soldiers could return home permanently. Wight wrote to his mother, "My name shall never go down to posterity as being the first one of that name ever playing the coward or shrunk from his duty." He continued, "It shall never be said of me that you gave birth to a son that would not respond promptly to the cause of his bleeding and ignored country."[10]

Given the men's attitudes, regimental desertion rates remained extremely low. Records of the 1st Mounted Rifles/1st Texas Cavalry for 1861–62 disclose a rate of only eight-tenths of 1 percent. At that time, the regiment was posted on the Texas frontier; despite restrictive leave regulations, the men generally could manage a quick visit home. If not, as in the case of some companies, the men knew that they were close to home and could provide for their families more easily in dire emergencies. During the latter stages of the war, when the regiment campaigned farther afield, surviving records indicate 72 deserters among the total regimental strength of 1,083, yielding a desertion rate of 6.7 percent for 1863–65. Explaining some of the absences, existing records prove that some soldiers absented themselves and returned. More than likely, others listed as deserters left for a short visit with family or friends and then returned to their companies. Several of those at one time recorded as deserters later appeared in prisoner of war or parolee records.[11]

The 1st Texas Cavalry displayed much lower rates of desertion in 1861–65 than the vast majority of other Confederate regiments. The 3rd Texas Cavalry came close, recording 93 desertions in a listed strength of 1,097, for a desertion rate of 8 percent. The 9th Texas Cavalry, notorious for unruly behavior, recorded many more desertions. On the night of September 3, 1863, alone, 31 enlisted men and one officer mounted up and rode away from the Ninth.[12]

As early as 1862, Robert E. Lee reported that deserters and stragglers deprived him of a third to a half of his force. During the war, North Carolina troops accounted for 20 percent of all Confederate desertions. At one point, staff officers of the Army of Tennessee estimated that one-third of their men were absent from duty; and in just one month of early 1865, Lee's Army of Northern Virginia lost 8 percent of its total strength to desertions. In a speech in September, 1864, Confederate President Jefferson Davis told an audience that two-thirds of the Confederate army was absent without leave.[13]

The 1st Texas Cavalry, from its inception as the 1st Regiment of Texas Mounted Rifles until the unit disbanded, functioned admirably, despite confronting immense disadvantages. As the first regiment from Texas to muster into the Confederate States Provisional Army, the regiment faced haphazard recruiting and funding policies on the part of both state and Confederate governments. Overcoming these impediments, regimental commanders managed to organize, equip, and train a unit that performed at a consistently high level throughout the Civil War. Although hampered by lack of funds, supplies, ammunition, and proper equipment, and constantly plagued by inhospitable terrain and bad weather, the regiment fulfilled its assigned missions.[14]

Initially, the mounted Texans assumed responsibility for a section of the frontier that, in 1850, had occupied all Texas Rangers and one-fourth of the U.S. Army. While commanding the Department of Texas, Brig. Gen. Earl Van Dorn, who had extensive experience on the Texas frontier while serving with the 2d U.S. Cavalry, recommended to the Confederate government that four regiments be assigned the duty allotted to the 1st Texas Mounted Rifles/1st Texas Cavalry. Challenged and pursued by relentless, hard-riding Texas horsemen, raiding Indians were prevented from roaming indiscriminately through, or sending war parties unhindered into, the settled regions of Texas. Throughout 1861 and into 1862, Indian raids decreased from the numbers reported in previous years. Wagon trains moved freely to deliver supplies, such as they were, along the trails between the regiment's outposts.[15]

Regimental commanders succeeded in maintaining between eight hundred and a thousand men on the frontier. For their successes, these men paid a price in killed and wounded, but the regiment stood firm in Texas's first hour of need in the Civil War. From the far-flung, lonely outposts of the Texas frontier, the regiment protected the state's citizenry from the ravages of marauding Indians and bandits. Armed bands of deserters, disaffected Unionists, and bushwhackers placed additional burdens upon the regiment. Unit commanders had to face not only external enemies but internal ones as well.[16]

Later, from the *brasada* along the Rio Grande up the Texas coast and into the mosquito-infested bayou country of Louisiana, whenever Union forces threatened to invade the state, they faced the resolute 1st Regiment of Texas Cavalry. Henry E. McCulloch, Augustus Buchel, and William O. Yager forged a cavalry unit that indisputably helped keep Texas from suffering the ravages of war that visited other states in the Confederacy. Texas's recovery after the war was a testament to the valorous service and the sacrifices rendered to the state by the regiment.[17]

Buchel exemplified the high caliber of leadership, courage, and fidelity demonstrated by the men who led the 1st Texas Cavalry. Viewed by some as a small, unassuming man, Buchel actually was quite complex, his quiet demeanor belying his fierce determination. A lifelong bachelor, he readily assumed the financial burden of his brother's family when Karl bled to death after being hit by a ricocheting ax. Known to his men as a disciplinarian, he exhibited constant fairness. Of discipline he said, "Make your discipline exact, impartial, and of universal application. . . . the supreme element is justice." Buchel employed punishment only as a last resort. All who knew him well expressed great respect for him. John Henry Brown, a personal friend, wrote that Buchel "had no enemies" and enjoyed the "most cordial friendship of the masses." Brown emphasized that "he was a man of honor and education."[18]

After Buchel died of multiple gunshot wounds on April 12, 1864, his men buried him at Mansfield, Louisiana; but Buchel's remains soon were reinterred at the state cemetery at Austin, where the state government erected a large marker at his grave. He received several other accolades for his devotion to both his men and his adopted state. George R. Kuykendall named his first son Augustus Buchel Kuykendall. Perhaps the highest honor, however, was awarded by Texas politicians. The state legislature demonstrated its appreciation for the regiment's fallen commander by naming a county after Brig. Gen. Augustus C. Buchel. On March 15, 1887, the legislature set aside part of Presidio County and named the territory Buchel County. The county, never completely organized, became part of Brewster County by act of the legislature in April, 1897. Thus the county, like its namesake and the exploits of the men of the 1st Texas Cavalry Regiment, lay hidden in the dust of history.[19]

NOTES

Regimental muster rolls (with personal information) and lists of equipment may be consulted via the Internet at: http://www.mcm.edu/academic/depts/grady/gmrfhome.htm.

Abbreviations

Barry Letters	Correspondence, 1861–1862, Box 2B42, James Buckner Barry Papers, Center for American History, University of Texas, Austin
Barry Orders	Confederate Army Orders, 1861–1865, Box 2B43, James Buckner Barry Papers, Center for American History, University of Texas, Austin
Bee Papers	Hamilton P. Bee Papers, Texas State Archives, Austin
Brown Papers	John Henry Brown Papers, Texas State Archives, Austin
Burleson Collection	Edward Burleson Collection, Center for American History, University of Texas, Austin
Compiled Service Records	Compiled Service Records of Confederate Soldiers, War Department Collection of Confederate Records, Record Group 109, National Archives and Record Service, Washington, D.C.
Davidson Papers	Sidney Green Davidson Papers, Box 2D50, Center for American History, University of Texas, Austin
King Papers	John R. King Papers, Texas State Archives, Austin
Kuykendall Diary	William Kuykendall, "Civil War Diary," in Kuykendall Family Papers, 1822–1991, Center for American History, University of Texas, Austin

Lenz Collection	Louis Lenz Collection, Center for American History, University of Texas, Austin
M323	Microfilmed Records of the 1st Texas Mounted Rifles and 1st Texas Cavalry Regiments, Compiled Service Records of Confederate Soldiers Who Served in Organizations from the State of Texas, War Department Collection of Confederate Records, Record Group 109, Microfilm Number M323, National Archives and Record Service, Washington, D.C.
McCulloch Collection	Henry E. McCulloch Collection, Texas State Archives, Austin
Muster Rolls	Muster Rolls and Unit Reports, 1st Texas Mounted Rifles and 1st Regiment of Texas Cavalry, War Department Collection of Confederate Records, Box 488, Record Group 109, National Archives and Record Service, Washington, D.C.
OR	*The War of Rebellion: A Compilation of the Official Records of the Union and Confederate Armies,* 4 series, 130 vols. (Washington, D.C.: Government Printing Office, 1880–1901). All references to *OR* are to Series I unless otherwise noted.
Stephens Letters	G. W. Stephens Letters, Confederate Research Center, Hill Junior College, Hillsboro, Texas
Stockdale Collection	Fletcher S. Stockdale Collection, Texas State Archives, Austin
Webb Diary	John Tyler Webb, "Civil War Diary," in Nancy Stevens Private Papers, Fort Worth, Texas

Preface

1. M323, Rolls 2–7; Clement A. Evans, ed., *Confederate Military History: A Library of the Confederate States in Seventeen Volumes: Written by Distinguished Men of the South,* vol. XV, 42–43; Mamie Yeary, comp., *Reminiscences of the Boys in Gray,* 341–43, 361–63, 636, 746–47; David Paul Smith, *Frontier Defense in the Civil War: Texas Rangers and Rebels,* 21–40; *OR,* vol. IX, 613–16.

2. M323, Roll 2; Special Orders No. 127, Dept. of Texas, New Mexico, and Arizona, May 2, 1863, in Muster Rolls.

3. M323, Rolls 2–4, 7; Special Orders No. 40, 1st Texas Mounted Rifles, June 18, 1861, in McCulloch Collection; Regimental Orders No. 10, 1st Texas Mounted Rifles, May 11, 1861, in Barry Orders; Carl L. Duaine, *The Dead Men Wore Boots: An Account of the 32nd Texas Volunteer Cavalry, CSA, 1862–1865*, 27–30, 49; Walter Lord, ed., *The Fremantle Diary: Being the Journal of Lieutenant Colonel James Arthur Lyon Fremantle, Coldstream Guards, on His Three Months in the Southern States*, 14–15; Kuykendall Diary, 4, 6, 10.

4. M323, Rolls 2–7. For a comparison of occupations, see James M. McPherson, *Battle Cry of Freedom: The Civil War Era*, 614; and Bell Irvin Wiley, *The Life of Johnny Reb: The Common Soldier of the Confederacy*, 17–18.

5. M323, Rolls 2–7.

6. M323, Rolls 2–7; Muster Rolls, 1st Texas Cavalry; Douglas John Cater, *As It Was: Reminiscences of a Soldier of the Third Texas Cavalry and the Nineteenth Louisiana Infantry*, 77, 84.

7. M323, Rolls 2–7; Richard B. Harwell, ed., *Destruction and Reconstruction: Personal Experiences of the Late War by Richard Taylor, Lieutenant General in the Confederate Army*, 190, 216; Kuykendall Diary, 4.

8. M323, Rolls 2–7; Yeary, *Reminiscences of Boys in Gray*, 341, 361, 363.

9. M323, Rolls 2–7; Yeary, *Reminiscences of Boys in Gray*, 341, 361, 363; David Smith, *Frontier Defense*, 168–69; Kuykendall Diary, 11.

Chapter 1. Genesis of a Regiment

1. Walter L. Buenger, *Secession and the Union in Texas*, 119–40; Evans, *Confederate Military History*, 15:13–22, 15:28; Ralph Wooster, *Texas and Texans in the Civil War*, 1–24.

2. Buenger, *Secession and the Union*, 141–58; Evans, *Confederate Military History*, 15:21–23, 15:43; Wooster, *Texas and Texans*, 1–24; J. J. Bowden, *The Exodus of Federal Troops from Texas, 1861*, 64–66; Allan Coleman Ashcraft, "Texas, 1860–1866: The Lone Star State in the Civil War."

3. Buenger, *Secession and the Union*, 141–58; Evans, *Confederate Military History*, 15:21–23, 15:43; Bowden, *Exodus of Federal Troops*, 64–66; Ron Tyler, ed., *The New Handbook of Texas*, 4:365; David Smith, *Frontier Defense*, 23–24; Wooster, *Texas and Texans*, 19, 27.

4. *OR*, vol. LIII, pt. I, 639–40; Allan C. Ashcraft, *Texas in the Civil War: A Resume History*, 7–8.

5. *OR*, vol. LIII, pt. I, 639–40; Wooster, *Texas and Texans*, 19; Ashcraft, *Texas in the Civil War*, 7–8; Bill Winsor, *Texas in the Confederacy: Military Installations, Economy, and People*, 14–15; Sidney Green Davidson to Mary Kuykendall Davidson (wife), Feb. 22, 1861, in Davidson Papers.

6. Buenger, *Secession and the Union*, 154; Evans, *Confederate Military History*, 15:24–27; Wooster, *Texas and Texans*, 16–18; Bowden, *Exodus of Federal Troops*, 48–63, 104–106; Tyler, *New Handbook of Texas*, 4:384.

7. *OR*, vol. LIII, pt. I, 639–40; Ashcraft, *Texas in the Civil War*, 7–8; S. G. Davidson to Mary Davidson, Feb. 22, 1861, in Davidson Papers.

8. *OR*, vol. LIII, pt. I, 639–40; Tyler, *New Handbook of Texas*, 5:1093; Ashcraft, *Texas in the Civil War*, 7–8; David Smith, *Frontier Defense*, 25.

9. *OR*, vol. LIII, pt. I, 639–40; Tyler, *New Handbook of Texas*, 5:1093; Ashcraft, *Texas in the Civil War*, 7–8; David Smith, *Frontier Defense*, 25.

10. *OR*, vol. LIII, pt. I, 640–42; S. G. Davidson to Mary Davidson, Mar. 4, 1861, in Davidson Papers; Wooster, *Texas and Texans*, 19.

11. S. G. Davidson to Mary Davidson, Mar. 10 and 29, 1861, in Davidson Papers.

12. *OR*, vol. LIII, pt. I, 641, 645; Henry E. McCulloch to James B. Barry, Mar. 7, 1861, in Barry Letters; David Smith, *Frontier Defense*, 26–28.

13. *OR*, vol. LIII, pt. I, 641, 645; James K. Greer, ed., *A Texas Ranger and Frontiersman: The Days of Buck Barry in Texas, 1845–1906*, 127; Wooster, *Texas and Texans*, 32.

14. *OR*, vol. LIII, pt. I, 640–42.

15. Ibid., pt. I, 641; S. G. Davidson to Mary Davidson, Mar. 22, 1861, in Davidson Papers.

16. *OR*, vol. LIII, pt. I, 640–42; S. G. Davidson to Mary Davidson, Apr. 6, 1861, in Davidson Papers.

17. *OR*, vol. LIII, pt. I, 639–41; Compiled Service Records, Henry E. McCulloch; Handbill, TDS, Apr. 6, 1894, in McCulloch Collection; Evans, *Confederate Military History*, 15:42–43.

18. Greer, *Texas Ranger*, 127–29.

19. M323, Rolls 2–7; *OR*, vol. LIII, pt. I, 639–40; Compiled Service Records, Henry E. McCulloch; Regimental Orders, Headquarters, Camp Colorado, Mar. 17, 1861, in Barry Orders; David Smith, *Frontier Defense*, 28–29. In the Unit Records and Reports for the 1st Regiment of Texas Mounted Rifles, this is the first date the regiment is mentioned as a Confederate unit versus a Texas state organization.

20. M323, Rolls 2–4; Evans, *Confederate Military History*, 15:43–44; Handbill, Apr. 6, 1894, in McCulloch Collection.

21. *OR*, vol. LIII, pt. I, 639–41; Evans, *Confederate Military History*, 15:43–44; Handbill, Apr. 6, 1894, in McCulloch Collection; A. W. Neville, *The History of Lamar County, Texas*, 114–15.

Chapter 2. "Good Riders and Crack Shots"

1. Handbill, TDS, Apr. 6, 1894, in McCulloch Collection.

2. M323, Rolls 2–4; Henry E. McCulloch to James B. Barry, Mar. 26, 1861, and

Milton Webb to Commander, Camp Cooper, Apr. 21, 1861, both in Barry Letters; John M. Elkins, written for Captain Elkins by Frank W. McCarty, *Indian Fighting on the Texas Frontier,* 92; Neville, *History of Lamar County,* 112.

3. Order No. 3, 1st Texas Mounted Rifles, Apr. 21, 1861, in Barry Orders; McCulloch to Barry, Mar. 27, 1861, in Barry Letters; Greer, *Texas Ranger,* 127–29; Notice, *Austin State Gazette,* Apr. 6, 1961, in Newspaper Files, Amon Carter Museum Library, Fort Worth, Tex. The pay of these troops equaled that of other Confederate volunteers. Pay and subsistence commenced when the companies reached their duty posts. The regimental commander hoped that the government would reimburse the cost of rations and forage required by the troops before they were mustered into service. The men enlisted for at least twelve months. McCulloch used "good marksmen" in his letter, while Barry used "crack shots" in his book. I chose Barry's term for flavor.

4. McCulloch to Barry, Mar. 27, 1861, in Barry Letters; Greer, *Texas Ranger,* 127–29.

5. M323, Rolls 2–4, Muster Rolls, 1st Texas Mounted Rifles; Regimental Orders No. 5, 1st Texas Mounted Rifles, Apr. 22, 1861, in Barry Orders; Handbill, TDS, Apr. 6, 1894, in McCulloch Collection; M323, Rolls 2–7. Initially H. W. Cook signed letters as quartermaster and commissary, but soon he was replaced by Washington L. Hill and John R. King.

6. Milton Webb to Commander, Camp Cooper, Apr. 21, 1861, in Barry Letters; Neville, *History of Lamar County,* 112–13. Men from Lamar, Fannin, Hunt, and Hopkins counties formed Webb's company.

7. McCulloch to Barry, Apr. 17, 1861, in Barry Letters; Regimental Orders No. 6, 1st Texas Mounted Rifles, Apr. 22, 1861, and Regimental Orders No. 11, 1st Texas Mounted Rifles, June 16, 1861, both in Barry Orders; M323, Rolls 2–4, Muster Rolls, 1st Texas Mounted Rifles; "George Washington Greer," *Albany (Tex.) Gazette,* n.d., in Camp Cooper file, Robert E. Nail Archives, Old Jail Art Center Museum, Albany, Tex.

8. "Captain Boggess," *Austin State Gazette,* Apr. 20, 1861, in Newspaper Files, Amon Carter Museum Library, Fort Worth, Tex.; Garland R. Farmer, *The Realm of Rusk County,* 45–46; Rusk County Genealogical Society, *Remembering Rusk County,* 11.

9. "U.S. Marshal H. E. McCulloch," *Austin State Gazette,* Feb. 9, 1861, in Newspaper Files, Amon Carter Museum Library, Fort Worth, Tex.; Tyler, *New Handbook of Texas,* 4:386.

10. "Pitts of Austin," *Houston Post,* n.d., and unidentified newspaper clipping, both in William A. Pitts Papers, Box 3C152, Center for American History, Univ. of Texas, Austin.

11. S. G. Davidson to Mary Davidson, Mar. 8, 1860, in Davidson Papers; S. G. Davidson to Mary Davidson, Apr. 6, 1861, in Davidson Papers; S. G. Davidson to Mary Davidson, May 10, 1861, in Davidson Papers; S. G. Davidson, Drawer 401–793, Folder 1, Index of Captains of Texas Units in Confederate Service,

Record Group 304, Comptroller Records, in Service and Payroll Records, Texas State Archives, Austin; Bertha Atkinson, *The History of Bell County, Texas*, 67–69, 123–25.

12. Neville, *History of Lamar County*, 112.

13. James B. Barry, Folder 1, Drawer 401–793, in Service and Payroll Records, Texas State Archives, Austin; Greer, *Texas Ranger*, 1–150; Tyler, *New Handbook of Texas*, 1:396–97.

14. Tyler, *New Handbook of Texas*, 1:838.

15. Thomas C. Frost, Folder 15, Box 401–724, in Service and Payroll Records, Texas State Archives, Austin; Ellis A. Davis, Edwin H. Grobe, et al., eds. and comps., *The New Encyclopedia of Texas*, 3:1534; Tyler, *New Handbook of Texas*, 3:3, 16.

16. Bowden, *Exodus of Federal Troops*, 78; *OR*, vol. LIII, pt. I, 639–41.

17. Bowden, *Exodus of Federal Troops*, 78; *OR*, vol. LIII, pt. I, 639–41.

18. Regimental Orders No. 6, 1st Texas Mounted Rifles, Apr. 22, 1961; Regimental Orders No. 10, 1st Texas Mounted Rifles, May 11, 1861; and Regimental Orders No. 11, 1st Texas Mounted Rifles, June 16, 1861; all in Barry Orders. The initial drawing went as follows: Fry, Company A; Pitts, Company B; Duke, Company C; Barry, Company D; Tobin, Company E; Nelson, Company F; Davidson, Company G; Frost, Company H; Boggess, Company K; Ashby, Company K; Milton Webb, no company listed. It was not until June that McCulloch dropped Duke and captains from Barry down advanced a letter. Then Webb received the designation and rank of Company K.

19. Regimental Orders No. 10, 1st Texas Mounted Rifles, May 11, 1861, in Barry Orders.

20. Thomas C. Frost to Barry, June 4, 1861, in Barry Letters; Compiled Service Records, James H. Fry; Evans, *Confederate Military History*, 15:42; *OR*, vol. IV, 97, 106; S. G. Davidson to Mary Davidson, Apr. 3, 1861, in Davidson Papers; Special Orders No. 51, 1st Texas Mounted Rifles, July 13, 1861, in Burleson Collection; M323, Rolls 2–4; David Smith, *Frontier Defense*, 31–32; Elkins, *Indian Fighting*, 88, 92.

21. Elkins, *Indian Fighting*, 92; Robert Pattison Felgar, "Texas in the War for Southern Independence, 1861–1865," 63–67; William Royston Geise, "Texas the First Year of the War, April 1861–April 1862: A Study of Organization and Command in the Trans-Mississippi West," *Military History of Texas and the Southwest* 13, no. 4 (1976): 32; David Smith, *Frontier Defense*, 32–33.

22. General Orders No. 5, Headquarters, Troops in Texas, May 13, 1861, in Barry Orders.

Chapter 3. "Chastising the Ruthless Savages"

1. Henry E. McCulloch to Earl Van Dorn, June 8, 1861, in King Papers.

2. Ibid.

3. Ibid.
4. Ibid.
5. Ibid.
6. Ibid.
7. Special Orders No. 40, 1st Texas Mounted Rifles, June 18, 1861, in Barry Orders; Special Orders No. 51, 1st Texas Mounted Rifles, July 13, 1861, in Burleson Collection; Henry E. McCulloch to Edward Burleson, July 22, 1861, in Burleson Collection; Milton M. Boggess to James B. Barry, June 29, 1861, in Barry Letters; Greer, *Texas Ranger*, 136–37.
8. Henry E. McCulloch to Van Dorn, June 8, 1861, in King Papers; Ernest Wallace and E. Adamson Hoebel, *The Comanches: Lords of the South Plains*, 20, 25–31; W. S. Nye, *Carbine and Lance: The Story of Old Fort Sill*, 6.
9. Special Orders No. 56, 1st Texas Mounted Rifles, July 12, 1861, in Burleson Collection; Special Orders No. 40, 1st Texas Mounted Rifles, June 18, 1861, in Barry Orders; M323, Rolls 2–7; Special Orders No. 51, 1st Texas Mounted Rifles, June 26, 1861, in Burleson Collection. Initially it was called Red River Station; McCulloch changed the name during the summer to honor Capt. James T. Jackson, who killed Capt. Elmer Ellsworth, 5th New York Zouaves, at Alexandria, Va., for "wantonly insulting the cause and flag of the Confederacy." Jackson was slain immediately by Ellsworth's followers.
10. Special Orders No. 40, 1st Texas Mounted Rifles, June 18, 1861, in Barry Orders; Special Orders No. 51, 1st Texas Mounted Rifles, June 26, 1861, and Special Orders No. 56, 1st Texas Mounted Rifles, July 12, 1861, both in Burleson Collection; Henry E. McCulloch to Regiment, Aug. 2, 1861, in Burleson Collection.
11. Special Orders No. 40, 1st Texas Mounted Rifles, June 18, 1861, in Barry Orders; William O. Yager to Barry, Sept. 12, 1861, in Barry Letters.
12. Special Orders No. 46, 1st Texas Mounted Rifles, June 17, 1861, and Special Orders No. 36, Dept. of Texas, July 3, 1861, both in King Papers.
13. Circular, Texas Mounted Riflemen, Aug. 2, 1861, in Barry Orders; S. G. Davidson to Mary Davidson, June 7, 1861, in Davidson Papers; *Belton (Tex.) Democrat*, July 12, 1861, in Davidson Papers; McCulloch to Regiment, Aug. 2, 1861, in Burleson Collection; Elkins, *Indian Fighting*, 92–95; Greer, *Texas Ranger*, 138–40.
14. Elkins, *Indian Fighting*, 93–95.
15. Circular, Texas Mounted Riflemen, Aug. 2, 1861, in Barry Orders; S. G. Davidson to Mary Davidson, June 7, 1861, in Davidson Papers; *Belton (Tex.) Democrat*, June 1, 1861, in Davidson Papers; McCulloch to Regiment, Aug. 2, 1861, in Burleson Collection; Elkins, *Indian Fighting*, 93–96; Greer, *Texas Ranger*, 138–40.
16. Circular, Texas Mounted Rifles, Aug. 2, 1861, in Barry Orders; *Belton (Tex.) Democrat*, July 12, 1861, in Davidson Papers; Elkins, *Indian Fighting*, 95–96.

17. Circular, Texas Mounted Rifles, Aug. 2, 1861, in Barry Orders; *Belton (Tex.) Democrat,* July 12, 1861, in Davidson Papers; Elkins, *Indian Fighting,* 95–96.

18. Circular, 1st Texas Mounted Riflemen, Aug. 2, 1861, in Barry Orders; McCulloch to Regiment, Aug. 2, 1861, in Burleson Collection; Greer, *Texas Ranger,* 137–40. The wounded men were: James McKee and William Kelly, mortally injured; Alfred Fletcher, G. S. Misner, and J. S. Parrish, badly wounded; William Johnson and William Fletcher, slightly wounded, the latter in three place.

19. Evans, *Confederate Military History,* 15:42; *OR,* vol. IV, 97, 106; Special Orders No. 51, 1st Texas Mounted Rifles, July 13, 1861, in Burleson Collection.

20. Special Orders No. 51, 1st Texas Mounted Rifles, July 13, 1861, in Burleson Collection; McCulloch to Burleson, July 22, 1861, in Burleson Collection; Greer, *Texas Ranger,* 136–37.

21. Burleson to McCulloch, Aug. 20, 1861, in Burleson Collection; David Smith, *Frontier Defense,* 34; Tyler, *New Handbook of Texas,* 3:241–32.

22. Burleson to McCulloch, Aug. 20, 1861, in Burleson Collection; David Smith, *Frontier Defense,* 37–38; Tyler, *New Handbook of Texas,* 3:241–42; Nye, *Carbine and Lance,* 29.

23. David Smith, *Frontier Defense,* 34–35.

24. Burleson to McCulloch, Aug. 20, 1861, in Burleson Collection; Greer, *Texas Ranger,* 138–40; Joseph Carrol McConnell, *The West Texas Frontier,* 2:51.

25. S. G. Davidson to Mary Davidson, May 4, 1861, in Davidson Papers; J. W. Wilbarger, *Indian Depredations in Texas: Reliable Accounts of Battle, Wars, Adventures, Forays, Murders, Massacres, etc. . . ,* 488–91, 501–502, 21–522; Elkins, *Indian Fighting,* 85–87; McConnell, *West Texas Frontier,* 2:51–52.

26. Wilbarger, *Indian Depredations,* 488–91, 501–502; Elkins, *Indian Fighting,* 85–87; McConnell, *West Texas Frontier,* 2:51–53.

27. Wilbarger, *Indian Depredations,* 488–91, 501–502, 521–22; Elkins, *Indian Fighting,* 85–87; McConnell, *West Texas Frontier,* 2:51–52.

28. Wilbarger, *Indian Depredations,* 488–91, 501–502, 521–22; Elkins, *Indian Fighting,* 85–87; McConnell, *West Texas Frontier,* 2:51–52.

29. Wilbarger, *Indian Depredations,* 488–91, 501–502, 521–22; Elkins, *Indian Fighting,* 85–87; McConnell, *West Texas Frontier,* 2:51–52.

30. Wilbarger, *Indian Depredations,* 488–91, 501–502, 521–22; Elkins, *Indian Fighting,* 85–87; McConnell, *West Texas Frontier,* 2:51–52.

31. Jess Marshal to Henry E. McCulloch, July 20, 1861, in Burleson Collection.

32. McCulloch to Burleson, Sept. 20, 1861, in Burleson Collection; Greer, *Texas Ranger,* 41.

33. Regimental Orders No. 17, 1st Texas Mounted Rifles, Aug. 6, 1861, in Barry Orders; David Smith, *Frontier Defense,* 38–39.

34. Regimental Orders No. 17, 1st Texas Mounted Rifles, Aug. 6, 1861, in Barry Orders; David Smith, *Frontier Defense,* 38–39.

35. Burleson to Barry, Aug. 21, 1861, in Barry Letters; Invoice, McCulloch to Barry, Aug. 28, 1861, in Barry Letters.

36. Burleson to Barry, Oct. 3, 1861, in Barry Letters.

37. Regimental Orders No. 19, 1st Texas Mounted Rifles, Nov. 30, 1861, in Burleson Collection; McCulloch to Barry, Nov. 27, 1861, in Barry Letters; Greer, *Texas Ranger,* 141–42.

38. Yager to Barry, Sept. 27, 1861, in Barry Letters; Yager to Barry, Oct. 10, 1861, in Barry Letters.

39. Yager to Barry, Sept. 27, 1861, and Burleson to Barry, Oct. 27, 1861, both in Barry Letters; McCulloch to Burleson, Sept. 20, 1861, and McCulloch to Burleson, Oct. 17, 1861, both in Burleson Collection; Greer, *Texas Ranger,* 141; Circular (number illegible), 1st Texas Mounted Rifles, Jan. 15, 1862, in Barry Orders; M323, Rolls 2–4.

40. McCulloch to Burleson, Oct. 19, 1861, in Burleson Collection; McCulloch to P. O. Herbert, Dec. 13, 1861, in M323, Roll 3; Regimental Orders No. 21, McCulloch's Mounted Riflemen, Dec. 21, 1861, in Barry Orders; Thomas C. Frost to Barry, Feb. 12, 1862, in Barry Letters; Regimental Orders No. 12, 1st Texas Mounted Rifles, Feb. 22, 1862, in Barry Orders; Election Results, 1st Texas Mounted Rifles, Feb. 22, 1862, and Election Results, Company C, Mar. 15, 1862, both in Barry Orders.

41. Yager to Barry, Nov. 18, 1861, in Barry Letters; Special Orders No. 1, 1st Texas Mounted Rifles, Jan. 8, 1862, in Barry Orders; *OR,* vol. IV, 150–52; McCulloch to Commander, Camp Colorado, Nov. 18, 1861, in Burleson Collection; Stephan Schwartz, *Twenty-two Months a Prisoner of War: A Narrative of Twenty-two Months' Imprisonment by the Confederates, in Texas, through General Twiggs' Treachery, Dating from April, 1861, to February, 1863,* 80, 92, 96–97.

42. Yager to Barry, Nov. 18, 1861, in Barry Letters; McCulloch to Commander, Camp Colorado, Nov. 18, 1861, in Burleson Collection; Special Orders No. 1, 1st Texas Mounted Rifles, Jan. 8, 1862, and Special Orders No. 23, 1st Texas Mounted Rifles, Apr. 12, 1862, both in Barry Orders.

43. *OR,* vol. IV, 151–52; Regimental Orders No. 1, 1st Texas Mounted Rifles, Jan. 7, 1862, and General Orders No. 11, Western Military District of Texas, n.d., both in Barry Orders.

44. Circular No. 3, 1st Texas Mounted Rifles, Nov. 9, 1861, and Circular (number illegible), 1st Texas Mounted Rifles, Jan. 15, 1862, both in Barry Orders.

45. Circular No. 3, 1st Texas Mounted Rifles, Nov. 9, 1861, and Circular (number illegible), 1st Texas Mounted Rifles, Jan. 15, 1862, both in Barry Orders.

46. T. Hill Ashby to Barry, Feb. 16, 1862, and Ashby to Barry, Feb. 18, 1862, both in Barry Letters.

47. Greer, *Texas Ranger,* 142–44.

Chapter 4. Frontier Life, "We Must Endure It"

1. M323, Rolls 2–7.
2. S. G. Davidson to Mary Davidson, Mar. 10, 1861, in Davidson Papers; Hazel Best Overton, ed., "Frontier Life of John Chadbourne Irwin," unpublished paper in Robert E. Nail Archives, Old Jail Art Center Museum, Albany, Tex.; Compiled Service Records, Capt. James M. Homsley; M323, Roll 3; Rupert Norval Richardson, *The Frontier of Northwest Texas, 1846 to 1876: Advance and Defense by the Pioneer Settlers of the Cross Timbers and Prairies,* 71, 95. Davidson may not have seen any ladies, but women lived at some posts. Requisitions for rations, wood, and straw for laundresses were discovered among regimental records.
3. S. G. Davidson to Mary Davidson, Mar. 10, 1861, in Davidson Papers; Overton, "Frontier Life of John Chadbourne Irwin,"; Compiled Service Records, Capt. James M. Homsley; M323, Roll 3; Richardson, *Frontier of Northwest Texas,* 71, 95.
4. Receipt for lumber, W. L. Hill, Jan. 27, 1862, in 1st Texas Cavalry Collection, Confederate Research Center, Hill Junior College, Hillsboro, Tex.; M323, Rolls 2–7; Henry E. McCulloch to Edward Burleson, Oct. 17, 1861, in Burleson Collection.
5. Compiled Service Records, James M. Homsley; M323, Rolls 2 and 3. Regimental records indicate that the coal shipped to camps was utilized only by unit blacksmiths, not for heating quarters. Some firewood also was used to make charcoal for blacksmiths' forges.
6. S. G. Davidson to Mary Davidson, Mar. 10, 1861, May 10, 1861, and May 21, 1861, all in Davidson Papers; Overton, "Frontier Life"; Richardson, *Frontier of Northwest Texas,* 161; Douglas Southall Freeman, *R. E. Lee: A Biography,* 1:367–68, 1:375–76; Robert E. Lee to Mrs. Lee (wife), Aug. 4, 1856, *West Texas Historical Association Year Book* 8 (June, 1932): 5–6.
7. Frederick Law Olmsted, *A Journey Through Texas; or, A Saddle-trip on the Southwestern Frontier: With a Statistical Appendix,* 308–309; Freeman, *R. E. Lee,* 1:363, 1:364; Richardson, *Frontier of Northwest Texas,* 162.
8. Olmsted, *Journey Through Texas,* 95–97, 247, 307; George R. Gautier, *Harder than Death: The Life of George R. Gautier: An Old Texan, Living at the Confederate Home, Austin, Texas,* 1, 3, 4–8; M323, Rolls 2–4; William Tecumseh Sherman, *Memoirs of General W. T. Sherman,* 883; Richardson, *Frontier of Northwest Texas,* 160; Emily Thacker, *The Vinegar Book,* 8, 10–11, 13. Although germ theory was not understood at the time, the disinfectant power of acidic vinegar killed some bacteria and microbes, thus preventing many infections in wounds.
9. Burleson to James B. Barry, Sept. 12, 1861, in Barry Letters; "Pitts of Austin," *Houston Post,* n.d., and unidentified newspaper article, both in William A. Pitts Papers, Box 3C152, Center for American History, Univ. of Texas, Austin;

Special Orders No. 40, June 18, 1861, and Regimental Orders No. 20, Dec. 5, 1861, both in Burleson Collection; S. G. Davidson to Mary Davidson, June 17, 1861, in Davidson Papers.

10. S. G. Davidson to Mary Davidson, Mar. 10, 1861; Mary Davidson to S. G. Davidson, Mar. 29, 1861; Mary Davidson to S. G. Davidson, Apr. 7, 1861; Mary Davidson to S. G. Davidson, Apr. 9, 1861; S. G. Davidson to Mary Davidson, May 10, 1861; S. G. Davidson to Mary Davidson, May 21, 1861; S. G. Davidson to Mary Davidson, June 1, 1861; S. G. Davidson to Mary Davidson, June 7, 1861; and S. G. Davidson to Mary Davidson, June 17, 1861, all in Davidson Papers.

11. General Orders No. 13, Dept. of Texas, July 3, 1861; General Orders No. 22, Dept. of Texas, Oct. 17, 1861; and General Orders No. 17, Adjutant and Inspector General's Office, Richmond, Va., Nov. 7, 1861; all in Barry Orders.

12. General Orders No. 22, Dept. of Texas, Oct. 17, 1861; General Orders No. 17, Adjutant and Inspector General's Office, Richmond, Va., Nov. 7, 1861; General Orders No. 200, Dept. of Texas, Dec. 2, 1861; and General Orders No. 5, Dept. of Texas, Jan. 25, 1862; all in Barry Orders.

13. Burleson to Barry, Sept. 12 and 19, 1861; McCulloch to Barry, Feb. 7, 1862; Thomas C. Frost to Barry, Feb. 12, 1862; all in Barry Letters.

14. Proceedings and Evidence of Court-Martial, Apr. 14, 1862, Fort Mason, Tex., in Barry Orders; M323, Roll 4.

15. M323, Rolls 2–4.

16. Ibid.

17. Thomas W. Cutrer, *Ben McCulloch and the Frontier Military Tradition*, 38–39; Special Orders No. 40, June 18, 1861, and Regimental Orders No. 20, Dec. 5, 1861, both in Burleson Collection; Regimental Orders No. 12, July 13, 1861, in Barry Orders; Gautier, *Harder than Death*, 8.

18. General Orders No. 3, Confederate War Office, Jan. 3, 1862, in Barry Orders.

19. General Orders No. 19, Dept. of Texas, Sept. 18, 1861; Regimental Orders No. 20, Dec. 3, 1861; General Orders No. 3, Confederate War Dept., Jan. 9, 1862; all in Barry Orders.

20. Special Orders No. 40, June 18, 1861; Regimental Orders No. 12, July 13, 1861; General Orders No. 19, Dept. of Texas, Sept. 18, 1861; and Regimental Orders No. 20, Dec. 3, 1861; all in Barry Orders.

21. Regimental Orders No. 20, Dec. 3, 1861, in Barry Orders.

22. Burleson to Barry, Oct. 3, 1861, and McCulloch to Barry, Oct. 27, 1861, both in Barry Letters.

23. Burleson to Barry, Oct. 3, 1861, and McCulloch to Barry, Oct. 27, 1861, both in Barry Letters; Regimental Orders No. 12, July 13, 1861, in Barry Orders.

24. McCulloch to Barry, Nov. 27, 1861, in Barry Letters.

25. Ibid.

26. Travis Hill Ashby to Barry, Feb. 16, 1962, in Barry Letters.

27. General Orders No. 18, Results of Court Martial, Dept. of Texas, Nov. 18, 1861,

in Barry Orders; M323, Rolls 2–4; General Orders No. 7, Headquarters Troops in Texas, May 22, 1861, in M323, Roll 3.

28. James M. Hill to P. O. Hebert, Dec. 18 and 31, 1861, in M323, Rolls 2 and 3.

29. M323, Rolls 2 and 3.

30. M323, Rolls 2 and 3.

31. M323, Rolls 2 and 3; Special Orders No. 165, May 1, 1861, M323 Rolls 2 and 3; James Hill to Hebert, Nov. 31, 1861, in M323, Roll 3.

32. General Orders No. 18, Dept. of Texas, Nov. 18, 1861, in Barry Orders; Compiled Service Records, Erasmus G. Freeman; M323, Rolls 2 and 4.

33. General Orders No. 18, Dept. of Texas, Nov. 18, 1861, in Barry Orders.

34. M323, Rolls 2–4.

35. Ashby to Barry, Feb. 18, 1862, and Frost to Barry, Feb. 22, 1862, both in Barry Letters. Special Orders No. 18, 1st Regiment of Mounted Rifles, Mar. 18, 1862, in Barry Orders. Frost to Barry, Mar. 19, 1862; Ashby to Barry, Apr. 4, 1862; and Frost to Barry (3 letters), Apr. 11, 1862; all in Barry Letters.

36. Muster Rolls, 1st Regiment of Texas Cavalry; *OR*, vol. IV, 151–52; Handbill, Apr. 8, 1862, in McCulloch Collection, Greer, *Texas Ranger*, 145; M323, Rolls 3 and 4.

37. Muster Rolls, 1st Regiment of Texas Mounted Rifles, M323, Rolls 2–4; *OR*, vol. IV, 151–52; Handbill, TDS, Apr. 8, 1862, in McCulloch Collection; Greer, *Texas Ranger*, 145; M323, Rolls 3 and 4. These reports and muster rolls indicate the direct lineage of companies that remained on active duty and later formed the nucleus of the 1st Regiment of Texas Cavalry.

Chapter 5. "They Are Permanently Located in the Soil of the Country"

1. Handbill, Apr. 6, 1894, in McCulloch Collection; Ashcraft, *Texas in the Civil War*, 9–11. The 1860 U.S. Census lists a William Yager residing in Maverick County. The 28-year-old man came from Baden (now part of Germany) and listed his occupation as professional soldier.

2. Compiled Service Records, William O. Yager; Kuykendall Diary, 6.

3. Compiled Service Records, William O. Yager; Kuykendall Diary, 6.

4. Compiled Service Records, William O. Yager; Kuykendall Diary, 6; M323, Rolls 2–4, 1st Regiment Texas Mounted Rifles; Bill Winsor, *Texas in the Confederacy*, 9, 32–33.

5. Compiled Service Records, William O. Yager; M323, Rolls 2–4, 1st Regiment Texas Mounted Rifles; *OR*, vol. IX, 483–84; Duaine, *Dead Men Wore Boots*, 33–34; Winsor, *Texas in the Confederacy*, 9, 32–33; Kuykendall Diary, 6.

6. Kuykendall Diary, 4–5.

7. Compiled Service Records, William O. Yager.

8. Ibid.; *OR*, vol. IX, 604; Lester N. Fitzhugh, "Saluria, Fort Esperanza, and Military Operations of the Texas Coast, 1861–1864," 76–77.

9. *OR,* vol. IX, 603–604; Compiled Service Records, William O. Yager; Fitzhugh, "Saluria, Fort Esperanza," 76–79. Undoubtedly there were other skirmishes with Union landing parties, but none appeared in available records.

10. *OR,* vol. IX, 603–604; Compiled Service Records, William O. Yager; Fitzhugh, "Saluria, Fort Esperanza," 76–79.

11. Kuykendall Diary, 5–6; Compiled Service Records, William O. Yager; *OR,* vol. IX, 484, 486, vol. XL, 851; M323, Rolls 2–7; Yeary, *Reminiscences of Boys in Gray,* 365, 368–69. Company B, before joining Yager's battalion, made up part of the defense force at Camp Aransas.

12. Kuykendall Diary, 7–8; *OR,* vol. IX, 484, 486; M323, Rolls 5–7; Yeary, *Reminiscences of Boys in Gray,* 365, 368–69; J. I. Campbell, "Reminiscences of a Private Soldier," 67; Duaine, *Dead Men Wore Boots,* 33–34.

13. Kuykendall Diary, 8.

14. Ibid., 10; M323, Rolls 5–7.

15. J. I. Campbell, "Reminiscences of a Private Soldier," 67; Kuykendall Diary, 9; *OR,* vol. XXVI, pt. II, 51, 67–69; Yeary, *Reminiscences of Boys in Gray,* 365, 368–69; Tyler, *New Handbook of Texas,* 2:526–27.

16. J. I. Campbell, "Reminiscences of a Private Soldier," 67; Kuykendall Diary, 9; *Galveston Weekly Free Man's Press,* July 25, 1868; "E. J. Davis," *Corpus Christi Caller-Times,* Jan. 18, 1959; Ina McQuaid, "Texas Cavalry in Union Army," *Dallas Morning News,* Nov. 12, 1953; "Reconstruction Governor: Hated Texan Lies with War Heroes," *San Antonio Express,* Feb. 3, 1958; Lord, *Fremantle Diary,* 13; *OR,* vol. XXVI, pt. II, 51, 67–69; Yeary, *Reminiscences of Boys in Gray,* 365, 368–69; Wooster, *Texas and Texans,* 111–12; Tyler, *New Handbook of Texas,* 2:526–27.

17. Kuykendall Diary, 9–10.

Chapter 6. "The Blackest Crime in Texas Warfare"

1. M323, Rolls 2–7; Compiled Service Records, Joseph Taylor; Randolph B. Campbell, *A Southern Community in Crisis: Harrison County, Texas, 1850 to 1880,* 100, 162, 164; Yeary, *Reminiscences of Boys in Gray,* 341, 361–63, 580; "Extra," *Tyler (Tex.) Reporter,* July 21, 1862; *Victoria (Tex.) Weekly Advocate,* Jan. 17 and 24, 1903, in Lenz Collection.

2. Compiled Service Records, Joseph Taylor; Joseph Taylor, Surgeon, to Company Commanders, Oct. 26, 1861, in King Papers; Randolph B. Campbell, *Southern Community,* 100, 162, 164; Yeary, *Reminiscences of Boys in Gray,* 341, 361–63, 580; "Extra," *Tyler (Tex.) Reporter,* July 21, 1862; M323, Rolls 2–4.

3. Terry G. Jordan, *German Seed in Texas Soil: Immigrant Farmers in Nineteenth-Century Texas,* 180–85; James Marten, *Texas Divided: Loyalty and Dissent in the Lone Star State, 1856–1874,* 107; William Paul Burrier, "The Civil War in the Texas Hill Country: The Battle of the Nueces and the Bushwhacker War," ix;

Frank W. Heintzen, "Fredericksburg, Texas, during the Civil War and Recon-struction," 19–21, 28; M323, Rolls 5–7.

4. Van der Stucken Family Records, vertical files, Pioneer Museum Library, Fredericksburg, Tex.; Tyler, *New Handbook of Texas*, 1:1022; M323, Rolls 6–7. Van der Stucken resigned his commission on Nov. 9, 1864, and moved to Antwerp, Belgium, on Jan. 31, 1865. His son, Frank Valentin, showed signs of being a music prodigy, and the elder van der Stucken wanted his son to study with the masters in Brussels and Antwerp. Additionally, he feared for his family. He and his brother, like many prominent Confederate sympathizers near Fredericksburg, suffered reprisals from local Unionists. Several were killed or their homes burned by bushwhackers.

5. Heintzen, "Fredericksburg during the Civil War," 21, 24–27.

6. Schwartz, *Twenty-two Months a Prisoner*, 133–37, 149–54; Heintzen, "Fred-ericksburg during the Civil War," 21, 24–27; Van der Stucken to J. S. Slaughter, chief-of-staff, Dept. of Texas, Feb. 29, 1864, in M323, Roll 7; Davis Bitton, ed., *The Reminiscences and Civil War Letters of Levi Lamoni Wight*, 25–26, 119; Burrier, "Civil War in the Hill Country," 7; Kenn Knopp, "Fredericksburg, Texas: Capital of the German Hills," pt. 1, ch. 4, 3–4. Twenty-eight years after his imprisonment, Schwartz mistakenly identified van der Stucken as Captain Stockton. Stockton obviously was van der Stucken, as Schwartz knew that the captain led a company recruited from farmers near Fredericksburg and that many of them had voiced doubts concerning "the rebellion."

7. Schwartz, *Twenty-two Months a Prisoner*, 133–37, 149–54; Heintzen, "Fredericksburg during the Civil War," 21, 24–27; Van der Stucken to J. S. Slaughter, chief-of-staff, Dept. of Texas, Feb. 29, 1864, in M323, Roll 7; Bitton, *Reminiscences and Civil War Letters Wight*, 25–26, 119; Burrier, "Civil War in the Hill Country," 7; Knopp, "Fredericksburg, Texas," pt. 1, ch. 4, 3–4.   8. Compiled Service Records, Joseph Taylor; Yeary, *Reminiscences of Boys in Gray*, 341, 361–63, 746–47; Evans, *Confederate Military History*, 15:69.

9. Compiled Service Records, Joseph Taylor; *OR*, vol. XV, 851; Olmsted, *Journey Through Texas*, 156–57; Yeary, *Reminiscences of Boys in Gray*, 341, 361–63, 746–47; Evans, *Confederate Military History*, 15:69. General Orders No. 13, Dept. of Texas, July 3, 1861; General Orders No. 22, Dept. of Texas, Oct. 17, 1861; and General Orders No. 17, Adjutant and Inspector General's Office, Richmond, Va., Nov. 7, 1861, all three in Barry Orders.

10. Guido E. Ransleben, *A Hundred Years of Comfort in Texas: A Centennial History*, 104–105; Marten, *Texas Divided*, 107, 113–15; Compiled Service Records, Joseph Taylor; M323, Roll 7; Burrier, "Civil War in the Hill Country," 51–52; Knopp, "Fredericksburg, Texas," pt. 1, ch. 4, 4; Wooster, *Texas and Texans*, 114; Robert W. Shook, "Battle of the Nueces, August 10, 1862," 31; Ernest Wallace, *Texas in Turmoil: The Saga of Texas, 1849–1875*, 134.

11. Henry E. McCulloch to Texas Governor, Mar. 27, 1862, in State Adjutant General Correspondence, Texas State Archives, Austin; *OR*, vol IX, 701–702, 704–706, vol. LIII, 445–55; Ransleben, *Hundred Years of Comfort*, 105; Burrier, "Civil War in the Hill Country," 51–52; Knopp, "Fredericksburg, Texas," pt. 1, ch. 4, 4; Wooster, *Texas and Texans*, 114; Shook, "Battle of the Nueces," 31.

12. Bitton, *Reminiscences and Letters of Wight*, 24–25; E. W. Williams, ed., *With the Border Ruffians: Memories of the Far West, 1852–1868*, 230–35; M323, Rolls 5–7; Marten, *Texas Divided*, 114–15; Heintzen, "Fredericksburg during the Civil War," 44–45; Ransleben, *Hundred Years of Comfort*, 105–106; Burrier, "Civil War in the Hill Country," 96–96, 99–101; Shook, "Battle of the Nueces," 31–36; *OR*, vol. IX, 613–16, vol, LIII, 454–55.

13. Bitton, *Reminiscences and Letters of Wight*, 24–25; Williams, *With Border Ruffians*, 230–35; M323, Rolls 5–7; Marten, *Texas Divided*, 114–15; Heintzen, "Fredericksburg during the Civil War," 44–45; Ransleben, *Hundred Years of Comfort*, 105–106; Burrier, "Civil War in the Hill Country," 96–96, 99–101; Shook, "Battle of the Nueces," 31–36; *OR*, vol. IX, 613–16, vol, LIII, 454–55.

14. *OR*, vol. LIII, 454–55; Williams, *With Border Ruffians*, 230–35; Heintzen, "Fredericksburg during the Civil War," 46; Burrier, "Civil War in the Hill Country," 99–101; Shook, "Battle of the Nueces," 31–36; *OR*, vol. IX, 613–16; Yeary, *Reminiscences of Boys in Gray*, 362.

15. Ransleben, *Hundred Years of Comfort*, 87–88, 90, 106–107; Burrier, "Civil War in the Hill Country," 116–17, 127–28; Williams, *With Border Ruffians*, 239–53; *OR*, vol. IX, 616–17; M323, Rolls 5–7; Shook, "Battle of the Nueces," 33–42. Lieutenant Williams probably remained in camp near Fredericksburg in command of the rear detachment of Taylor's cavalry.

16. Williams, *With Border Ruffians*, 239–53; Ransleben, *Hundred Years of Comfort*, 91, 96–97, 107–108; Shook, "Battle of the Nueces," 33–42; Burrier, "Civil War in the Hill Country," 141–42, 185; Yeary, *Reminiscences of Boys in Gray*, 362; *OR*, vol. IX, 613–16.

17. *OR*, vol. IX, 613–16; Williams, *With Border Ruffians*, 239–53; Ransleben, *Hundred Years of Comfort*; 110; Shook, "Battle of the Nueces," 33–42; Burrier, "Civil War in the Hill Country," 138–42.

18. John W. Sansom, "The German Citizens Were Loyal to the Union," 12; Williams, *With Border Ruffians*, 239–53; Ransleben, *Hundred Years of Comfort*, 91, 97, 103, 109, 117; Shook, "Battle of the Nueces," 33–42; Burrier, "Civil War in the Hill Country," 143–47; *OR*, vol. IX, 613–16. John Sansom did not write his account until 1905; thus his recollections, like those of many others, may have become distorted over time.

19. Ransleben, *Hundred Years of Comfort*, 88, 91, 93, 97, 99, 110, 114–15; Burrier, "Civil War in the Hill Country," 147–49; *OR*, vol. IX, 613–16. Nine of those who abandoned their comrades in the camp later were apprehended and executed by state troops.

20. Williams, *With Border Ruffians*, 239–53; Ransleben, *Hundred Years of Comfort*, 97; Burrier, "Civil War in the Hill Country," 154–58; *OR*, vol. IX, 613–14. Several more Germans may have been with the horses and so escaped the final assaults. None of the several accounts of the battle is clear on this point.

21. Williams, *With Border Ruffians*, 239–53; Ransleben, *Hundred Years of Comfort*, 88, 92, 97, 99, 111–12; Burrier, "Civil War in the Hill Country," 150–59; *OR*, vol. IX, 613–16.

22. Williams, *With Border Ruffians*, 251; Ransleben, *Hundred Years of Comfort*, 88, 93–94, 112, 114; Burrier, "Civil War in the Hill Country," 169–70, 173–76; *OR*, vol. IX, 613–14. In his account of the period, Williams called Duff by the name "Dunn" and Lilly by the name "Luck," further confusing matters.

23. *OR*, vol. IX, 614–16; Williams, *With Border Ruffians*, 239–53; Ransleben, *Hundred Years of Comfort*, 79, 93, 113–15; Shook, "Battle of the Nueces," 42; Burrier, "Civil War in the Hill Country," 169, 175–84.

24. Ella Lonn, *Foreigners in the Confederacy*, 430; Don H. Biggers, *German Pioneers in Texas: A Brief History of Their Hardships, Struggles and Achievements*, 57–72; Ransleben, *Hundred Years of Comfort*, 90–98; Williams, *With Border Ruffians*, 239–53; Burrier, "Civil War in the Hill Country," 116, 117, 130, 156–58, 183–84; M323, Rolls 5–7; McCulloch to Capt. John R. King, May 16, 1861, in King Papers; *OR*, vol. IX, 616–17; Stephen B. Oates, *Confederate Cavalry West of the River*, 71–73.

25. Lonn, *Foreigners in the Confederacy*, 430; T. R. Fehrenbach, *Lone Star: A History of Texas and the Texans*, 363–64; Sansom, "German Citizens Were Loyal"; *OR*, vol. IX, 615–16; Williams, *With Border Ruffians*, 239–53; Ransleben, *Hundred Years of Comfort*, 112, 117–18; *San Antonio Herald*, Aug. 20, 1862, in Texana-Genealogy Dept., San Antonio Public Library, San Antonio, Tex.; *San Antonio Semi-Weekly News*, Aug. 25, 1862, in Texana-Genealogy Dept., San Antonio Public Library; Burrier, "Civil War in the Hill Country," 116, 117, 130, 156–58, 183–84.

26. *OR*, vol. IX, 615–16; Williams, *With Border Ruffians*, 239–53; Ransleben, *Hundred Years of Comfort*, 112, 117–18; *San Antonio Herald*, Aug. 20, 1862, in Texana-Genealogy Dept., San Antonio Public Library, San Antonio, Tex.; *San Antonio Semi-Weekly News*, Aug. 25, 1862, in Texana-Genealogy Dept., San Antonio Public Library; Burrier, "Civil War in the Hill Country," 116, 117, 130, 156–58, 183–84.

27. *OR*, vol. IX, 615–16, vol. LIII, 455; Williams, *With Border Ruffians*, 250–51; Ransleben, *Hundred Years of Comfort*, 88, 90; Burrier, "Civil War in the Hill Country," 169–70, 263–65.

28. Compiled Service Records, Joseph Taylor; Department Headquarters of Texas, New Mexico, and Arizona, Special Orders No. 127, May 2, 1863, in Muster Rolls, 1st Regiment of Texas Cavalry; Yeary, *Reminiscences of Boys in Gray*, 341, 361–63, 746–47; M323, Rolls 5–7; Ransleben, *Hundred Years of Comfort*, 93, 114.

29. Compiled Service Records, Joseph Taylor; Department Headquarters of Texas, New Mexico, and Arizona, Special Orders No. 127, May 2, 1863, in Muster Rolls, 1st Regiment of Texas Cavalry; Yeary, *Reminiscences of Boys in Gray*, 341, 361–63, 746–47; M323, Rolls 5–7; Ransleben, *Hundred Years of Comfort*, 93, 114.

30. Compiled Service Records, James N. Harris; M323, Roll 6.

31. Compiled Service Records, Joseph Taylor; Department Headquarters of Texas, New Mexico, and Arizona, Special Orders No. 127, May 2, 1863, in Muster Rolls, 1st Regiment of Texas Cavalry; Yeary, *Reminiscences of Boys in Gray*, 341, 361–63, 746–47; Bill Winsor, *Texas in the Confederacy*, 12. Carricitas Lake is spelled four different ways. "Carricitas" seems most prominent.

Chapter 7. Bullets, Beans, Stalwart Men, and Sturdy Steeds

1. Recruiting Officer to Augustus Buchel, May 25, 1861, in Lenz Collection; *OR*, vol. IV, 131; Evans, *Confederate Military History*, 15:56–69; Wooster, *Texas and Texans*, 31–32; Ashcraft, *Texas in the Civil War*, 9–11.

2. Evans, *Confederate Military History*, 15:56–69; M323, Rolls 2–7; Bowden, *Exodus of Federal Troops*, 73; Wooster, *Texas and Texans*, 31–32; Ashcraft, *Texas in the Civil War*, 9–11.

3. Albert Burton Moore, *Conscription and Conflict in the Confederacy*, 12–26, 52–113; Evans, *Confederate Military History*, 15:68; *Tyler (Tex.) Reporter*, June 11 and 24, 1862; Circular, Aug. 5, 1862, in McCulloch Collection.

4. Evans, *Confederate Military History*, 15:60, 68–69.

5. Ibid., 61; Joseph E. Chance, *The Second Texas Infantry from Shiloh to Vicksburg*, 179; Oates, *Confederate Cavalry*, 26–27; Wooster, *Texas and Texans*, 31.

6. Evans, *Confederate Military History*, 15:61; Chance, *Second Texas Infantry*, 179; Oates, *Confederate Cavalry*, 34–35, 51; M323, Rolls 5–7.

7. Muster Rolls, M323, Rolls 2–7, 1st Regiment of Texas Cavalry; *OR*, vol. IV, 106–107; Yeary, *Reminiscences of Boys in Gray*, 27, 258–59, 320, 340, 341, 343, 361, 580, 636, 746–47, 777; J. I. Campbell, "Reminiscences of a Private Soldier," 67; Harwell, *Destruction and Reconstruction*, 190; M323, Rolls 5–7.

8. M323, Rolls 5–7; Muster Rolls, 1st Regiment of Texas Cavalry; Lenz to Unknown, Apr. 12, 1862, in Lenz Collection.

9. Circular, Aug. 5, 1862, in McCulloch Collection; Oates, *Confederate Cavalry*, 48, 68.

10. Wiley, *Life of Johnny Reb*, 15–16; Buenger, *Secession and the Union*, 119–21.

11. Rudolph L. Biesele, *The German Settlements in Texas, 1831–1861*, 205–206; Marten, *Texas Divided*, 22, 106; Terry Jordan, *German Seed*, 180–84; Circular, Aug. 5, 1862, in McCulloch Collection; Harwell, *Destruction and Reconstruction*, 190.

12. Biesele, *German Settlements in Texas*, 205–206; Terry Jordan, *German Seed*, 180–84.

13. Marcus J. Wright, comp., *Texas in the War, 1861–1865*, 18–19, Wooster, *Texas and Texans*, 28–29; Oates, *Confederate Cavalry*, 9, 30, 51–52; Anne J. Bailey, *Between the Enemy and Texas: Parson's Texas Cavalry in the Civil War*, 29. A company

comprised the basic unit of the cavalry, which followed the infantry model. A full company called for 115 men and officers. A captain commanded the company, with 3 lieutenants, 9 noncommissioned officers (a first or orderly sergeant; 2d, 3rd, and 4th sergeants; and corporals), two musicians (fifer or bugler), and 100 privates.

14. *OR,* vol. XV, 851, vol. XXVI, pt. II, 564; M323, Rolls 2–7; Muster Rolls, 1st Regiment of Texas Cavalry; Oates, *Confederate Cavalry,* 51–52, 181, app. B.

15. Evans, *Confederate Military History,* 15:112–13; Oates, *Confederate Cavalry,* 56–57; M323, Rolls 2–7; Kuykendall Diary, 16, 36.

16. *OR,* vol. XV, 986–88, vol. LIII, pt. I, 870–71.

17. Olmsted, *Journey Through Texas,* 247; Don Worcester, *The Spanish Mustang: From the Plains of Andalusia to the Plains of Texas,* 39–42, 44–47, 54; Bowden, *Exodus of Federal Troops,* 30; Oates, *Confederate Cavalry,* 75–84.

18. Olmsted, *Journey Through Texas,* 247; Worcester, *Spanish Mustang,* 39–42, 44–47, 54; Bowden, *Exodus of Federal Troops,* 30; Oates, *Confederate Cavalry,* 75–84.

19. Olmsted, *Journey Through Texas,* 247; Worcester, *Spanish Mustang,* 39–42, 44–47, 54; Bowden, *Exodus of Federal Troops,* 30; Oates, *Confederate Cavalry,* 75–84.

20. M323, Rolls 2–7; Oates, *Confederate Cavalry,* 30, 62–66, 83; Cater, *As It Was,* 73.

21. M323, Rolls 2–7; Oates, *Confederate Cavalry,* 30, 62–66, 83; Cater, *As It Was,* 73.

22. Worcester, *Spanish Mustang,* 39–44; Lord, *Fremantle Diary,* 11; Bowden, *Exodus of Federal Troops,* 30–31; Oates, *Confederate Cavalry,* 80–84.

23. Worcester, *Spanish Mustang,* 39–44; Lord, *Fremantle Diary,* 11; Bowden, *Exodus of Federal Troops,* 30–31; Oates, *Confederate Cavalry,* 80–84.

24. M323, Rolls 2–7; *OR,* vol. LIII, pt. II, 641.

25. M323, Rolls 2–7; *OR,* vol. LIII, pt. II, 641.

26. Compiled Service Records, Henry E. McCulloch; Compiled Service Records, James A. White; *OR,* vol. LIII, pt. II, 641; Evans, *Confederate Military History,* 15:56; Cater, *As It Was,* 84–85. L. B. Northrop to John R. King, Sept. 4, 1861, and Mar. 5, 1862; and McCulloch to King, Dec. 19, 1861; all in King Papers. M323, Rolls 2–7.

27. Oates, *Confederate Cavalry,* 80–81; Cater, *As It Was,* 84; Lord, *Fremantle Diary,* 11; Winsor, *Texas in the Confederacy,* 84.

28. Bitton, *Reminiscences and Letters of Wight,* 23; Oates, *Confederate Cavalry,* 81–85; M323, Rolls 2–7; Evans, *Confederate Military History,* 15:113.

29. Oates, *Confederate Cavalry,* 81–85; Evans, *Confederate Military History,* 15:113.

30. Oates, *Confederate Cavalry,* 62–66; Evans, *Confederate Military History,* 15:55; Bowden, *Exodus of Federal Troops,* 6–25.

31. General Orders No. 40, May 17, 1862, in McCulloch Collection; M323, Rolls 2–7.

32. Ordnance Receipt, Sept. 22, 1862, in 1st Texas Cavalry Collection, Confederate Research Center, Hill Junior College, Hillsboro, Tex.; McCulloch to King, May 16, 1861, in King Papers; Evans, *Confederate Military History,* 15:116–17; Oates, *Confederate Cavalry,* 67–68, 79–81.

33. Evans, *Confederate Military History*, 15:116–17; Kuykendall Diary; Muster Rolls, 1st Texas Cavalry; P. S. Hagy, "Military Operations of the Lower Trans-Mississippi Dept., 1863–1864," 545; Oates, *Confederate Cavalry*, 67–68, 79–81; Cater, *As It Was*, 77. The report obviously was incomplete, given the number of revolvers reported. Previous receipts prove that the regiment carried a larger number of both Army and Navy model Colt revolvers. Additionally, privately owned weapons were not reported.

34. Evans, *Confederate Military History*, 15:116–17; Kuykendall Diary; Muster Rolls, 1st Texas Cavalry; Hagy, "Military Operations," 545; Oates, *Confederate Cavalry*, 67–68, 79–81; Cater, *As It Was*, 77; Charles S. Lee, "400 Guns," *Texas Gun Collector* (Fall, 1994): 70–73.

35. McCulloch to James Buckner Barry, Mar. 27, 1861, in Barry Letters; Robert L. Wilson, *Colt: An American Legend*, 16, 23, 27, 30, 45–47, 96–97, 104, 106; Alden Hatch, *Remington Arms in American History*, 356–57; M323, Rolls 2–7.

36. Cater, *As It Was*, 75, 77; M323, Rolls 2–7; Winsor, *Texas in the Confederacy*, 84.

37. M323, Rolls 2–7. Extracts are from several companies, but they indicate amounts of ammunition issued to company-sized units.

38. Cater, *As It Was*, 75, 77; M323, Rolls 2–7; Winsor, *Texas in the Confederacy*, 84.

39. M323, Rolls 2–7; *OR*, vol. XXXIV, pt. I, 354, 357, 369, 451–52, 567–68, 593–94, 607–608, 617; Harwell, *Destruction and Reconstruction*, 182–83; John W. Spencer, *Terrell's Texas Cavalry*, 1; Norman D. Brown, ed., *Journey to Pleasant Hill: The Civil War Letters of Captain Elijah P. Petty, Walker's Texas Division, CSA*, 405.

40. General Orders No. 6, June 11, 1862, in Compiled Service Records, Henry E. McCulloch; M323, Roll 3; Northrop to King, Nov. 26, 1861, in King Papers.

41. Special Orders No. 4, Headquarters San Antonio, Apr. 20, 1861; Chief of Commissary and Subsistence, Dept. of Texas, to Capt. John R. King, May 24, 1861; Special Orders No. 41, 1st Texas Mounted Rifles, June 18, 1861; Office of Chief Commissary, Dept. of Texas, to King, Aug. 10, 1861; D. C. Thomas to King, Oct. 29, 1861; W. L. Baylor to King, Nov. 5, 1862; Pvt. James O. Mills to King, Nov. 16, 1961; James H. Price to King, Dec. 7, 1861; and McCulloch to King, Dec. 21, 1861. All the above are in King Papers.

42. Cater, *As It Was*, 84; Oates, *Confederate Cavalry*, 55; Kuykendall Diary, 24.

43. Maj. Lackfield Mackin to King, May 24, 1861; Circular, Confederate War Dept., Richmond, Va., July, 1861; and McCulloch to King, Nov. 2, 1861, all three in King Papers. Oates, *Confederate Cavalry*, 55.

44. M323, Rolls 5 and 6.

45. Evans, *Confederate Military History*, 15:114; John D. Winters, *The Civil War in Louisiana*, 319, 322–23; Oates, *Confederate Cavalry*, 52–54.

46. Depot Quartermaster to Farmers and Planters, Oct. 2, 1863, in McCulloch Collection; Evans, *Confederate Military History*, 15:112, 15:114; Oates, *Confederate Cavalry*, 52, 54–56; Sherman, *Memoirs*, 882. San Antonio became the supply depot for Texas because the main trade and supply route for the western

Confederacy became the overland route from San Antonio to Matamoros, Mexico. The Mexican town contained several merchant houses that exchanged cotton for crucial war materiel. To safeguard this route, to control border violence, and to intercept Unionists and shirkers attempting to cross the Rio Grande, the Confederacy and Texas maintained troops along the supply routes and on the international border.

47. General Orders No. 6, June 11, 1862, in Compiled Service Records, Henry E. McCulloch; Cater, *As It Was,* 84; Rebecca W. Smith and Marion Mullins, eds., "The Diary of H. C. Medford, Confederate Soldier, 1864," 206–12; Oates, *Confederate Cavalry,* 55.

48. *OR,* vol. IV, pt. I, 126; Evans, *Confederate Military History,* 15:113; S. G. Davidson to Mary Davidson, Mar. 4, 1861, in Davidson Papers; Cater, *As It Was,* 73, Oates, *Confederate Cavalry,* 56–57; Winsor, *Texas in the Confederacy,* 85.

49. Lord, *Fremantle Diary,* 7–9, 35; Bitton, *Reminiscences and Letters of Wight,* 23; Quartermaster Receipts, 1st Texas Cavalry Collection, Confederate Research Center, Hill Junior College, Hillsboro, Texas; General Orders No. 4, Confederate War Dept., Jan. 24, 1862, in Barry Orders; Evans, *Confederate Military History,* 15:113; Oates, *Confederate Cavalry,* 56–57; Winsor, *Texas in the Confederacy,* 85.

50. Lord, *Fremantle Diary,* 7–9, 35; Bitton, *Reminiscences and Letters of Wight,* 23; Quartermaster Receipts, 1st Texas Cavalry Collection, Confederate Research Center, Hill Junior College, Hillsboro, Texas; General Orders No. 4, Confederate War Dept., Jan. 24, 1862, in Barry Orders; Evans, *Confederate Military History,* 15:113; Oates, *Confederate Cavalry,* 56–57; Winsor, *Texas in the Confederacy,* 85.

51. Lord, *Fremantle Diary,* 7–9, 35; Bitton, *Reminiscences and Letters of Wight,* 23; Quartermaster Receipts, 1st Texas Cavalry Collection, Confederate Research Center, Hill Junior College, Hillsboro, Texas; General Orders No. 4, Confederate War Dept., Jan. 24, 1862, in Barry Orders; Evans, *Confederate Military History,* 15:113; Oates, *Confederate Cavalry,* 56–57; Winsor, *Texas in the Confederacy,* 85.

52. McCulloch to Edward Burleson, Sept. 20, 1861, in Burleson Collection; Evans, *Confederate Military History,* 15:114; Oates, *Confederate Cavalry,* 56–57.

53. Regimental Orders No. 20, Dec. 5, 1861, in Burleson Collection; Muster Rolls, 1st Regiment of Texas Cavalry; General Orders No. 40, Headquarters, Trans-Mississippi Dept., n.d., in Compiled Service Records, James A. White; Certificate, Aug. 10, 1863, in 1st Texas Cavalry Collection, Confederate Research Center, Hill Junior College, Hillsboro, Tex.; Evans, *Confederate Military History,* 15:112.

54. Kuykendall Diary, 4–10; Cater, *As It Was,* 85, 130; Harwell, *Destruction and Reconstruction,* 183; Rebecca Smith and Mullins, "Diary of H. C. Medford," 211.

55. M323, Rolls 2–7; Yeary, *Reminiscences of Boys in Gray,* 636; Wooster, *Texas and*

Texans, 32; Bowden, *Exodus of Federal Troops,* 30; Harwell, *Destruction and Reconstruction,* 183; Duaine, *Dead Men Wore Boots,* 53.

Chapter 8. "A Gallant, Efficient, and Meritorious Officer"

1. Muster Rolls, 1st Regiment of Texas Cavalry; M323, Rolls 2–7.
2. Special Orders No. 127, May 2, 1863, in Muster Rolls, 1st Regiment of Texas Cavalry; Departmental [Texas] Headquarters to Headquarters, 1st Division, Goliad, July 2, 1863, 1st Regiment of Texas Cavalry, Muster Rolls; Evans, *Confederate Military History,* 15:54; Yeary, *Reminiscences of Boys in Gray,* 341, 361–63, 636, 746–47; Kuykendall Diary, 10–11.
3. J. I. Campbell, "Reminiscences of a Private Soldier," 67; Lt. Gov. Fletcher S. Stockdale, "Eulogy of Buchel," May 10, 1865, in Stockdale Collection; John Henry Brown to Unknown, n.d., in Brown Papers. According to letters written by Fletcher S. Stockdale, John Henry Brown, and others who knew him, Buchel had a mastery of English but spoke with an accent that made him somewhat self-conscious, so generally he spoke quietly.
4. Birth Certificate, Oct. 8, 1813, and Lenz to Unknown, Apr. 12, 1862, both in Lenz Collection; John Henry Brown to Unknown, n.d., in Brown Papers; Stockdale, "Eulogy of Buchel." Disagreements exist over the actual birth date and year—his birth certificate is dated October 8, but a translation from the French indicates that Buchel was born the day before. Buchel actually was a French citizen at birth. The area in which he was born, Canton of Oppenheim, Department of Mont-tonnerre, came under French control as a result of the treaty that ended the Thirty Years War. The Province of Hesse came into being while Buchel was a child.
5. "Augustus Buchel," *Victoria (Tex.) Weekly Advocate,* Jan. 17 and 24, 1903; Lenz to Unknown, Apr. 12, 1862; and Spanish Certificate, Feb. 1, 1838, all in Lenz Collection. Stockdale, "Eulogy of Buchel."
6. Lenz to Unknown, Apr. 12, 1862, and Visa, Letter of Transmit No. 461, Feb. 13, 1845, Embassy of Grand Duchy of Hessen, Royal Imperial Austrian Court, both in Lenz Collection; John Henry Brown to Unknown, n.d., in Brown Papers; "Augustus Buchel," *Victoria (Tex.) Weekly Advocate,* Jan. 17 and 24, 1903, in Lenz Collection; Stockdale, "Eulogy of Buchel."
7. Lenz to Unknown, Apr. 12, 1862, and Visa, Letter of Transmit No. 461, Feb. 13, 1845, Embassy of Grand Duchy of Hesse, Royal Imperial Austrian Court, both in Lenz Collection; John Henry Brown to Unknown, n.d., in Brown Papers; "Augustus Buchel," *Victoria (Tex.) Weekly Advocate,* Jan. 17 and 24, 1903, in Lenz Collection; Stockdale, "Eulogy of Buchel"; (French) Captains Colemann, Chazot, and Piteaux to French Ambassador to Spain, Mar. 20, 1845, and Naturalization Certificate, Sept. 27, 1852, both in Lenz Collection; Lord, *Fremantle Diary,* 16; Spencer, *Terrell's Texas Cavalry,* 72.

8. Augustus Buchel, Mexican War Service Records, National Archives and Record Service, Washington, D.C.; John Henry Brown to Unknown, n.d., in Brown Papers; Stockdale, "Eulogy of Buchel"; "Augustus Buchel," *Victoria (Tex.) Weekly Advocate,* Jan. 17 and 24, 1903, in Lenz Collection; Biesele, *German Settlements in Texas,* 193–94.

9. John Henry Brown to Unknown, n.d., in Brown Papers; Stockdale, "Eulogy of Buchel"; "Augustus Buchel," *Victoria (Tex.) Weekly Advocate,* Jan. 17 and 24, 1903, in Lenz Collection.

10. Stockdale to Buchel, Jan. 31, 1860, in Lenz Collection; John Henry Brown to Unknown, n.d., in Brown Papers; Stockdale, "Eulogy of Buchel"; "Augustus Buchel," *Indianola (Tex.) Bulletin,* n.d., in Lenz Collection.

11. Stockdale, "Eulogy of Buchel"; Receipt, Stockdale to H. Runge, Mar. 28, 1861, in Stockdale Collection; Gov. Edward Clark to Buchel, Apr. 7, 1861, in Lenz Collection; Wooster, *Texas and Texans,* 24–27.

12. Texas State Certificate, Apr. 18, 1861; State Adjutant General to Buchel, May 25, 1861; and State Adjutant General to Buchel, July 11, 1861 [Buchel is referred to as colonel]; all in Lenz Collection.

13. Compiled Service Records, Augustus Buchel; Evans, *Confederate Military History,* 15:54, 56; *OR,* vol. IV, 116–17, 164–65; Allan C. Ashcraft, "Fort Brown, Texas, in 1861," 243–44.

14. General Orders No. 28, in *OR,* vol. XV, 986–88; Ashcraft, "Fort Brown, Texas," 243–44.

15. *OR,* vol. IV, 149–52; *OR,* ser. II, vol. II, 1407–1408.

16. *OR,* vol. IV, 151–55, 164–66; Buchel to Don Albino López, in *OR,* vol. XV, 924; Compiled Service Records, Augustus Buchel.

17. *OR,* vol. XXVI, pt. II, 72–73, 99, 165; Regimental Return, Aug., 1863, in Muster Rolls, 1st Regiment of Texas Cavalry; Kuykendall Diary, 10.

18. *OR,* vol. XXVI, pt. II, 72–73, 99, 165; Regimental Return, Aug., 1863, in Muster Rolls, 1st Regiment of Texas Cavalry; Kuykendall Diary, 10.

19. Kuykendall Diary, 11; M323, Roll 6.

20. *OR,* vol. XXVI, pt. II, 72–63, 99, 165; Regimental Return, Aug., 1863, in Muster Rolls, 1st Regiment of Texas Cavalry.

21. Kuykendall Diary, 11–12.

22. David C. Edmonds, *Yankee Autumn in Acadiana: A Narrative of the Great Texas Overland Expedition through Southwestern Louisiana, October–December, 1863,* 3–5; *OR,* vol. XXVI, pt. II, 333; Harwell, *Destruction and Reconstruction,* 180; Robert Underwood Johnson and Clarence Clough Buel, eds., *Battles and Leaders of the Civil War,* rev. ed., 4:345–46; Tyler, *New Handbook of Texas,* 2:692–93; Winsor, *Texas in the Confederacy,* 131–32; Ludwell H. Johnson, *Red River Campaign: Politics and Cotton in the Civil War,* 37.

23. Richard Lowe, *The Texas Overland Expedition of 1863,* 31; Edmonds, *Yankee Autumn,* 6; *OR,* vol. XXVI, pt. II, 333; Harwell, *Destruction and Reconstruction,*

180; Robert Johnson and Buel, *Battles and Leaders,* 4:346; Winsor, *Texas in the Confederacy,* 131–32.

24. Kuykendall Diary, 13; M323, Rolls 5–7.

25. Kuykendall Diary, 13–14.

26. Bitton, *Reminiscences and Letters of Wight,* 128–29; Kuykendall Diary, 14.

27. *OR,* vol. XXVI, pt. II, 247–48, 281; Hagy, "Military Operations," 545.

28. *OR,* vol. XXVI, pt. II, 333, 336–37.

29. Ibid.; Kuykendall Diary, 14; M323, Rolls 5–7; Winters, *Civil War in Louisiana,* 320–21.

30. Kuykendall Diary, 15; *OR,* vol. XXVI, pt. II, 333, 336–37.

31. *OR,* vol. XXVI, pt. II, 346–47, 350.

32. Kuykendall Diary, 15.

33. Ibid.

34. *OR,* vol. XXVI, pt. II, 345–46; *OR,* vol. LIII, 902.

35. Bitton, *Reminiscences and Letters of Wight,* 130–34; *OR,* vol. XXVI, pt. II, 345–46; *OR,* vol. LIII, 902.

36. Bitton, *Reminiscences and Letters of Wight,* 130–34; Kuykendall Diary, 15–16; *OR,* vol. XXVI, pt. II, 318–21; *OR,* vol. LIII, 902.

37. Bitton, *Reminiscences and Letters of Wight,* 130–34; Kuykendall Diary, 15–16; *OR,* vol. XXVI, pt. II, 318–21, 345–46; *OR,* vol. LIII, 902.

38. Bitton, *Reminiscences and Letters of Wight,* 130–34; Kuykendall Diary, 15–16; *OR,* vol. XXVI, pt. II, 318–21, 345–46; *OR,* vol. LIII, 902.

39. *OR,* vol. XXVI, pt. II, 318–21, 345–46; *OR,* vol. LIII, 902.

40. *OR,* vol. XXVI, pt. II, 318–21, 345–46; *OR,* vol. LIII, 902.

41. *OR,* vol XXVI, pt. II, 318–21, 345–46; *OR,* vol. LIII, 351, 361, 363, 366–67; Edmonds, *Yankee Autumn,* 114–15.

42. *OR,* vol. XXVI, pt. II, 318–21, 345–46; *OR,* vol. LIII, 351, 361, 363, 366–67.

43. *OR,* vol. XXVI, pt. II, 318–21, 345–46; *OR,* vol. LIII, 351, 361, 363, 366–67.

44. Kuykendall Diary, 15; Bitton, *Reminiscences and Letters of Wight,* 135–36; Muster Rolls, 1st Regiment of Texas Cavalry; Compiled Service Records, William O. Yager; Compiled Service Records, Joseph Taylor; Compiled Service Records, Robert A. Myers; M323, Rolls 5–7; *OR,* vol. XXVI, pt. II, 361, 370, 376. The regimental returns for October also list five artillery pieces as absent from the regiment. Departmental records and regimental returns contradict one another—the departmental records list ten companies present, while the regimental returns record only five. Yager's records prove that he was at Brownsville, but his battalion must have been at Niblett's Bluff, as indicated by the presence of some of his company commanders (Beaumont, for example).

45. Kuykendall Diary, 15; Bitton, *Reminiscences and Letters of Wight,* 135–36; Muster Rolls, 1st Regiment of Texas Cavalry; Compiled Service Records, William O. Yager; Compiled Service Records, Joseph Taylor; Compiled Service Records, Robert A. Myers; M323, Rolls 5–7; *OR,* vol. XXVI, pt. II, 361, 370, 376.

46. Edmonds, *Yankee Autumn*, 214–15, 236, 251–53, 272–95; Lowe, *Texas Overland Expedition*, 48–62; *OR*, vol. XXVI, pt. II, 370, 379–80, 390.

47. Lowe, *Texas Overland Expedition*, 63–79, 80–100, 108; Edmonds, *Yankee Autumn*, 251–52, 272–95; *OR*, vol XXVI, pt. II, 390–92, 400, 415; Wooster, *Texas and Texans*, 93–94; John Henry Brown, *History of Texas from 1685 to 1892*, 2:424; Winsor, *Texas in the Confederacy*, 132.

48. *OR*, vol. XXVI, pt. II, 370, 379–80, 390; Winsor, *Texas in the Confederacy*, 132.

49. *OR*, vol. XXVI, pt. II, 370, 379–80, 390; Edmonds, *Yankee Autumn*, 392–93; Winsor, *Texas in the Confederacy*, 132; Robert Johnson and Buel, *Battles and Leaders*, 4:346; Wooster, *Texas and Texans*, 91.

50. *OR*, vol. XXVI, pt. II, 370, 379–80, 390; Edmonds, *Yankee Autumn*, 392–93; Winsor, *Texas in the Confederacy*, 132; Robert Johnson and Buel, *Battles and Leaders*, 4:346; Wooster, *Texas and Texans*, 91.

Chapter 9. "With Minnié Balls Flying"

1. M323, Rolls 2–7; *OR*, vol. XXVI, pt. II, 407, 436, 467, 473, 500, 509.

2. Kuykendall Diary, 16; Duaine, *Dead Men Wore Boots*, 47; *OR*, vol. XXVI, pt. II, 407, 436, 467, 473, 500, 509; M323, Rolls 5–7.

3. Kuykendall Diary, 16.

4. *OR*, vol. XXVI, pt. II, 407, 436, 467, 473, 500, 509; M323, Rolls 5–7.

5. Kuykendall Diary, 16; Duaine, *Dead Men Wore Boots*, 47; *OR*, vol. XXVI, pt. II, 407, 436, 467, 473, 500, 509; M323, Rolls 5–7.

6. *OR*, vol. XXVI, pt. II, 436, 467, 473, 500, 509.

7. *OR*, vol. XXVI, pt. II, 527; Winsor, *Texas in the Confederacy*, 133.

8. *OR*, vol. XXVI, pt. II, 527; Winsor, *Texas in the Confederacy*, 133.

9. Kuykendall Diary, 16; Bitton, *Reminiscences and Letters of Wight*, 30; *OR*, vol. XXVI, pt. II, 481–85.

10. Kuykendall Diary, 16; Bitton, *Reminiscences and Letters of Wight*, 30; *OR*, vol. XXVI, pt. II, 481–85.

11. Kuykendall Diary, 16; Bitton, *Reminiscences and Letters of Wight*, 30; *OR*, vol. XXVI, pt. II, 481–85.

12. Kuykendall Diary, 16–17; *OR*, vol. XXVI, pt. II, 481–85.

13. Kuykendall Diary, 16–17; Winsor, *Texas in the Confederacy*, 133; *OR*, vol. XXVI, pt. II, 481–85.

14. *OR*, vol. XXVI, pt. II, 481–86.

15. Ibid.; Kuykendall Diary, 17; Winsor, *Texas in the Confederacy*, 133. Accounts of the sizes of the opposing forces disagree. Estimates of the Confederates range from 60 to 1,000 and of the Union from 100 to over 300. In any case, the action must have been heavy, as Colonel Hesseltine won the Medal of Honor for his participation in it.

16. Kuykendall Diary, 17–18; Winsor, *Texas in the Confederacy,* 133–34; *OR,* vol. XXIV, pt. II, 815.

17. Kuykendall Diary, 17–18; Winsor, *Texas in the Confederacy,* 133–34; *OR,* vol. XXIV, pt. II, 815.

18. Bitton, *Reminiscences and Letters of Wight,* 30; Kuykendall Diary, 17; Morning Reports, 1st Regiment of Texas Cavalry, in Muster Rolls; *OR,* vol. XXVI, pt. II, 564; *OR,* vol. XXIV, pt. II, 837, 839; Winsor, *Texas in the Confederacy,* 134; M323, Rolls 5–7. Compiled Service Records show several men sick in the hospital and some deaths, but surviving records officially attribute only three deaths to measles.

19. Bitton, *Reminiscences and Letters of Wight,* 30; Kuykendall Diary, 17; Morning Reports, 1st Regiment of Texas Cavalry, in Muster Rolls; *OR,* vol. XXVI, pt. II, 564; *OR,* vol. XXIV, pt. II, 837, 839; Winsor, *Texas in the Confederacy,* 134; M323, Rolls 5–7.

20. Kuykendall Diary, 17–18.

21. *OR,* vol. XXIV, pt. II, 899, 913–16, 932; Winsor, *Texas in the Confederacy,* 134.

22. *OR,* vol. XXIV, pt. II, 899, 913–16, 932; Winsor, *Texas in the Confederacy,* 134.

23. *OR,* vol. XXIV, pt. II, 1003, 1004, 1006.

24. *OR,* vol. XXIV, pt. II, 638–39; Winsor, *Texas in the Confederacy,* 134; Evans, *Confederate Military History,* 15:123; M323, Rolls 5–7.

25. Evans, *Confederate Military History,* 15:119–20; *OR,* vol. XXIV, pt. II, 1004; Ludwell H. Johnson, *Red River Campaign,* 45–48; John Henry Brown, *History of Texas,* 2:424.

Chapter 10. "Our Time Is at Hand"

1. James K. Ewer, *The Third Massachusetts Cavalry in the War for the Union,* 142; Ludwell H. Johnson, *Red River Campaign,* 118; Harwell, *Destruction and Reconstruction,* 182–89; T. Michael Parrish, *Richard Taylor: Soldier Prince of Dixie,* 317–18; Winters, *Civil War in Louisiana,* 329.

2. *OR,* vol. XXXIV, pt. I, 606, 635–36, vol. XXIV, pt. II, 1004; Robert Johnson and Buel, *Battles and Leaders,* 4:345–47, 4:349–60; Evans, *Confederate Military History,* 15:119–20; John Henry Brown, *History of Texas,* 424; Sherman, *Memoirs,* 424–26; Winters, *Civil War in Louisiana,* 325–26; Ludwell H. Johnson, *Red River Campaign,* 4, 5, 100, 120–21. Sherman had hoped to lead the expedition, as he had taught at the Louisiana Seminary of Learning at Alexandria before the war. In the end, however, he loaned Banks A. J. Smith's corps of 10,000 men for 30 days, although Smith's men were not returned in the time agreed upon.

3. [John Tyler] Webb Diary, 7; Robert Johnson and Buel, *Battles and Leaders,* 4:345–47, 349–50; Ludwell H. Johnson, *Red River Campaign,* 100, 120–21.

4. Parrish, *Richard Taylor*, 319–20; Ludwell H. Johnson, *Red River Campaign*, 4, 5, 100, 120–21; Robert Johnson and Buel, *Battles and Leaders*, 4:345–47, 4:349–50; Evans, *Confederate Military History*, 15:119–20; John Henry Brown, *History of Texas*, 2:424; Sherman, *Memoirs*, 424–26; Edwin C. Bearss, ed., *A Louisiana Confederate: Diary of Felix Pierre Poche*, 95, 97; Winters, *Civil War in Louisiana*, 325–26.

5. Webb Diary, 7; *OR*, vol. XXXIV, pt. I, 358; Ewer, *Third Massachusetts Cavalry*, 133, 137; Robert Johnson and Buel, *Battles and Leaders*, 4:350–51; Ludwell H. Johnson, *Red River Campaign*, 115–17, 125; Winters, *Civil War in Louisiana*, 334–35, 337–38.

6. *OR*, vol. XXXIV, pt. I, 358; Ewer, *Third Massachusetts Cavalry*, 133, 137; Robert Johnson and Buel, *Battles and Leaders*, 4:350–51; Ludwell H. Johnson, *Red River Campaign*, 115–17, 125; Winters, *Civil War in Louisiana*, 334–35, 337–38.

7. Evans, *Confederate Military History*, 15:205; *OR*, vol. XXIV, pt. I, 449–50, 562–63, 607; M323, Rolls 5–7; Bitton, *Reminiscences and Letters of Wight*, 150, 157; Xavier Blanchard DeBray, "A Sketch of DeBray's 26th Regiment of Texas Cavalry," 153; Rebecca Smith and Mullins, "Diary of H. C. Medford," 211–12; Bearss, *Louisiana Confederate*, 103; Harwell, *Destruction and Reconstruction*, 191–92; Parrish, *Richard Taylor*, 337; Robert Johnson and Buel, *Battles and Leaders*, 4:369–70; Ludwell H. Johnson, *Red River Campaign*, 116, 119–20; Winters, *Civil War in Louisiana*, 327; Wooster, *Texas and Texans*, 139; Spencer, *Terrell's Texas Cavalry*, 13. All of the 1st Texas Cavalry did not join Bee's brigade. Magruder had sent Capt. James A. Ware and an undetermined number of his men to Fort Duncan, near Eagle Pass, to search for deserters. Although he had orders from Buchel to join the regiment as soon as possible, Ware and his detachment remained near Eagle Pass until at least August, 1864. Ludwell H. Johnson makes the same error as Ella Lonn and many others, asserting that the 1st Regiment of Texas Cavalry was a German regiment. Although many members of the regiment were of German descent, the majority were not of German origin.

8. Webb Diary, 8; Bitton, *Reminiscences and Letters of Wight*, 31, 152–53; *OR*, vol. XXXIV, pt. I, 449–59, 562–63, 607; Evans, *Confederate Military History*, 15:205; Harwell, *Destruction and Reconstruction*, 191–92; Ludwell H. Johnson, *Red River Campaign*, 124–25; Ewer, *Third Massachusetts Cavalry*, 143.

9. Evans, *Confederate Military History*, 15:205; *OR*, vol. XXXIV, pt. I, 562–63, 607; Harwell, *Destruction and Reconstruction*, 192; Rebecca Smith and Mullins, "Diary of H. C. Medford," 214–15; Spencer, *Terrell's Texas Cavalry*, 13.

10. Evans, *Confederate Military History*, 15:205; *OR*, vol. XXXIV, pt. I, 562–63, 607; Harwell, *Destruction and Reconstruction*, 192; Rebecca Smith and Mullins, "Diary of H. C. Medford," 214–15; Spencer, *Terrell's Texas Cavalry*, 13.

11. *OR*, vol. XXIV, pt. I, 450–52, 607–608; Harwell, *Destruction and Reconstruction*, 192; Evans, *Confederate Military History*, 13:128, 13:135–36; Robert Johnson and

Buel, *Battles and Leaders,* 4:353; Winters, *Civil War in Louisiana,* 341; Ewer, *Third Massachusetts Cavalry,* 144; Spencer, *Terrell's Texas Cavalry,* 13–14.

12. Bitton, *Reminiscences and Letters of Wight,* 32; Ewer, *Third Massachusetts Cavalry,* 144; Winters, *Civil War in Louisiana,* 341.

13. Bitton, *Reminiscences and Letters of Wight,* 32; Ewer, *Third Massachusetts Cavalry,* 144; Winters, *Civil War in Louisiana,* 341.

14. *OR,* vol. XXXIV, pt. 1, 330, 563, 606; Evans, *Confederate Military History,* 13:135–36, 15:133, 15:201; Ewer, *Third Massachusetts Cavalry,* 146; Robert Johnson and Buel, *Battles and Leaders,* 4:352; Harwell, *Destruction and Reconstruction,* 192–95; DeBray, "DeBray's 26th Regiment," 157–60; Winters, *Civil War in Louisiana,* 339–40.

15. *OR,* vol. XXIV, pt. I, 563, 606; Evans, *Confederate Military History,* 13:135–36, 15:133, 15:201; Robert Johnson and Buel, *Battles and Leaders,* 4:352; Harwell, *Destruction and Reconstruction,* 192–95; DeBray, "DeBray's 26th Regiment," 157–60; Winters, *Civil War in Louisiana,* 339–40; Parrish, *Richard Taylor,* 341; Spencer, *Terrell's Texas Cavalry,* 16–17.

16. Muster Rolls, 1st Texas Regiment of Texas Cavalry; *OR,* vol. XXXIV, pt. I, 452–53, 476, 564–65, 607; Evans, *Confederate Military History,* 13:135–36, 15:201–202; Harwell, *Destruction and Reconstruction,* 197–99; Yeary, *Reminiscences of Boys in Gray,* 258–59; Winters, *Civil War in Louisiana,* 340–42; Duaine, *Dead Men Wore Boots,* 54–55; Bearss, *Louisiana Confederate,* 106; Parrish, *Richard Taylor,* 341–42; Spencer, *Terrell's Texas Cavalry,* 18, 166; Robert Johnson and Buel, *Battles and Leaders,* 4:353, 4:367.

17. Bitton, *Reminiscences and Letters of Wight,* 30–32; *OR,* vol. XXXIV, pt. I, 563, 606; Evans, *Confederate Military History,* 13:135–36, 15:133, 15:201; Harwell, *Destruction and Reconstruction,* 192–95; Alvin M. Josephy, Jr., *The Civil War in the American West,* 201; Spencer, *Terrell's Texas Cavalry,* 16–17.

18. Muster Rolls, 1st Regiment of Texas Cavalry; *OR,* vol. XXXIV, pt. I, 452–53, 476, 564–65, 607; Robert Johnson and Buel, *Battles and Leaders,* 4:353; Evans, *Confederate Military History,* 13:135–36, 15:201–202; Harwell, *Destruction and Reconstruction,* 197–99; Bearss, *Louisiana Confederate,* 107; Yeary, *Reminiscences of Boys in Gray,* 258–59; Parrish, *Richard Taylor,* 343–44, 346; Winters, *Civil War in Louisiana,* 342–43.

19. Muster Rolls, 1st Regiment of Texas Cavalry; *OR,* vol. XXXIV, pt. I, 452–53, 476, 564–65, 607; Evans, *Confederate Military History,* 13:135–36, 15:201–202; Harwell, *Destruction and Reconstruction,* 197–99; Yeary, *Reminiscences of Boys in Gray,* 258–59; Winters, *Civil War in Louisiana,* 342–43.

20. Ewer, *Third Massachusetts Cavalry,* 148–49; Peter Biegel, *History of the Second Battalion, Duryee Zouaves, 165th Regiment, New York Volunteer Infantry,* 26–27; Muster Rolls, 1st Regiment of Texas Cavalry; *OR,* vol. XXXIV, pt. I, 453, 476, 564–65, 606–607; Evans, *Confederate Military History,* 15:201–202; Harwell, *Destruction and Reconstruction,* 197–99; Yeary, *Reminiscences of Boys in Gray,* 258–59; Winters, *Civil War in Louisiana,* 343.

21. Rebecca Smith and Mullins, "Diary of H. C. Medford," 218; Ludwell H. Johnson, *Red River Campaign*, 136–37; Ewer, *Third Massachusetts Cavalry*, 148–49; Muster Rolls, 1st Regiment of Texas Cavalry; *OR*, vol. XXXIV, pt. I, 452–53, 476, 564–65, 607; Evans, *Confederate Military History*, 13:135–36, 15:201–202; DeBray, "DeBray's 26th Regiment," 158; Harwell, *Destruction and Reconstruction*, 197–99; Robert Johnson and Buel, *Battles and Leaders*, 4:353.

22. Ludwell H. Johnson, *Red River Campaign*, 137–38; Yeary, *Reminiscences of Boys in Gray*, 627; *OR*, vol. XXXIV, pt I, 330, 452–53, 476, 564–65, 607; Evans, *Confederate Military History*, 13:135–36, 15:201–202; DeBray, "DeBray's 26th Regiment," 158; Winters, *Civil War in Louisiana*, 344–45; Ewer, *Third Massachusetts Cavalry*, 150–52; Spencer, *Terrell's Texas Cavalry*, 18; Parrish, *Richard Taylor*, 349.

23. Ludwell H. Johnson, *Red River Campaign*, 137–38; Yeary, *Reminiscences of Boys in Gray*, 258–59, 746–47; *OR*, vol. XXIV, pt. I, 330, 452–53, 476, 564–65, 607; Evans, *Confederate Military History*, 13:135–36, 15:201–202; Ewer, *Third Massachusetts Cavalry*, 151–53; Parrish, *Richard Taylor*, 350–52; *OR*, vol. XXXIV, pt. I, 476, 564–65, 606–607; DeBray, "DeBray's 26th Regiment," 158; Harwell, *Destruction and Reconstruction*, 197–99; Winters, *Civil War in Louisiana*, 345–46; Ewer, *Third Massachusetts Cavalry*, 150–52; Spencer, *Terrell's Texas Cavalry*, 18; Parrish, *Richard Taylor*, 349.

24. Ludwell H. Johnson, *Red River Campaign*, 138–40; Yeary, *Reminiscences of Boys in Gray*, 258–59, 746–57; Rebecca Smith and Mullins, "Diary of H. C. Medford," 218–19; Ewer, *Third Massachusetts Cavalry*, 151–53; Parrish, *Richard Taylor*, 350–52; *OR*, vol. XXIV, pt. I, 476, 564–65, 606–607; Robert Johnson and Buel, *Battles and Leaders*, 4:354, 4:367; Evans, *Confederate Military History*, 15:201–202; Harwell, *Destruction and Reconstruction*, 164, 197–99; DeBray, "DeBray's 26th Regiment," 157–58; M323, Rolls 5–7; Winters, *Civil War in Louisiana*, 345–46; Josephy, *Civil War in the West*, 205–206.

25. Ludwell H. Johnson, *Red River Campaign*, 138–40; Yeary, *Reminiscences of Boys in Gray*, 258–59, 746–57; Rebecca Smith and Mullins, "Diary of H. C. Medford," 218–19; Ewer, *Third Massachusetts Cavalry*, 151–53; Parrish, *Richard Taylor*, 350–52; *OR*, vol. XXIV, pt. I, 476, 564–65, 606–607; Robert Johnson and Buel, *Battles and Leaders*, 4:354, 4:367; Evans, *Confederate Military History*, 15:201–202; Harwell, *Destruction and Reconstruction*, 164, 197–99; DeBray, "DeBray's 26th Regiment," 157–58; M323, Rolls 5–7; Winters, *Civil War in Louisiana*, 345–46; Josephy, *Civil War in the West*, 205–206.

26. Bitton, *Reminiscences and Letters of Wight*, 32; Yeary, *Reminiscences of Boys in Gray*, 258–59, 746–57; *OR*, vol. XXIV, pt. I, pp., 476, 564–65, 606–607; Robert Johnson and Buel, *Battles and Leaders*, 4:354, 4:367; Evans, *Confederate Military History*, 15:201–202; DeBray, "DeBray's 26th Regiment," 157–58; M323, Rolls 5–7; Spencer, *Terrell's Texas Cavalry*, 18, 166.

27. Rebecca Smith and Mullins, "Diary of H. C. Medford," 220–21; Kuykendall

Diary, 20; Yeary, *Reminiscences of Boys in Gray,* 746–47; Ludwell H. Johnson, *Red River Campaign,* 152–53; *OR,* vol. XXXIV, pt. I, 565–67, 607–608; Harwell, *Destruction and Reconstruction,* 198–99; Hamilton P. Bee, "Battle of Pleasant Hill—An Error Corrected," *Southern Historical Society Papers* 8 (1880): 184; Robert Johnson and Buel, *Battles and Leaders,* 4:354; Spencer, *Terrell's Texas Cavalry,* 33.

28. Bitton, *Reminiscences and Letters of Wight,* 153; DeBray, "DeBray's 26th Regiment," 158; Yeary, *Reminiscences of Boys in Gray,* 746–47; Ludwell H. Johnson, *Red River Campaign,* 146 and 147; *OR,* vol. XXIV, pt. I, 565–67, 607–608; Harwell, *Destruction and Reconstruction,* 198–99; Bee, "Battle of Pleasant Hill," 184–85; Winters, *Civil War in Louisiana,* 348; Spencer, *Terrell's Texas Cavalry,* 33.

29. Yeary, *Reminiscences of Boys in Gray,* 746–47; Ludwell H. Johnson, *Red River Campaign,* 148–50; *OR,* vol. XXXIV, pt. I, 353, 565–67, 607–608; Harwell, *Destruction and Reconstruction,* 198–99; Spencer, *Terrell's Texas Cavalry,* 33.

30. Ludwell H. Johnson, *Red River Campaign,* 148–50; *OR,* vol. XXXIV, pt. I, 353, 565–67, 607–608; Spencer, *Terrell's Texas Cavalry,* 33; Harwell, *Destruction and Reconstruction,* 198–99; Robert Johnson and Buel, *Battles and Leaders,* 4:354–55.

31. Yeary, *Reminiscences of Boys in Gray,* 746–47; Ludwell H. Johnson, *Red River Campaign,* 154–56; *OR,* vol. XXXIV, pt. I, 565–67, 607–608; Harwell, *Destruction and Reconstruction,* 198–99; Spencer, *Terrell's Texas Cavalry,* 33–34; Josephy, *Civil War in the West,* 206–207.

32. *OR,* vol. XXIV, pt. I, 353–55, 452, 566–67, 608; Evans, *Confederate Military History,* 15:203–204; Harwell, *Destruction and Reconstruction,* 199–200; Ludwell H. Johnson, *Red River Campaign,* 155–56.

33. Bitton, *Reminiscences and Letters of Wight,* 32; Robert Johnson and Buel, *Battles and Leaders,* 4:355; *OR,* vol. XXXIV, pt. I, 353–55, 452, 566–67, 608; Evans, *Confederate Military History,* 15:203–204; Harwell, *Destruction and Reconstruction,* 199–200; Ludwell H. Johnson, *Red River Campaign,* 155–56.

34. Yeary, *Reminiscences of Boys in Gray,* 361–63, 746–47; Bitton, *Reminiscences and Letters of Wight,* 32–33; Compiled Service Records, Augustus Buchel; *OR,* vol. XXXIV, pt. I, 357, 369, 451–52, 567–568, 607–608, 617; Evans, *Confederate Military History,* 13:204–205; Harwell, *Destruction and Reconstruction,* 190, 204; Norman D. Brown, *Journey to Pleasant Hill,* 405–406; M323, Roll 5; Robert Johnson and Buel, *Battles and Leaders,* 4:355, 4:371–72.

35. Norman D. Brown, *Journey to Pleasant Hill,* 405–406; Yeary, *Reminiscences of Boys in Gray,* 362–63, 746–47; Ludwell H. Johnson, *Red River Campaign,* 156; Parrish, *Richard Taylor,* 359; *OR,* vol. XXXIV, pt. I, 354, 357, 369, 451–52, 567–68, 607–608, 617; Evans, *Confederate Military History,* 13:204–205; Harwell, *Destruction and Reconstruction,* 190, 204.

36. Norman D. Brown, *Journey to Pleasant Hill,* 405–406; DeBray, "DeBray's 26th Regiment," 159; Ewer, *Third Massachusetts Cavalry,* 158; Rebecca Smith and Mullins, "Diary of H. C. Medford," 222; Yeary, *Reminiscences of Boys in Gray,*

362–63, 746–47; Ludwell H. Johnson, *Red River Campaign*, 155–57; Compiled Service Records, Augustus Buchel; *OR*, vol. XXXIV, pt. I, 354–57, 363, 451–52, 567–68, 607–608, 617; Evans, *Confederate Military History*, 13:204–205; Harwell, *Destruction and Reconstruction*, 190, 204; Spencer, *Terrell's Texas Cavalry*, 34–35.

37. Norman D. Brown, *Journey to Pleasant Hill*, 405–406; DeBray, "DeBray's 26th Regiment," 159; Ewer, *Third Massachusetts Cavalry*, 158; Rebecca Smith and Mullins, "Diary of H. C. Medford," 222; Yeary, *Reminiscences of Boys in Gray*, 362–63, 746–47; Ludwell H. Johnson, *Red River Campaign*, 155–57; Compiled Service Records, Augustus Buchel; *OR*, vol. XXXIV, pt. I, 354–57, 363, 451–52, 567–68, 607–608, 617; Evans, *Confederate Military History*, 13:204–205; Harwell, *Destruction and Reconstruction*, 190, 204; Spencer, *Terrell's Texas Cavalry*, 34–35.

38. Yeary, *Reminiscences of Boys in Gray*, 362–63, 746–47; Ludwell H. Johnson, *Red River Campaign*, 156; Compiled Service Records, Augustus Buchel; *OR*, XXXIV, pt. I, 355, 357, 451–52, 567–68, 607–608, 617; Evans, *Confederate Military History*, 13:204–205; Harwell, *Destruction and Reconstruction*, 190, 204; Norman D. Brown, *Journey to Pleasant Hill*, 405–406. Union soldiers mistakenly reported that the downed officer was Brig. Gen. Arthur P. Bagby.

39. Bitton, *Reminiscences and Letters of Wight*, 33; Yeary, *Reminiscences of Boys in Gray*, 362–63, 746–47; Harwell, *Destruction and Reconstruction*, 190–204; Ludwell H. Johnson, *Red River Campaign*, 156–57; Compiled Service Records, Augustus Buchel; *OR*, vol. XXXIV, pt. I, 355–57, 369, 451–52, 567–68, 607–608, 617; Evans, *Confederate Military History*, 13:204–205; Norman D. Brown, *Journey to Pleasant Hill*, 405–406; Emma Morrill Shirley, "Major Buchel: The Man History Forgot."

40. Bitton, *Reminiscences and Letters of Wight*, 33; Yeary, *Reminiscences of Boys in Gray*, 362–63, 746–47; Harwell, *Destruction and Reconstruction*, 190–204; Ludwell H. Johnson, *Red River Campaign*, 156–57; Compiled Service Records, Augustus Buchel; *OR*, vol. XXXIV, pt. I, 355–57, 369, 451–52, 567–68, 607–608, 617; Evans, *Confederate Military History*, 13:204–205; Norman D. Brown, *Journey to Pleasant Hill*, 405–406; Emma Morrill Shirley, "Major Buchel: The Man History Forgot."

41. *OR*, vol. XXIV, pt. I, 453, 567–68; Norman D. Brown, *Journey to Pleasant Hill*, 406–407; Evans, *Confederate Military History*, 15:138–40; Harwell, *Destruction and Reconstruction*, 205; Robert Johnson and Buel, *Battles and Leaders*, 4:355, 4:372; Ludwell H. Johnson, *Red River Campaign*, 160.

42. Ludwell H. Johnson, *Red River Campaign*, 158–62; Robert Johnson and Buel, *Battles and Leaders*, 4:355–56; Norman D. Brown, *Journey to Pleasant Hill*, 406–407; *OR*, vol. XXXIV, pt. I, 336, 453, 567–68; Evans, *Confederate Military History*, 13:138–40; Harwell, *Destruction and Reconstruction*, 205.

43. *OR*, vol. XXXIV, pt. I, 336, 453, 567–68; Norman D. Brown, *Journey to Pleasant Hill*, 406–407; Evans, *Confederate Military History*, 13:138–40; Harwell, *Destruction and Reconstruction*, 205; Robert Johnson and Buel, *Battles and Leaders*, 4:355–56; Ludwell H. Johnson, *Red River Campaign*, 158–62.

44. Ludwell H. Johnson, *Red River Campaign*, 159–62; Harwell, *Destruction and Reconstruction*, 190, 204; Yeary, *Reminiscences of Boys in Gray*, 362–63, 746–47; Norman D. Brown, *Journey to Pleasant Hill*, 405–406; Spencer, *Terrell's Texas Cavalry*, 34–35; *OR*, vol. XXXIV, pt. I, 355–57, 362–63, 451–52, 567–68, 607–608, 617; Evans, *Confederate Military History*, 13:204–205.

45. G. W. Stephens to James Robertson, Apr. 12, 1864, in Stephens Letters; Ludwell H. Johnson, *Red River Campaign*, 159–62; Winters, *Civil War in Louisiana*, 354; Bee, "Battle of Pleasant Hill," 185; *OR*, vol. XXXIV, pt. I, 355–56, 363, 453, 568, 609, 653; Harwell, *Destruction and Reconstruction*, 206.

46. Stephens to Robertson, Apr. 12, 1864, in Stephens Letters; Ludwell H. Johnson, *Red River Campaign*, 159–62; Winters, *Civil War in Louisiana*, 354; Bee, "Battle of Pleasant Hill," 185; *OR*, vol. XXXIV, pt. I, 355–56, 363, 453, 568, 609, 653; Harwell, *Destruction and Reconstruction*, 206.

47. Bitton, *Reminiscences and Letters of Wight*, 32, 154; Yeary, *Reminiscences of Boys in Gray*, 362–63; Ludwell H. Johnson, *Red River Campaign*, 163–64; Stephens to Robertson, Apr. 12, 1864, in Stephens Letters; DeBray, "DeBray's 26th Regiment," 159; *OR*, vol. XXXIV, pt. I, 453, 568, 609, 653; Harwell, *Destruction and Reconstruction*, 206; Bee, "Battle of Pleasant Hill," 185–86; Robert Johnson and Buel, *Battles and Leaders*, 4:356–57, 4:372.

48. Bitton, *Reminiscences and Letters of Wight*, 32, 154; Yeary, *Reminiscences of Boys in Gray*, 362–63; Ludwell H. Johnson, *Red River Campaign*, 163–64; Stephens to Robertson, Apr. 12, 1864, in Stephens Letters; DeBray, "DeBray's 26th Regiment," 159; *OR*, vol. XXXIV, pt. I, 453, 568, 609, 653; Harwell, *Destruction and Reconstruction*, 206; Bee, "Battle of Pleasant Hill," 185–86; Robert Johnson and Buel, *Battles and Leaders*, 4:356–57, 4:372.

49. Rebecca Smith and Mullins, "Diary of H. C. Medford," 222; Yeary, *Reminiscences of Boys in Gray*, 747; Bitton, *Reminiscences and Letters of Wight*, 33; Bee, "Battle of Pleasant Hill," 185–86; Stephens to Robertson, Apr. 12, 1864, in Stephens Letters; *OR*, vol. XXXIV, pt. I, 568–69, 608–609; Robert Johnson and Buel, *Battles and Leaders*, 4:372; Harwell, *Destruction and Reconstruction*, 208.

50. Stephens to Robertson, Apr. 12, 1864, in Stephens Letters; R. W. H. Jordan to Miss Mattie, Apr., 1864, in R. W. H. Jordan Letters, Confederate Research Center, Hillsboro, Tex.; Louis A. Bringier to Stel (wife), Apr. 15, 1864, in Louis A. Bringier Papers, Box 2, Personal Correspondence File March–May 1864, Hill Memorial Library, Louisiana State Univ., Baton Rouge; Ludwell H. Johnson, *Red River Campaign*, 164–65, 169–70; Rebecca Smith and Mullins, "Diary of H. C. Medford," 224–25; Bearss, *Louisiana Confederate*, 111; Yeary, *Reminiscences of Boys in Gray*, 341, 747; *OR*, vol. XXXIV, pt. I, 568–69, 608–609; Robert Johnson and Buel, *Battles and Leaders*, 4:372; Harwell, *Destruction and Reconstruction*, 208; Bee, "Battle of Pleasant Hill," 185–86; Thomas L. Livermore, *Numbers and Losses in the Civil War in America, 1861–1865*, 109–10; Wooster, *Texas and Texans*, 144.

51. Stephens to Robertson, Apr. 12, 1864, in Stephens Letters; Jordan to Miss Mattie, Apr., 1864, in R. W. H. Jordan Letters; Bringier to Stel, Apr. 15, 1864, in Louis A. Bringier Papers; Ludwell H. Johnson, *Red River Campaign*, 164–65, 169–70; Rebecca Smith and Mullins, "Diary of H. C. Medford," 224–25; Bearss, *Louisiana Confederate*, 111; Yeary, *Reminiscences of Boys in Gray*, 341, 747; *OR*, vol. XXXIV, pt. I, 568–69, 608–609; Robert Johnson and Buel, *Battles and Leaders*, 4:372; Harwell, *Destruction and Reconstruction*, 208; Bee, "Battle of Pleasant Hill," 185–86; Livermore, *Numbers and Losses*, 109–10; Wooster, *Texas and Texans*, 144.

52. Kuykendall Diary, 20; Bitton, *Reminiscences and Letters of Wight*, 153–54; Alwyn Barr, "Texas Losses in the Red River Campaign, 1864," 105; M323, Roll 6.

53. Kuykendall Diary, 20; Bitton, *Reminiscences and Letters of Wight*, 153–54; Alwyn Barr, "Texas Losses in the Red River Campaign, 1864," 105; M323, Roll 6. The lieutenant could have been either George or Matthew Kuykendall. Both were in Bigham's unit.

54. Rebecca Smith and Mullins, "Diary of H. C. Medford," 223–24, 225; Bitton, *Reminiscences and Letters of Wight*, 155; Bearss, *Louisiana Confederate*, 111; Harwell, *Destruction and Reconstruction*, 207; Bee, "Battle of Pleasant Hill," 186; B. P. Gallaway, ed., *The Dark Corner of the Confederacy: Accounts of Civil War Texas as Told by Contemporaries*, 20; Winters, *Civil War in Louisiana*, 356–57; Ashcraft, *Texas in the Civil War*, 23–24; Robert Johnson and Buel, *Battles and Leaders*, 4:367; *OR*, vol. XXXIV, pt. I, 453, 569, 609. Banks reported his losses until Apr. 26 as 3,980 total, with 289 killed, 1,541 wounded, and 2,150 missing, "a large portion . . . captured."

55. Yeary, *Reminiscences of Boys in Gray*, 627; Biegel, *History of Duryee Zouaves*, 27, 81–82; Gallaway, *Dark Corner of the Confederacy*, 20; Ashcraft, *Texas in the Civil War*, 23–24; Harwell, *Destruction and Reconstruction*, 207; *OR*, vol. XXXIV, pt. I, 453, 569, 609.

Chapter 11. "The Limits of Endurance Have Been Reached"

1. Webb Diary, 8–9; Bitton, *Reminiscences and Letters of Wight*, 32, 159; *OR*, vol. XXXIV, pt. I, 346, 614; Harwell, *Destruction and Reconstruction*, 210–12; Robert Johnson and Buel, *Battles and Leaders*, 4:373.

2. Webb Diary, 9; Rebecca Smith and Mullins, "Diary of H. C. Medford," 228–29; *OR*, vol. XXXIV, pt. I, 358, 614; Harwell, *Destruction and Reconstruction*, 210–12; Robert Johnson and Buel, *Battles and Leaders*, 4:373; John D. Winters, *Civil War in Louisiana*, 357–58; Ludwell H. Johnson, *Red River Campaign*, 219–20.

3. Kuykendall Diary, 21–23.

4. Ibid.

5. Ibid. Evidently Dickey recovered his mount and saddle or secured another from the company.

6. John A. Wharton to Hamilton P. Bee, June 30, 1864, and Bee to Brig. Gen. W. R. Boggs, Aug. 17, 1864, both in Bee Papers; Ludwell H. Johnson, *Red River Campaign,* 242; Harwell, *Destruction and Reconstruction,* 218–19; DeBray, "DeBray's 26th Regiment," 160–62.

7. Kuykendall Diary, 23–24; *OR,* vol. XXXIV, pt. I, 610.

8. Kuykendall Diary, 23–24; *OR,* vol. XXXIV, pt. I, 610.

9. Kuykendall Diary, 25–27; Bee to Boggs, Aug. 17, 1864, in Bee Papers; Ludwell H. Johnson, *Red River Campaign,* 221–28; *OR,* vol. XXXIV, pt. I, 610, 612; Harwell, *Destruction and Reconstruction,* 218–19; DeBray, "DeBray's 26th Regiment," 160–62; Robert Johnson and Buel, *Battles and Leaders,* 4:357; *OR,* vol. XXXIV, pt. IV, 357.

10. Bee to Boggs, Aug. 17, 1864, in Bee Papers; Ludwell H. Johnson, *Red River Campaign,* 221–28; Harwell, *Destruction and Reconstruction,* 218–19; DeBray, "DeBray's 26th Regiment," 160–62; Robert Johnson and Buel, *Battles and Leaders,* 4:357; *OR,* vol. XXXIV, pt. I, 610–11, 613.

11. *OR,* vol. XXXIV, pt. I, 611, 613; DeBray, "DeBray's 26th Regiment," 160–61; Wharton to Bee, June 30, 1864, in Bee Papers; Bee to Boggs, Aug. 17, 1864, in Bee Papers; Harwell, *Destruction and Reconstruction,* 218–19; Ludwell H. Johnson, *Red River Campaign,* 227–34.

12. Kuykendall Diary, 27–30; Bee to Boggs, Aug. 17, 1864, in Bee Papers; Harwell, *Destruction and Reconstruction,* 226–29; *OR,* vol. XXXIV, pt. I, 580–81, 611, 613–14; DeBray, "DeBray's 26th Regiment," 162–63; Robert Johnson and Buel, *Battles and Leaders,* 4:357–58.

13. Duaine, *Dead Men Wore Boots,* 75; Webb Diary, 9; Ludwell H. Johnson, *Red River Campaign,* 229–35; Winters, *Civil War in Louisiana,* 363–65; Harwell, *Destruction and Reconstruction,* 226–29; DeBray, "DeBray's 26th Regiment," 162–63; Robert Johnson and Buel, *Battles and Leaders,* 4:357–58; *OR,* vol. XXXIV, pt. I, 580–81.

14. Kuykendall Diary, 30–31; Yeary, *Reminiscences of Boys in Gray,* 363.

15. Webb Diary, 9–10; Duaine, *Dead Men Wore Boots,* 77; Ludwell H. Johnson, *Red River Campaign,* 238–41, 254, 257–60; Winters, *Civil War in Louisiana,* 367–71; DeBray, "DeBray's 26th Regiment," 161; Harwell, *Destruction and Reconstruction,* 197–98, 226–29; Robert Johnson and Buel, *Battles and Leaders,* 4:358.

16. Bitton, *Reminiscences and Letters of Wight,* 159–60; Kuykendall Diary, 31–33; Yeary, *Reminiscences of Boys in Gray,* 341; *OR,* vol. XXIV, pt. I, 583. Taylor's men captured large quantities of supplies at Mansfield, but Walker's and Churchill's departing infantry took their share to Arkansas. By this time, Taylor's command had consumed most of its remaining rations.

17. Bitton, *Reminiscences and Letters of Wight,* 159–60; Kuykendall Diary, 31–33; Yeary, *Reminiscences of Boys in Gray,* 341; *OR,* vol. XXIV, pt. I, 583.

18. Kuykendall Diary, 31–32.

19. Ibid., 32–33.

20. Ludwell H. Johnson, *Red River Campaign*, 238–41, 254, 257–60; Winters, *Civil War in Louisiana*, 367–71; DeBray, "DeBray's 26th Regiment," 161; Harwell, *Destruction and Reconstruction*, 226–29; Robert Johnson and Buel, *Battles and Leaders*, 4:58; *OR*, vol. XXXIV, pt. I, 587, 589–91, 612. On May 14, 1864, Taylor relieved Bee of command and placed Bagby in charge of Bee's division.

21. Kuykendall Diary, 33–34.

22. Ibid.

23. Ibid., 34–35.

24. Kuykendall Diary, 36; M323, Rolls 5–7.

25. Ludwell H. Johnson, *Red River Campaign*, 248–49; Winters, *Civil War in Louisiana*, 367–69; Robert Johnson and Buel, *Battles and Leaders*, 4:257–58.

26. Yeary, *Reminiscences of Boys in Gray*, 341; Ludwell H. Johnson, *Red River Campaign*, 235–36, 238–41, 257–58, 262–66, 270; Winters, *Civil War in Louisiana*, 370–74; *OR*, vol. XXXIV, pt. I, 592; Harwell, *Destruction and Reconstruction*, 226–29.

27. Gallaway, *Dark Corner of the Confederacy*, 20; Duaine, *Dead Men Wore Boots*, 78; Ludwell H. Johnson, *Red River Campaign*, 260–61; Parrish, *Richard Taylor*, 384; *OR*, vol. XXXIV, pt. I, 453, 569, 609; Harwell, *Destruction and Reconstruction*, 207.

28. Kuykendall Diary, 36; Webb Diary, 12; Yeary, *Reminiscences of Boys in Gray*, 341; Ludwell H. Johnson, *Red River Campaign*, 272–64; *OR*, vol. XXXIV, pt. I, 278, 332, 359, 592–94, 630–31; Evans, *Confederate Military History*, 15:208; M323, Rolls 5–7; Harwell, *Destruction and Reconstruction*, 229–32.

29. Bearss, *Louisiana Confederate*, 122; Ludwell H. Johnson, *Red River Campaign*, 272–74; Winters, *Civil War in Louisiana*, 264–75; *OR*, vol. XXXIV, pt. I, 278; *OR*, vol. XXIV, pt. I, 593–94; Evans, *Confederate Military History*, 15:208; Harwell, *Destruction and Reconstruction*, 229–32; Spencer, *Terrell's Texas Cavalry*, 48–49.

30. Bitton, *Reminiscences and Letters of Wight*, 35; Ludwell H. Johnson, *Red River Campaign*, 275–76; Winters, *Civil War in Louisiana*, 376–77; *OR*, vol. XXXIV, pt. I, 193, 320, 325, 330, 347–49, 352, 357–58, 361, 364, 367–68, 372, 466–67, 594, 595, 624, 627, 631; Evans, *Confederate Military History*, 15:208; Harwell, *Destruction and Reconstruction*, 229–32; Robert Johnson and Buel, *Battles and Leaders*, 4:359. Confederate losses are difficult to determine exactly, due to the paucity of surviving records.

31. Winters, *Civil War in Louisiana*, 377; Robert Johnson and Buel, *Battles and Leaders*, 4:367–68. Banks reported that his losses on the retreat from Alexandria approximated 165 killed, 650 wounded, and 450 captured or missing. Taylor reported that his army numbered 13,000 at its greatest strength. After Pleasant Hill, it was reduced to 5,200, and "our total loss [during the entire campaign] in killed wounded and missing was 3976."

32. Bitton, *Reminiscences and Letters of Wight*, 163; Spencer, *Terrell's Texas Cavalry*, 50–55.
33. Compiled Service Records, William O. Yager; Spencer, *Terrell's Texas Cavalry*, 50–55.
34. Compiled Service Records, William O. Yager; Spencer, *Terrell's Texas Cavalry*, 50–55.
35. Bitton, *Reminiscences and Letters of Wight*, 164–65, 174, 177–79; Compiled Service Records, William O. Yager; Spencer, *Terrell's Texas Cavalry*, 55–56. Wight reported an engagement between a 40-man detachment from the regiment led by Major Beaumont and 37 Union troops. According to Wight, the Texans "killed 2 and captyered [*sic*] 35," without losing a man. Where this skirmish took place is unclear.
36. Bitton, *Reminiscences and Letters of Wight*, 165–66, 174–78.
37. Ibid., 173–75; *OR*, vol. XLVIII, pt. I, 1389–90; *OR*, vol. XLIX, pt. I, 877; M323, Rolls 5–7. Wight's letters home indicate that a detachment from the regiment participated in operations against Jayhawkers in Saint Landry Parish, Louisiana, in early 1865. Compiled Service Records contain several instances of prisoners of war listed as members of the 1st Texas Cavalry who were captured east of the Mississippi River, but most of these were captured near Franklin, Tennessee, in December, 1864. There is no substantiation of the 1st Texas Cavalry serving in this region in any capacity.
38. Bitton, *Reminiscences and Letters of Wight*, 173–75; *OR*, vol. XLVIII, pt. I, 1389–90; *OR*, vol. XLIX, pt. I, 877; M323, Rolls 5–7.

Chapter 12. "A Tribute to the Cavalry Branch of the Service"

1. Muster Rolls, 1st Regiment of Texas Cavalry; Harwell, *Destruction and Reconstruction*, 271–72; Oates, *Confederate Cavalry*, 155, 159–60, 170; Spencer, *Terrell's Texas Cavalry*, 55–56.
2. Muster Rolls, 1st Regiment of Texas Cavalry; Harwell, *Destruction and Reconstruction*, 271–72; Oates, *Confederate Cavalry*, 155, 159–60, 170; Spencer, *Terrell's Texas Cavalry*, 55–56; Yeary, *Reminiscences of Boys in Gray*, 341, 363.
3. Kuykendall Diary, 6; "Pitts of Austin," *Houston Post*, n.d., and unidentified newspaper article, both in William A. Pitts Papers, Box 3C152, Center for American History, Univ. of Texas, Austin; Yeary, *Reminiscences of Boys in Gray*, 362–63, 746–47; Ludwell H. Johnson, *Red River Campaign*, 156; Compiled Service Records, William O. Yager; Evans, *Confederate Military History*, 15:85–88.
4. Parrish, *Richard Taylor*, 348; Harwell, *Destruction and Reconstruction*, 189–90, 216; Duaine, *Dead Men Wore Boots*, 21, 29–30; Yeary, *Reminiscences of Boys in Gray*, 448–49; Robert A. Newell to Sara Newell (wife), Mar., 1863, in Robert A. Newell Papers, Louisiana and Lower Mississippi Collection, Louisiana State Univ. Library, Baton Rouge; Evans, *Confederate Military History*, 15:135–36.

5. *OR,* vol. XXXIV, pt. I, 609, 614, 616.

6. Harwell, *Destruction and Reconstruction,* 190, 216; Yeary, *Reminiscences of Boys in Gray,* 362–63; M323, Rolls 2–7; Evans, *Confederate Military History,* 15:135–36.

7. Biesele, *German Settlements in Texas,* 205–207; Terry Jordan, *German Seed,* 30–33; Wooster, *Texas and Texans,* 114; Knopp, "Fredericksburg, Texas," pt. 1, ch. 4, 4–5; Muster Rolls, 1st Regiment of Texas Cavalry; Handbill, TDS, Apr. 6, 1894, in McCulloch Collection; Harwell, *Destruction and Reconstruction,* 190; Yeary, *Reminiscences of Boys in Gray,* 777; Jerry D. Thompson, ed., *Westward the Texans: The Civil War Journal of William Randolph Howell,* 25–28; John Henry Brown to Unknown, n.d., in Brown Papers; Chance, *Second Texas Infantry,* 179–80.

8. M323, Rolls 2–7.

9. Ibid.; Terry G. Jordan, *Trails to Texas: Southern Roots of Western Cattle Ranching,* 80, 127; Grady McWhiney, *Cracker Culture: Celtic Ways in the Old South,* 52–55, 61–62, 89.

10. M323, Rolls 2–7; Bitton, *Reminiscences and Letters of Wight,* 175–79.

11. M323, Rolls 2–7; Bitton, *Reminiscences and Letters of Wight,* 175–79; General Orders No. 13, Dept. of Texas, in Barry Orders. Regimental muster rolls and quarterly reports for 1861–62 are almost complete. From 1862 to 1864, the records have gaps. After February, 1864, records are incomplete and, in some instances, missing entirely. Surviving documents list deserters' places of birth as: Northern States, 9; Border States, 6; Texas, 5; Other Southern States, 16; Ireland, 2; France, 1; Germany, 6; England, 2; Scotland, 1; Mexico, 9; and Unknown, 15.

12. M323, Rolls 2–7; Bitton, *Reminiscences and Letters of Wight,* 175–79; Douglas Hale, *The Third Texas Cavalry in the Civil War,* 40, 192–96; Wiley, *Life of Johnny Reb,* 144–45; McPherson, *Battle Cry,* 440, 612–13, 820–21; Richard N. Current, ed., *Encyclopedia of the Confederacy,* 2:467–69.

13. M323, Rolls 2–7; Bitton, *Reminiscences and Letters of Wight,* 175–79; Hale, *The Third Texas Cavalry in the Civil War,* 40, 192–96; Wiley, *Life of Johnny Reb,* 144–45; McPherson, *Battle Cry,* 440, 612–13, 820–21; Current, *Encyclopedia of the Confederacy,* 2:467–69.

14. Handbill, TDS, Apr. 6, 1894, in McCulloch Collection; David Smith, *Frontier Defense,* 29–31, 37–39, 168–73.

15. Handbill, TDS, Apr. 6, 1894, in McCulloch Collection; David Smith, *Frontier Defense,* 29–31, 37–39, 168–73.

16. Handbill, TDS, Apr. 6, 1894, in McCulloch Collection; David Smith, *Frontier Defense,* 29–31, 37–39, 168–73.

17. Handbill, TDS, Apr. 6, 1894, in McCulloch Collection; David Smith, *Frontier Defense,* 29–31, 37–39, 168–73.

18. Stockdale, "Eulogy of Buchel"; John Henry Brown to Unknown, n.d., in Brown Collection; Private Papers of J. M. Buchel (grandnephew of A. Buchel), Hilltop Lakes, Tex.; J. M. Buchel, interview by author, Hilltop Lakes, Tex.,

June, 1993; Buchel to Julie [niece], Feb. 12, 1862 [translated from German], and E. Buchel to Otto Buchel, May 18, 1870 [translated from German], both in Lenz Collection; Lord, *Fremantle Diary,* 14–15; Shirley, "Major Buchel."

19. Kuykendall Diary, 7; Tyler, *New Handbook of Texas,* 1:799–800. The Confederate government never officially promoted Buchel to brigadier general. In fact, he may have been promoted by orders from the Trans-Mississippi Department. Several other officers who commanded brigades received promotion to brigadier general from Lt. Gen. E. Kirby Smith. These included Arthur P. Bagby, Xavier B. DeBray, Wilburn H. King, and Horace Randal. However, no Confederate orders survive promoting Buchel. Other officers and his men referred to him as general in several documents. The rank on his tombstone in the Texas State Cemetery in Austin is brigadier general.

BIBLIOGRAPHY

Documentary Sources

Banks, Nathaniel P. Letterbook. Box 2326, Hill Memorial Library, Louisiana State University, Baton Rouge.

Barry, James Buckner. Correspondence, 1861–1862. Box 2B42, Center for American History, University of Texas, Austin.

———Confederate Army Orders, 1861–1865. Box 2B43, Center for American History, University of Texas, Austin.

Bee, Hamilton, P. Papers. Texas State Archives, Austin.

Bringier, Louis A. Papers. Box 2, Personal Correspondence File, March–May, 1864. Hill Memorial Library, Louisiana State University, Baton Rouge.

Brown, John Henry. Papers. Texas State Archives, Austin.

Buchel, Augustus. Papers. Personal Collection of J. M. Buchel, Hilltop Lakes, Texas.

Burleson, Edward. Collection. Center for American History, University of Texas, Austin.

Camp Cooper. File. Robert E. Nail Archives, Old Jail Art Center Museum, Albany, Texas.

Civil War Papers. Louisiana Historical Association Collections, Folder 16, Box 9, Manuscript Collection 55B, Manuscript Department, Howard-Tilton Memorial Library, Tulane University, New Orleans, Louisiana.

Davidson, Sidney Green. Papers. Box 2D50, Center for American History, University of Texas, Austin.

First Texas Cavalry Collection. Confederate Research Center, Hill Junior College, Hillsboro, Texas.

Garland, J. D. Papers. Special Collections, Group 153, Hill Memorial Library, Louisiana State University, Baton Rouge.

Hardin, N. J. Fair. "Notes on the Red River Campaign." Boxes 8–10, Group No. 1014, Hill Memorial Library, Louisiana State University, Baton Rouge.

Index of Captains of Texas Units in Confederate State Service. Comptroller Records, Service and Payroll Records, Record Group 304, Texas State Archives, Austin.

Jordan, R. W. H. Letters. Confederate Research Center, Hill Junior
    College, Hillsboro, Texas.

King, John R. Papers. Texas State Archives, Austin.

Kuykendall, William. Civil War Diary. In Kuykendall Family Papers, 1822–
    1991, Center for American History, University of Texas, Austin.

Lenz, Louis. Collection. Box 3H168, Center for American History,
    University of Texas, Austin.

McCulloch, Henry E. Collection. Texas State Archives, Austin.

Moncure, John C. Papers. In N. J. Fair Hardin Collections, Special
    Collections, Hill Memorial Library, Louisiana State University, Baton
    Rouge.

Newell, Robert A. Papers. No. 653, Louisiana and Lower Mississippi
    Collection, Hill Memorial Library, Louisiana State University, Baton
    Rouge.

Pension Records. Confederate Veterans. Texas State Archives, Austin.

Pitts, William A. Papers. Box 3C152, Center for American History,
    University of Texas, Austin.

State of Texas. Adjutant General. Correspondence. Texas State Archives,
    Austin.

Stephens, G. W. Letters. Confederate Research Center, Hill Junior
    College, Hillsboro, Texas.

Stevens, Nancy. Private Papers. Fort Worth, Texas.

Stockdale, Fletcher S. Collection. Texas State Archives, Austin.

Tyson, Robert A. Diary. Box 1693, Hill Memorial Library, Louisiana State
    University, Baton Rouge.

U.S. Census Bureau. Eighth Census of the U.S. (1860). Population
    Schedules of the National Archives Microfilm Publication. Microcopy
    653, Texas, Volume 7, Roll 1300. Washington, D.C., 1967.

U.S. War Department. Collection of Confederate Records.

———. Ashby, Travis H. National Archives and Record Service, Washington, D.C.

———. Boggess, Milton M. National Archives and Record Service,
    Washington, D.C.

———. Buchel, Augustus. National Archives and Record Service,
    Washington, D.C.

———. Compiled Service Records of Confederate Soldiers. Record
    Group 109, National Archives and Record Service, Washington, D.C.

———. Fry, James H. National Archives and Record Service, Washington,
    D.C.

———. Hill, Washington L. National Archives and Record Service,
    Washington, D.C.

———. Homsley, James M. National Archives and Record Service,
    Washington, D.C.

———. McCulloch, Henry E. National Archives and Record Service, Washington, D.C.

———. McGowan, William Joseph. National Archives and Record Service, Washington, D.C.

———. Microfilmed Records of the 1st Texas Mounted Rifles and 1st Texas Cavalry Regiments, Compiled Service Records of Confederate Soldiers Who Served in Organizations from the State of Texas, Record Group 109, Microfilm Number M323, National Archives and Record Service, Washington, D.C.

———. Muster Rolls and Unit Reports, 1st Regiment of Texas Cavalry (Buchel's). Box 488, Record Group 109, National Archives and Record Service, Washington, D.C.

———. Muster Rolls and Unit Reports, 1st Texas Mounted Rifles. Box 488, Record Group 109, National Archives and Record Service, Washington, D.C.

———. Myers, Robert A. National Archives and Record Service, Washington, D.C.

———. Taylor, Joseph. National Archives and Record Service, Washington, D.C.

———. White, James A. National Archives and Record Service, Washington, D.C.

———. Yager, William O. National Archives and Record Service, Washington, D.C.

Van der Stucken Family. Records. Vertical Files, Pioneer Museum Library, Fredericksburg, Texas.

Whitney, William H. Letters. Groups 1043 and 1046, Correspondence from 1864, Hill Memorial Library, Louisiana State University, Baton Rouge.

Books

Ashcraft, Allan C. *Texas in the Civil War: A Résumé History.* Austin: Texas Civil War Centennial Commission, 1962.

Atkinson, Bertha. *The History of Bell County, Texas.* N.p.: Bell County Historical Society, 1970.

Bailey, Ann J. *Between the Enemy and Texas: Parson's Texas Cavalry in the Civil War.* Fort Worth: Texas Christian University Press, 1989.

Barkley, Mary Starr. *History of Travis County and Austin, 1839–1899.* Waco, Tex.: Texian Press, 1963.

Barron, S. B. *Lone Star Defenders.* Waco, Tex.: W. M. Morrison, 1908.

Bearss, Edwin C., ed. *A Louisiana Confederate: Diary of Felix Pierre Poche.* Translated by Eugena Watson. Natchitoches, La.: Louisiana Studies Institute, Northwestern State University, 1972.

Biegel, Peter. *History of the Second Battalion, Duryee Zouaves, 165th Regiment, New York Volunteer Infantry.* Rev. ed. New York: N.p., 1903.

Biesele, Rudolph L. *The History of the German Settlements in Texas, 1831–1861.* Austin: Von Boeckmann–Jones Press, 1930.

Biggers, Don H. *German Pioneers in Texas: A Brief History of Their Hardships, Struggles and Achievements.* Fredericksburg, Tex.: Fredericksburg Publishing Company, 1983.

Bitton, Davis, ed. *The Reminiscences and Civil War Letters of Levi Lamoni Wight.* Salt Lake City: University of Utah Press, 1970.

Bosque County History Book Committee, comp. *Bosque County: Land and People.* Meridian, Tex.: N.p., 1985.

Bowden, J. J. *The Exodus of Federal Troops from Texas, 1861.* Austin: Eakin Press, 1986.

Brown, John Henry. *History of Texas from 1685 to 1892.* 2 volumes. Austin: L. E. Daniell Publishers, 1892.

———. *Indian Wars and Pioneers of Texas.* Austin: Texas State Archives. 189?. Reprint, Austin: L. E. Daniell Publishers, 1988.

Brown, Norman D., ed. *Journey to Pleasant Hill: The Civil War Letters of Captain Elijah P. Petty, Walker's Texas Division, CSA.* San Antonio: Institute of Texan Cultures, 1982.

Buenger, Walter L. *Secession and the Union in Texas.* Austin: University of Texas Press, 1984.

Campbell, Randolph B. *A Southern Community in Crisis: Harrison County, Texas, 1850 to 1880.* Austin: Texas State Historical Association, 1983.

Cater, Douglas John. *As It Was: Reminiscences of a Soldier of the Third Texas Cavalry and the Nineteenth Louisiana Infantry.* Austin: Statehouse Press, 1990.

Chance, Joseph E. *The Second Texas Infantry from Shiloh to Vicksburg.* Austin: Eakin Press, 1984.

Chrisman, Brutus Clay. *Early Days in Callahan County.* Abilene, Tex.: Abilene Printing and Stationery Company, 1966.

Crute, Joseph, Jr. *Units of the Confederate States Army.* Midlothian, Va.: Derwent Books, 1987.

Current, Richard N., ed. *Encyclopedia of the Confederacy.* New York: Simon and Schuster, 1993.

Cutrer, Thomas W. *Ben McCulloch and the Frontier Military Tradition.* Chapel Hill: University of North Carolina Press, 1993.

Davis, Ellis A. et al., comps. and eds. *The New Encyclopedia of Texas.* Dallas: Texas Development Bureau, n.d.

Duaine, Carl L. *The Dead Men Wore Boots: An Account of the 32nd Texas Volunteer Cavalry, CSA, 1862–1865.* Austin: San Felipe Press, 1966.

Edmonds, David C. *Yankee Autumn in Acadiana: A Narrative of the Great*

Texas Overland Expedition Through Southwestern Louisiana, October–December, 1863. Lafayette, La.: Acadiana Press, 1979.

Elkins, John M. *Indian Fighting on the Texas Frontier.* Written for Captain Elkins by Frank W. McCarty. Amarillo, Tex.: Russell and Cockrell, 1929.

Evans, Clement A., ed. *Confederate Military History: A Library of the Confederate States in Seventeen Volumes: Written by Distinguished Men of the South.* Atlanta, Ga.: Confederate Publishing Company, 1899. Reprint, Wilmington, N.C.: Broadfoot Publishing Co., 1988.

Ewer, James K. *The Third Massachusetts Cavalry in the War for the Union.* Maplewood, Mass.: Wm. G. J. Perry Press, 1903.

Farmer, Garland R. *The Realm of Rusk County.* Henderson, Tex.: Henderson Times, 1951.

Fehrenbach, T. R. *Lone Star: A History of Texas and the Texans.* New York: Collier Books Division of Macmillan Publishing Co., 1968.

Freeman, Douglas Southall. *R. E. Lee: A Biography.* 4 volumes. New York: Charles Scribner's Sons, 1942.

Gallaway, B. P. *The Ragged Rebel: A Common Soldier in W. H. Parson's Texas Cavalry, 1861–1865.* Austin: University of Texas Press, 1988.

———, ed. *The Dark Corner of the Confederacy: Accounts of Civil War Texas as Told by Contemporaries.* Dubuque, Iowa: Kendall-Hunt Publishing Company, 1972.

Gautier, George R. *Harder then Death: The Life of George R. Gautier, an Old Texan Living at the Confederate Home, Austin, Texas.* Austin: N.p, 1902.

Goyne, Minetta Altgelt. *Lone Star and Double Eagle: Civil War Letters of a German Family.* Fort Worth: Texas Christian University Press, 1982.

Greer, James K., ed. *A Texas Ranger and Frontiersman: The Days of Buck Barry in Texas, 1845–1906.* Dallas: Southwest Press, 1932.

Hale, Douglas. *The Third Texas Cavalry in the Civil War.* Norman: University of Oklahoma Press, 1993.

Harwell, Richard B., ed. *Destruction and Reconstruction: Personal Experiences of the Late War, by Richard Taylor, Lieutenant General in the Confederate Army.* New York: Longmans, Green and Company, 1955.

Hatch, Alden. *Remington Arms in American History.* New York: Rinehart and Company, 1956.

Henderson, Harry McCorry. *Texas in the Confederacy.* San Antonio: Naylor Company, 1955.

Horton, Louise. *Samuel Bell Maxey: A Biography.* Austin: University of Texas Press, 1974.

Inemire, Francis Terry. *Guadalupe County Marriage Records, 1847–1874.* San Antonio: G. McLin, 1985.

Johnson, Ludwell H. *Red River Campaign: Politics and Cotton in the Civil*

War. Baltimore, Md.: Johns Hopkins University Press, 1958. Reprint, Kent, Ohio: Kent State University Press, 1993.

Johnson, Robert Underwood, and Clarence Clough Buel, eds. *Battles and Leaders of the Civil War.* Rev. ed. 4 volumes. Secaucus, N.J.: Books Sales, Inc., 1984.

Jordan, Terry G. *German Seed in Texas Soil: Immigrant Farmers in Nineteenth-Century Texas.* Austin: University of Texas Press, 1966.

————*Trails to Texas: Southern Roots of Western Cattle Ranching.* Lincoln: University of Nebraska Press, 1981.

Josephy, Alvin M., Jr. *The Civil War in the American West.* New York: Alfred A. Knopf, 1991.

Ledbetter, Barbara Neal. *Fort Belknap Frontier Saga: Indians, Negroes, and Anglo Americans on the Texas Frontier.* Burnet, Tex.: Eakin Press, 1982.

Livermore, Thomas L. *Numbers and Losses in the Civil War in America, 1861–1865.* Bloomington: Indiana University Press, 1957.

Lonn, Ella. *Foreigners in the Confederacy.* Chapel Hill: University of North Carolina Press, 1940.

Lord, Walter, ed. *The Fremantle Diary: Being the Journal of Lieutenant Colonel James Arthur Lyon Fremantle, Coldstream Guards, on His Three Months in the Southern States.* Boston: Little, Brown and Company, 1954.

Lowe, Richard. *The Texas Overland Expedition of 1863.* Abilene, Tex.: McWhiney Foundation Press, 1998.

Malsch, Brownson. *Indianola: Mother of Western Texas.* Austin: Statehouse Press, 1988.

Marten, James. *Texas Divided: Loyalty and Dissent in the Lone Star State, 1856–1874.* Lexington: University Press of Kentucky, 1990.

McConnell, Joseph Carrol. *The West Texas Frontier.* Volume 2. Jacksboro, Tex.: Gazette Print, 1939.

McPherson, James M. *Battle Cry of Freedom: The Civil War Era.* New York: Oxford University Press, 1988.

McWhiney, Grady. *Cracker Culture: Celtic Ways in the Old South.* Tuscaloosa: University of Alabama Press, 1981.

Moore, Albert Burton. *Conscription and Conflict in the Confederacy.* New York: Macmillan, 1924. Reprint, Columbia: University of South Carolina Press, 1996.

Neville, A. W. *The History of Lamar County, Texas.* Paris, Tex.: North Texas Publishing Company, 1937.

Nye, W. S. *Carbine and Lance: The Story of Old Fort Sill.* Norman: University of Oklahoma Press, 1943.

Oates, Stephen B. *Confederate Cavalry West of the River.* Austin: University of Texas Press, 1961.

Olmsted, Frederick Law. *A Journey Through Texas; or, A Saddle-trip on the Southwestern Frontier; with a Statistical Appendix.* New York: Dix, Edwards and Company, 1857.

Paddock, B. B., ed. *A Twentieth-Century History and Biographical Record of North and West Texas.* 3 volumes. Chicago: Lewis Publishing Company, 1906.

Parrish, T. Michael. *Richard Taylor: Soldier Prince of Dixie.* Chapel Hill: University of North Carolina Press, 1992.

Pruitt, Jakey L., and Scott Black. *Civil War Letters, 1861 to 1865: A Glimpse of the War Between the States.* Austin: Eakin Press, 1985.

Ransleben, Guido E. *A Hundred Years of Comfort in Texas: A Centennial History.* San Antonio: Naylor Company, 1954.

Richardson, Rupert Norval. *The Frontier of Northwest Texas, 1846 to 1876: Advance and Defense by the Pioneer Settlers of the Cross Timbers and Prairies.* Glendale, Ill.: Arthur H. Clark Company, 1963.

Rusk County Genealogical Society. *Remembering Rusk County.* Dallas: Curtis Media Corporation, 1992.

Schwartz, Stephan. *Twenty-two Months a Prisoner of War: A Narrative of Twenty-two Months' Imprisonment by the Confederates, in Texas, through General Twiggs' Treachery, Dating from April, 1861, to February, 1863.* St. Louis, Mo.: A. F. Nelson Publishing Company, 1892.

Sherman, William Tecumseh. *Memoirs of General W. T. Sherman.* New York: Library of America, 1990.

Sisakis, Stewart. *Compendium of the Confederate Armies: Texas.* New York: Facts on File, 1995.

Smith, David Paul. *Frontier Defense in the Civil War: Texas Rangers and Rebels.* College Station: Texas A&M University Press, 1992.

Sowell, A. J. *Rangers and Pioneers of Texas.* 1884. Reprint, Austin: Statehouse Press, 1991.

Spencer, John W. *Terrell's Texas Cavalry.* Austin: Eakin Press, 1982.

Thacker, Emily. *The Vinegar Book.* Canton, Ohio: Tresco Publishers, 1995.

Thompson, Jerry D., ed. *Westward the Texans: The Civil War Journal of William Randolph Howell.* El Paso: Texas Western Press, 1990.

Tyler, Ron, ed. *The New Handbook of Texas.* 6 volumes. Austin: Texas State Historical Association, 1996.

Wallace, Ernest. *Texas in Turmoil: The Saga of Texas, 1849–1875.* Austin: Steck-Vaughn, 1965.

Wallace, Ernest, and E. Adamson Hoebel. *The Comanches: Lords of the South Plains.* Norman: University of Oklahoma Press, 1952.

The War of Rebellion: A Compilation of the Official Records of the Union and Confederate Armies. 4 series, 130 vols. Washington, D.C.: Government Printing Office, 1880–1901.

West Texas Historical Association Yearbook. Volume 8. Abilene, Tex.: N.p., 1932.

Wiley, Bell Irvin. *The Life of Johnny Reb: The Common Soldier of the Confederacy.* Baton Rouge: Louisiana State University Press, 1943. Reissued, 1978.

Wilbarger, J. W. *Indian Depredation in Texas: Reliable Accounts of Battles, Wars, Adventures, Forays, Murders, Massacres, etc. . . .* Austin: Hutchings Printing House, 1889.

Williams, E. W., ed. *With the Border Ruffians: Memories of the Far West, 1852 to 1868.* Toronto: The Musson Book Co., Ltd, 1919.

Wilson, Robert L. *Colt: An American Legend.* New York: Abbeville Press, 1939.

Winsor, Bill. *Texas in the Confederacy: Military Installations, Economics, and People.* Hillsboro, Tex.: Hill Junior College Press, 1978.

Winters, John D. *The Civil War in Louisiana.* Baton Rouge: Louisiana State University Press, 1963.

Wooster, Ralph A., ed. *Lone Star Blue and Gray: Essays on Texas in the Civil War.* Austin: Texas State Historical Association, 1995.

———. *Texas and Texans in the Civil War.* Austin: Eakin Press, 1995.

Worcester, Don. *The Spanish Mustang: From the Plains of Andalusia to the Prairies of Texas.* El Paso: Texas Western Press, 1986.

Wright, Marcus J., comp. *Texas in the War, 1861–1865.* Hillsboro, Tex.: Hill Junior College Press, 1965.

Yeary, Mamie, comp. *Reminiscences of the Boys in Gray.* Dallas: Smith and Lamar Publishing House, 1912.

Articles and Periodicals

Ashcraft, Allan C. "Fort Brown, Texas, in 1861." *Texas Military History* 3, no. 4 (Winter, 1963): 243–47.

Austin State Gazette. February, 1861–June, 1865. Newspaper Holdings, Amon Carter Museum Library, Fort Worth, Texas.

Barr, Alwyn. "Texas Losses in the Red River Campaign, 1864." *Texas Military History* 3, no. 2 (Summer, 1963): 103–110.

Bee, Hamilton P. "Battle of Pleasant Hill—An Error Corrected." *Southern Historical Society Papers* 8 (1880): 184–86. Reprint, Richmond, Virginia: Broadfoot Publishing Company, 1990.

Burroughs, Sara. "Immigrant Soldier Fought for Texas." *Houston Post,* May 10, 1964. In Vertical Files, Center for American History, University of Texas, Austin.

Campbell, J. I. "Reminiscences of a Private Soldier." *Confederate Veteran* 21, no. 2 (February, 1913): 67.

"Colonel H. E. McCulloch to the People of Texas." *Clarksville (Tex.) Standard,* October 26, 1861. In Newspaper Holdings, Amon Carter Museum Library, Fort Worth, Texas.

"Colonel McCulloch's Call." *Austin State Gazette,* January 4, 1862. In Newspaper Holdings, Amon Carter Museum Library, Fort Worth, Texas.

"Convention Elects E. J. Davis President." *San Antonio Daily Express News,* June 3, 1868. In Vertical Files, Center for American History, University of Texas, Austin.

DeBray, Xavier Blanchard. "A Sketch of the History of DeBray's 26th Regiment of Texas Cavalry." *Southern Historical Society's Papers* 12 (January–December, 1885): 547–54. Reprint, Richmond, Va.: Broadfoot Publishing Company, 1990.

"E. J. Davis." *Corpus Christi Caller-Times,* January 18, 1959. In Vertical Files, Center for American History, University of Texas, Austin.

"Edmund J. Davis." *Galveston Weekly Freemans Press,* July 25, 1868. In Vertical Files, Center for American History, University of Texas, Austin.

"Famed Conductor and Composer Born in Old Home." *Fredericksburg (Tex.) Standard,* March 3, 1976. In Vertical Files, Center for American History, University of Texas, Austin.

"The Fighting Population of Travis County." *Austin State Gazette,* February 15, 1862. In Newspaper Holdings, Amon Carter Museum Library, Fort Worth, Texas.

Fitzhugh, Lester N. "Saluria, Fort Esperanza, and Military Operations of the Texas Coast, 1861–1864." *Southwestern Historical Quarterly* 61, no. 1 (July, 1957): 66–100.

"Forgotten Grave Hides Famous Texas Great." *Austin Statesman,* August 29, 1934. In Vertical Files, Center for American History, University of Texas, Austin.

"From the Coast." *Austin Tri-Weekly Gazette,* January 22, 1864. In Newspaper Holdings, Amon Carter Museum Library, Fort Worth, Texas.

Geise, William Royston. "Texas [in] the First Year of the War, April 1861–April 1862: A Study of Organization and Command in the Trans-Mississippi West." *Military History of Texas and the Southwest* 13, no. 4 (1976): 30–41.

Hagy, P. S. "Military Operations of the Lower Trans-Mississippi Department, 1863–64." *Confederate Veteran* 24, no. 12 (December, 1916): 545.

Jones, Allen W. "Military Events in Texas During the Civil War, 1861–1865." *Southwestern Historical Quarterly* 64, no. 1 (July, 1960): 126–30.

Lee, Charles S. "Four Hundred Guns." *Texas Gun Collector* (Fall, 1994): 70–73.

McQuaid, Ina. "Texas Cavalry in Union Army." *Dallas Morning News,* November 12, 1953. In Vertical Files, Center for American History, University of Texas, Austin.

"Organization of the Army." *Austin State Gazette.* December 28, 1863. In Newspaper Holdings, Amon Carter Museum Library, Fort Worth, Texas.

"Reconstruction Governor: Hated Texan Lies with War Heroes." *San Antonio Express,* February 3, 1958. In Vertical Files, Center for American History, University of Texas, Austin.

San Antonio Herald, August 20, 1862. Texana-Genealogy Department, San Antonio Public Library, San Antonio, Texas.

San Antonio Semi-Weekly News, August 25, 1862. Texana-Genealogy Department, San Antonio Public Library, San Antonio, Texas.

Sansom, John W. "The German Citizens Were Loyal to the Union." *Hunter's Magazine* 2, no. 1 (November, 1911): 12. In Sansom File, Institute of Texan Cultures, San Antonio.

Shirley, Emma Morrill. "Major Buchel: The Man History Forgot." *Dallas Morning News,* January 27, 1929. Center for American History, University of Texas, Austin.

Shook, Robert W. "The Battle of the Nueces, August 10, 1862." *Southwestern Historical Quarterly* 66, no. 1 (1962–63): 31–42.

Smith, Rebecca W., and Marion Mullins, eds. "The Diary of H. C. Medford, Confederate Soldier, 1864." *Southwestern Historical Quarterly* 34 (1930–31): 203–30.

"Texas' Only GOP Governor Released." *Dallas Morning News,* November 9, 1978. In Vertical Files, Center for American History, University of Texas, Austin.

Dissertations, Theses, and Unpublished Papers

Ashcraft, Allan Coleman. "Texas, 1860–1866: The Lone Star State in the Civil War." Ph.D. dissertation, Columbia University, 1960.

Burrier, William Paul. "The Civil War in the Texas Hill Country: The Battle of the Nueces and the Bushwhacker War." Unpublished paper, 1995. Leakey, Texas.

Felgar, Robert Pattison. "Texas in the War for Southern Independence, 1861–1865." M.A. thesis, University of Texas at Austin, 1935.

Heintzen, Frank W. "Fredericksburg, Texas, during the Civil War and Reconstruction." M.A. thesis, St. Mary's University, San Antonio, 1944.

Knopp, Kenn. "Fredericksburg, Texas: Capital of the German Hills." Unpublished paper, 1995. Fredericksburg, Texas.

Overton, Hazel Best, ed. "Frontier Life of John Chadbourne Irwin." Unpublished paper, 1960?. In Robert E. Nail Archives, Old Jail Art Center Museum, Albany, Texas.

Walter, John S. "Histories of Texas Units in the Civil War." Unpublished paper, 1981. In Confederate Research Center, Hill Junior College, Hillsboro, Texas.

INDEX